WINDOWS

LINA GHOTMEH
LARS MÜLLER PUBLISHERS

OF LIGHT

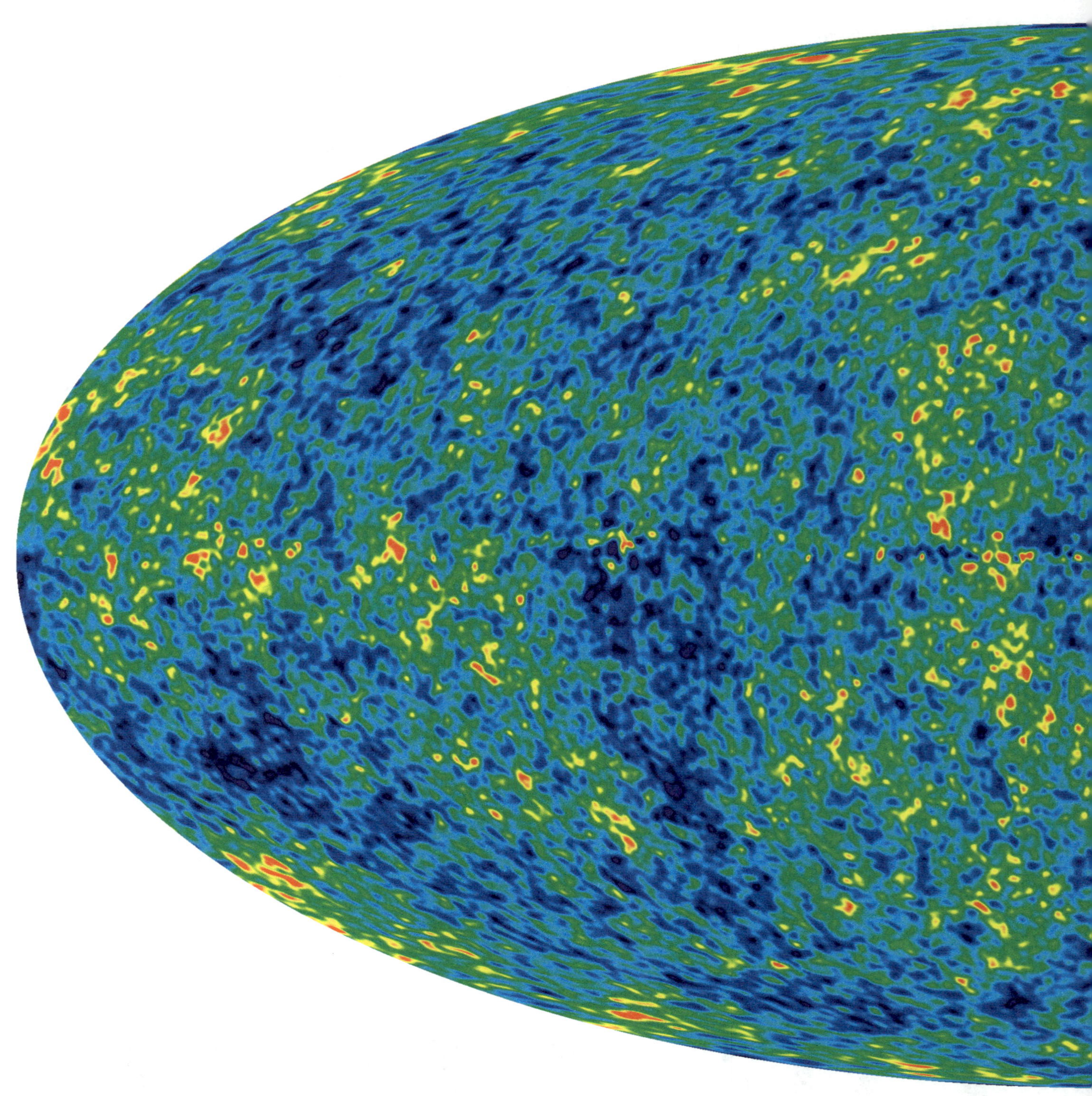

This image represents nine years of data compiled into the universe's "baby photo," capturing it when it was 380,000 years old. Displayed in varied colours, this map shows miniscule temperature variations in the cosmic microwave background (CMB)—the pervasive radiation that fills the universe from a time when the universe finally cooled down enough for particles of light (photons) to travel freely through space. These fluctuations are not just remnants, they are the oldest light we can observe—also termed the echo of Big Bang.

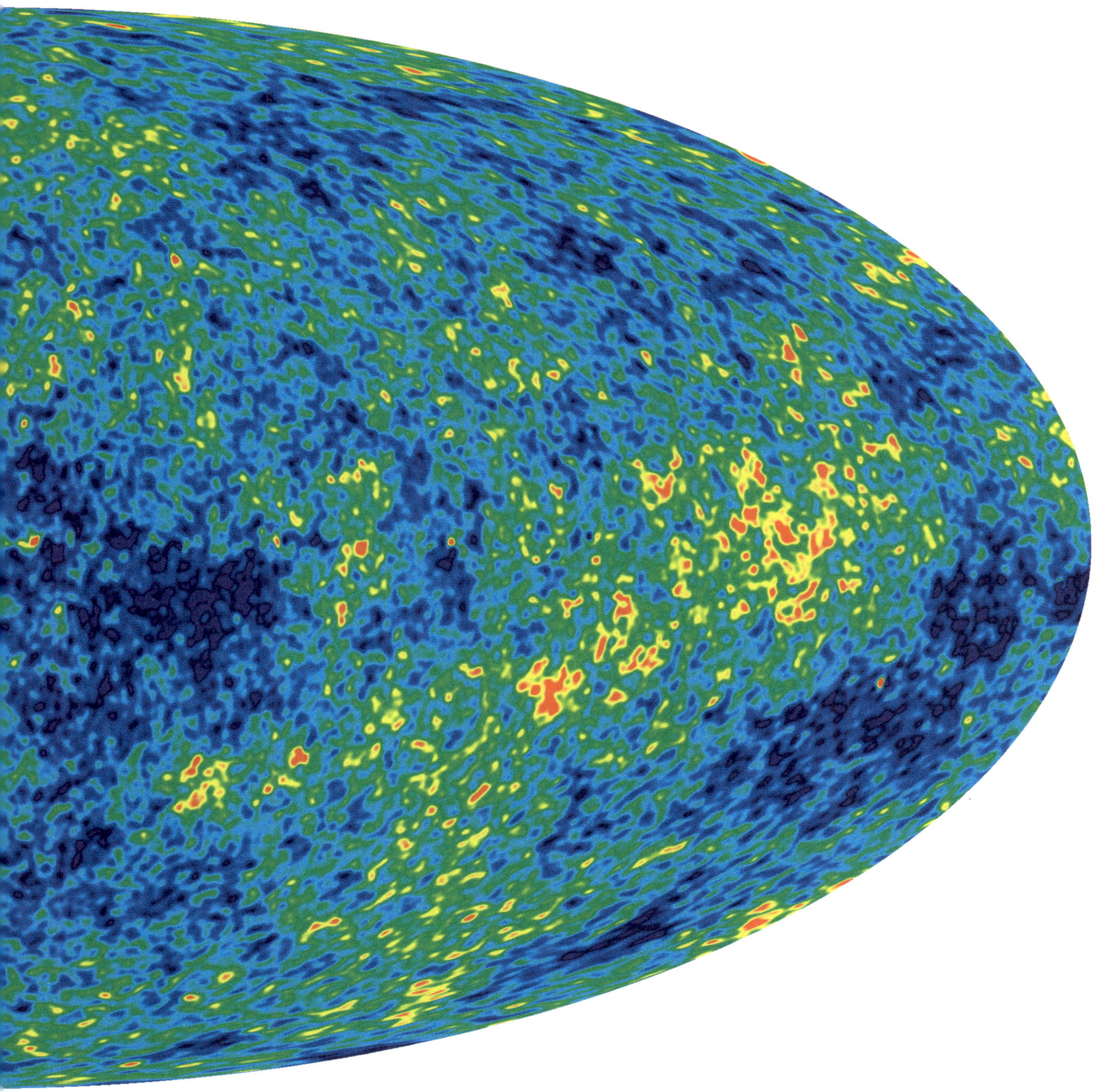

FOREWORD

"يا أيُّها البرق الّذي تَلمعُ

مِن أيِّ أكنافِ الحِمى تَسطعُ"

"O lightning that shines,

From which haven do you shine?"

Attributed to Suhrawardi, author of *Hayakal al-Nur*
(*The Shape of Light*)

The discovery of the cosmic microwave background (CMB) provides us with the oldest light we can detect, originating from a time when the universe had cooled enough for photons to move freely. This microwave radiation pervades space, living as the afterglow of the Big Bang and offering profound insights into the universe's early moments and its subsequent evolution over billions of years. As the oldest map in the universe, it provides a clear window into the early cosmos.

Windows of Light explores light as if unearthing an artefact. The first chapter, "Archeology of Light," examines both light and darkness across three integrated themes: origins of light, surveying light, and capturing light. Light and darkness permeate everything, from the birth of our sun to solar worship, cyanobacteria, luminescent fungi, travelling obelisks, observatories, the magic lantern, and the impact of Las Vegas and Starlink on our skies. Since the scope of information on light and darkness is limitless, the research, too, remains perpetually unfinished. Presented as fieldnotes, it spans diverse cultures that have created countless artefacts, myths, innovations, and theories related to light. While official historic records often marginalised less dominant or non-Western cultures, *Windows of Light* endeavours to bring diverse knowledges forward by highlighting shared ideas, both written and visual, in a non-linear chronology to create a common ground for new perspectives. Remarkably, similarities and near identical icons appear, centuries apart, in the most disparate places across the planet. This cross-generational exchange of inspirations helps trace a more diversified narrative about light from 4.6 billion years ago to the present day.

As cities have expanded through capitalist development, artificial light has become pervasive, disrupting ecosystems as well as cultural and social structures—darkness is often hard to come by in urban environments today. This calls for more appreciation and protection of both light and darkness as essential components of our shared urban heritage. While modern cities create a dependence on electric light, access to it is not always reliable or fairly distributed. The second chapter, "Without Light," documents the electricity crisis in Beirut—an example of energy inequity where access to light remains a privilege rather than a right. The chapter unfolds as a photographic essay of the city and of *Stone Garden*, a project realised by my practice, Lina Ghotmeh – Architecture, near the port of Beirut. The essay therefore captures *Stone Garden* both during its construction and after the 2020 port explosion. By photographing the city from the building's interior, through the frame of the window, the essay reminds us that architecture is a means of measuring light.

The concluding chapter, "Material Light," presents a series of ink drawings I created during the publication, which serve as personal and contemplative notes on the nature of light, water, and the natural world. By echoing the book's initial imagery of the sun and its flares, the ink as a medium is not only a means of expression but also a tool for understanding light's materiality through the tangible act of creating by hand.

Windows of Light delves into how light and darkness—cultural forces that resonate across time and space—impact our environment, shape our perception of the world, and define our role within it.

LINA GHOTMEH

SUMMARY

ARCHEOLOGY

Origins of Light
Surveying Light
Capturing Light

OF LIGHT

|

WITHOUT

Beirut - Laurian Ghiniţoiu
Stone Garden - Lina Ghotmeh

LIGHT

|

MATERIAL

Flows - Lina Ghotmeh

LIGHT

GLOW – SHINI(NG)

GLEAM

LIGHT – GLEAM

MOONLIGHT – GLEAM

ILLUMINATION – MOONLIGHT

LUMINARE

→ LUMIÈRE → LUX

FULGENT – LUCENT – PHOTIC – NOCTILUCENT

CHIAROSCURO – CELESTIAL

DAZZLING

{ ٱلله نور ٱلسموت وٱلأرض مثل نوره كمشكوة فيها مصباح ٱلمصباح في زجاجة ٱلزجاجة كأنها كوكب

توهّج

لمعة

بدر

والله بكل شيء عليم } [النور: 35]

نُور

الشُّعاع

الإشعاع

G – BRIGHT – RADIANCE – BEAM OF LIGHT – ILLU

SPECTRAL – PENUMBRA

(LATIN)

LUMEN

LUMINO

LUMIÈRE

The French *lumière* is derived from the Latin "lūminaria", meaning "star" or "torch" and originating from lūmen, which refers to "light," "flame," or "daylight." Dating from around 1100 CE, the term lumière encompasses not only the physical aspect of light but also symbolises advancement, knowledge, and innovation. Les Lumières ("The Lights") refers to a European philosophical movement that started in the late seventeenth-century. Influenced by thinkers like René Descartes, Baruch de Spinoza, John Locke, Pierre Bayle, and Isaac Newton, this movement spread throughout Europe, peaking in eighteenth-century France–the era known as *Le siècle des Lumières* (the Age of Enlightenment).

Unlike the translations of other European languages that suggest enlightenment comes from an external source, the French interpretation emphasises enlightenment originating from within oneself.

Le mot « lumière » est dérivé du latin « lūminaria », qui signifie « étoile » ou « torche », et provient de « lūmen », qui signifie « lumière », « flamme » ou « lumière du jour ». Apparu vers 1100 de notre ère, le terme « lumière » englobe non seulement l'aspect physique de la lumière mais symbolise également le progrès, la connaissance et l'innovation. « Les Lumières » fait référence à un mouvement philosophique européen qui a émergé à la fin du XVIIᵉ siècle. Influencé par des penseurs comme René Descartes, Baruch de Spinoza, John Locke, Pierre Bayle et Isaac Newton, ce mouvement s'est répandu à travers l'Europe, atteignant son apogée en France au XVIIIᵉ siècle, période dite Le siècle des Lumières.

Contrairement aux traductions d'autres langues européennes qui suggèrent que l'illumination vient d'une source externe, l'interprétation française met l'accent sur une illumination provenant de l'intérieur de soi.

نور

Al-nur (النور) refers to a metaphysical dimension of light, representing both the origin and culmination of light. It encompasses both the physical and metaphysical realms, as well as concepts of lightness and darkness in space. Al-nur in its essential form is gentle and spiritual, devoid of reflection, shadow, burning, or harm. It manifests as pure radiance, illuminating everything around it, both sensually and morally. It is also used to describe a supreme being as "the light of the heavens and the earth," casting images of the absolute onto the human soul.

النور يشير إلى بُعد ميتافيزيقي للضوء، يمثل كلاً من أصل الضوء وذروته. يشمل كلا من العوالم المادية والميتافيزيقية، وكذلك مفاهيم النور والظلام في الفضاء. النور في صورته الأساسية لطيف وروحاني، خال من الانعكاس، والظل، والحرق، أو الأذى. يتجّلى كشعاع نقي، ينير كل شيء من حوله، حسيًا ومعنويًا. يُستخدم أيضًا لوصف كائن أسمى باعتباره "نور السماوات والأرض"، ملقيًا صور المطلق على النفس البشرية.

TIMELINE

BCE —

4.6 billion years ago

Sun starts emitting light.

3.8 billion years ago

Evidence of microbial life.

2.4 billion years ago

Cyanobacteria evolved.

5500 BCE

Armenia's Carahunge, one of the oldest megalithic sites.

3500 BCE

Obelisks erected to honour sun deities.

3100-1600 BCE

Stonehenge constructed.

1300 BCE

Earliest sundial found in Egypt's Valley of the Kings.

600 BCE

Thales discovered static electricity with amber and silk.

300 BCE

Euclid writes *Optics*.

CE —

150 CE

Ptolemy writes *The Almagest*.

964 CE

Abd al-Rahman al-Sufi documents the Andromeda Galaxy.

984 CE

Ibn Sahl writes on optical properties of lenses.

1000 —

1011-1021

Alhazen writes a seven-volume treatise on optics.

1100 —

1186

Shahab al-Din Suhrawardi founds Illuminationism.

1200 —

1250

Roger Bacon explores light reflection.

1259

Maragheh Observatory established.

1400 —

1425

Ulugh Beg builds an observatory in Samarkand.

1442

Beijing Observatory founded.

1500 —

1543

Copernicus proposes heliocentric model.

1600 —

1608

Hans Lippershey applies for the first telescope patent.

1609

Galileo constructs his own telescope.

1621

Snell's Law of Refraction discovered.

1660

Otto von Guericke demonstrates a vacuum and static electricity.

1667

Public lighting established in Paris.

1700 –

1676:
Ole Roemer measures the speed of light.

1724:
Jantar Mantar built by Maharaja Jai Singh II.

1752:
Benjamin Franklin's kite experiment with electricity.

1800 –

1800:
Alessandro Volta invents the first electric battery.

1808
Sir Humphry Davy invents the arc lamp.

1826
Georg Ohm defines Ohm's Law.

1839
Daguerre invents the daguerreotype process.

1840
First astronomical photographs by Draper.

1841:
James Prescott Joule shows energy conservation in circuits.

1860
Maxwell presents the electromagnetic field theory.

1878
Charles Brush develops an arc lamp powered by a generator.

1881
The electric streetcar invented by Werner von Siemens.

1900 –

1883
Nikola Tesla invents the Tesla coil.

1897
Joseph John Thomson discovers the electron.

1901
Discovery of the Antikythera Mechanism.

1912
Introduction of animated electric signs by Douglas Leigh.

1960
Theodore Harold Maiman demonstrates the first laser.

1962
Invention of light-emitting diodes by Nick Holonyak.

1985
Completion of the Hubble Telescope frame.

1990
First image taken with the Hubble Telescope.

1991
Hubble's first images of Jupiter released.

1993
Hubble takes major step in determining universe's age.

1994
Existence of supermassive black holes confirmed.

1995
Star birth seen in the Eagle Nebula.

2000 –

1996
Hubble Deep Field image, the deepest and most detailed view of the universe at the time.

1996
First image of a star's surface released.

2006
Direct proof of dark matter observed.

2010
Cosmic lens used for the first time to probe dark energy.

SYMBOLS

SOLAR
BEAIVI
EARLY PRIMITIVE SYMBOL OF SUN
AKHET
SUN WHEEL IN THE
CRESCENT OF THE MOON

ZIA SUN
I'ITOI
ASHUR SUN CROSS
CADDO SOLAR CROSS
SUN WHEEL
AZTEC SUN
OWIA KOKROKO
SŁONECZKO
TRISKELION
BASQUE CROSS
DHARMA CHAKRA
SUN CROSS
SUN WHEEL
SUN KACHINA
BORJGALI
DAISY

ARCHEOLOGY
OF LIGHT

ORIGINS OF LIGHT

*ANCIENT ORGANISMS, DEEP-SEA COLONIES,
LUMINESCENT FUNGI, FIREFLY LAMPS,
AND SOLAR EXPRESSIONS: PART 1 EXPLORES
THE ORIGINS OF LIGHT.*

أصول الضوء

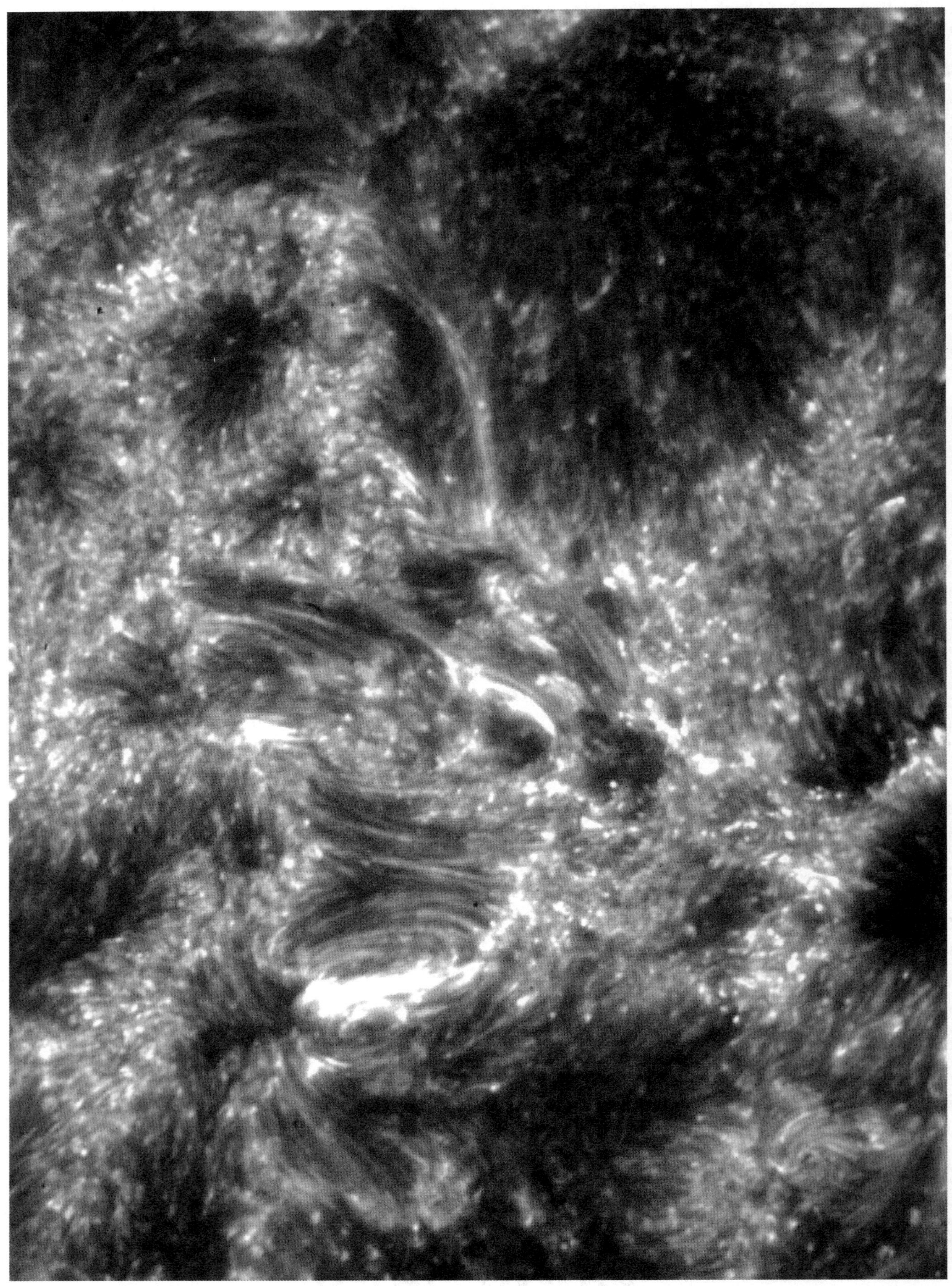

001

002

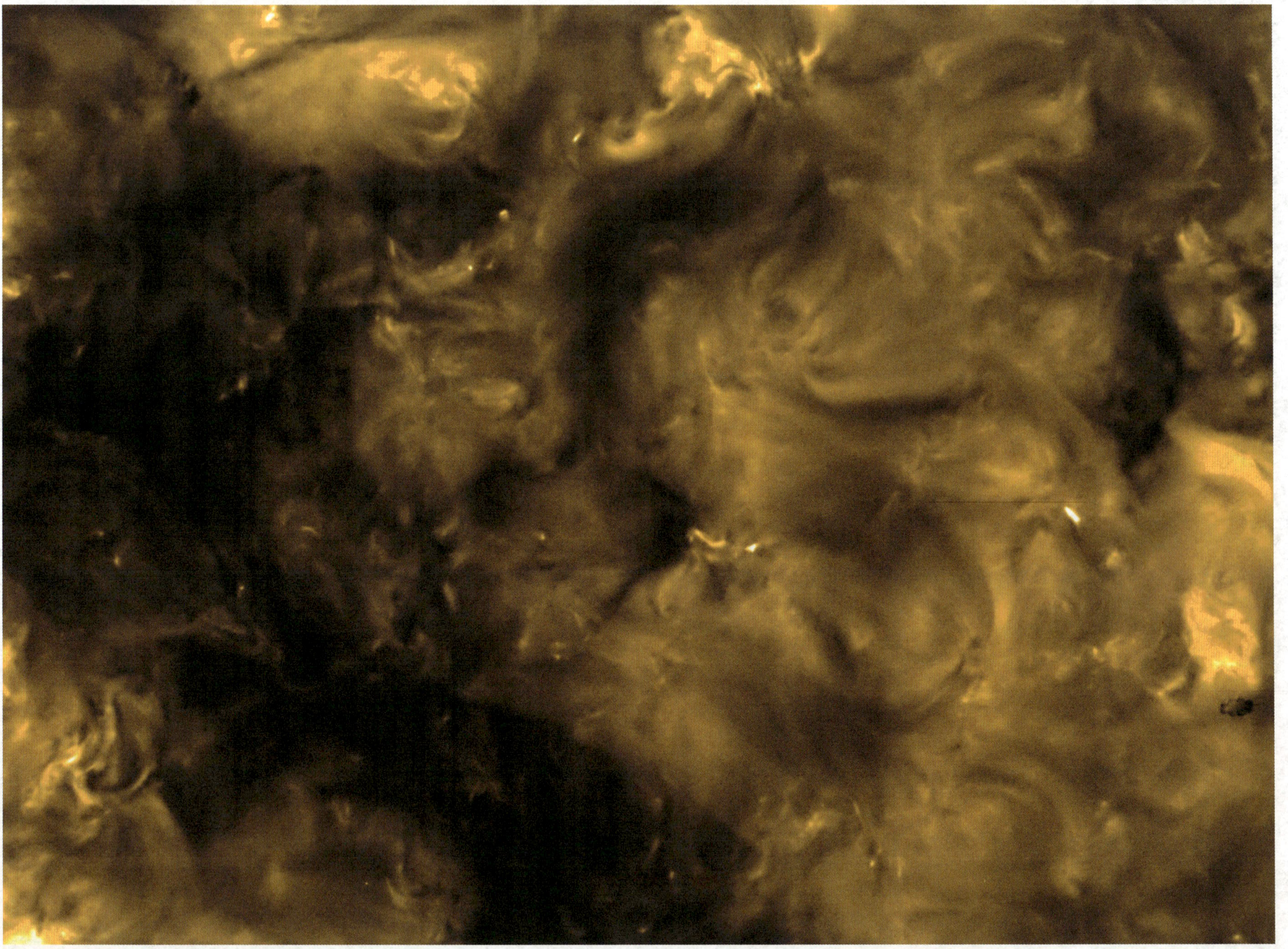

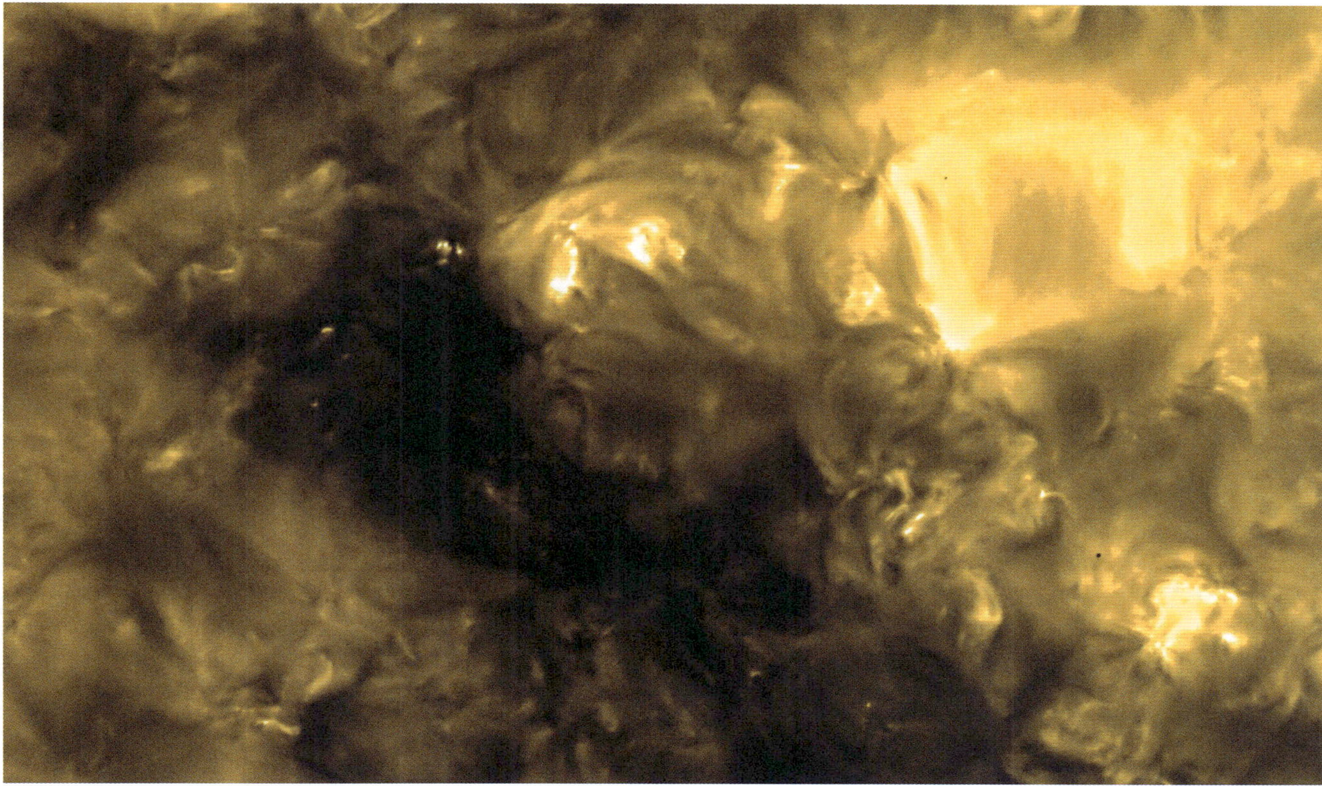

004

001
Magnetic loops of plasma at the surface of the sun.

002
As temperatures neared absolute zero (minus 273 degrees Celsius), gravitational forces began to compact gas into an interstellar cloud. This cloud eventually collapsed inward, forming a glowing hot sphere of plasma known as a protostar.

003
Over the next 30 million years, this young star matured, reaching a high enough pressure and temperature to sustain nuclear reactions. This is the Sun. It has been emitting light since its formation approximately 4.6 billion years ago.

004
Looking deep into the inferno of the Sun, beneath its outer layer of chaotic hot plasma, sits the core, about 650,000 kilometres below the surface. Although one might assume it to be a calm interior when compared to the fiery outer layers, the core is the hottest region of the solar system, with a temperature that soars to around 15 million degrees Celsius.

005

005
These extreme conditions facilitate a rare event crucial to sustaining the Sun's power: nuclear fusion. In this process, hydrogen atoms merge to form helium and release vast amounts of energy. The photons created during fusion take more than 100,000 years to make their way from the core toward the surface of the Sun. Once nearly there, they then reach the surface of the Earth within less than ten minutes.

006
A single scoop of a hand net in a natural body of water captures a diverse array of organisms, from photosynthetic cyanobacteria and diatoms to zooplankton, like fish eggs and crab larvae. These creatures represent the variety of life adrift in the planktonic community, some residing permanently and others temporarily. Like terrestrial plants, phytoplankton harness sunlight to produce energy through photosynthesis. Single-celled organisms in the ocean contribute to over half of earth's productivity and generate most of its oxygen.

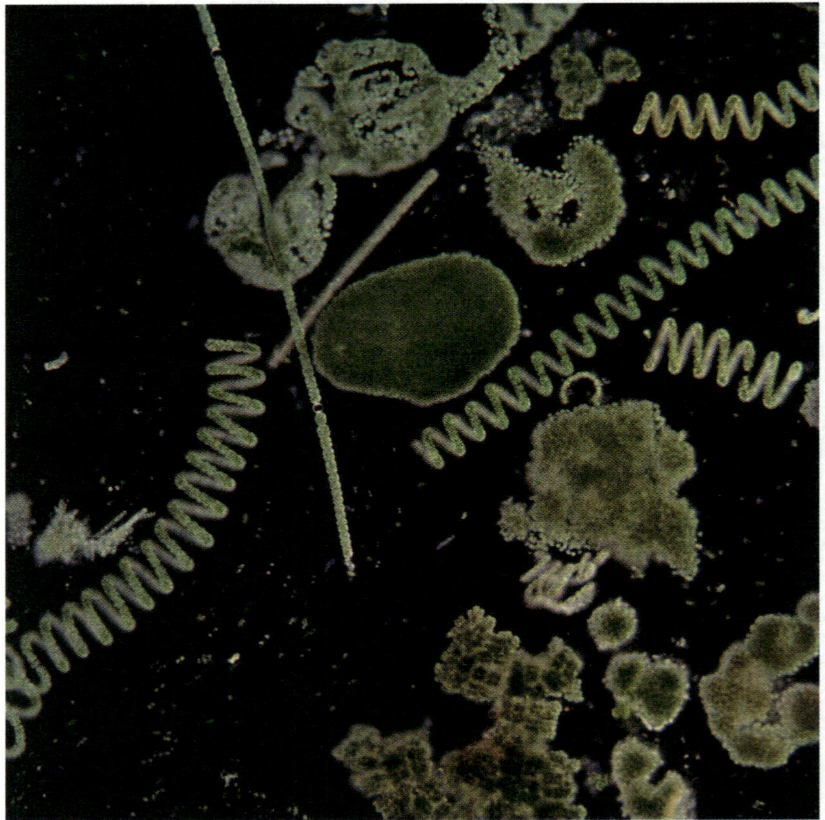

006

007

008

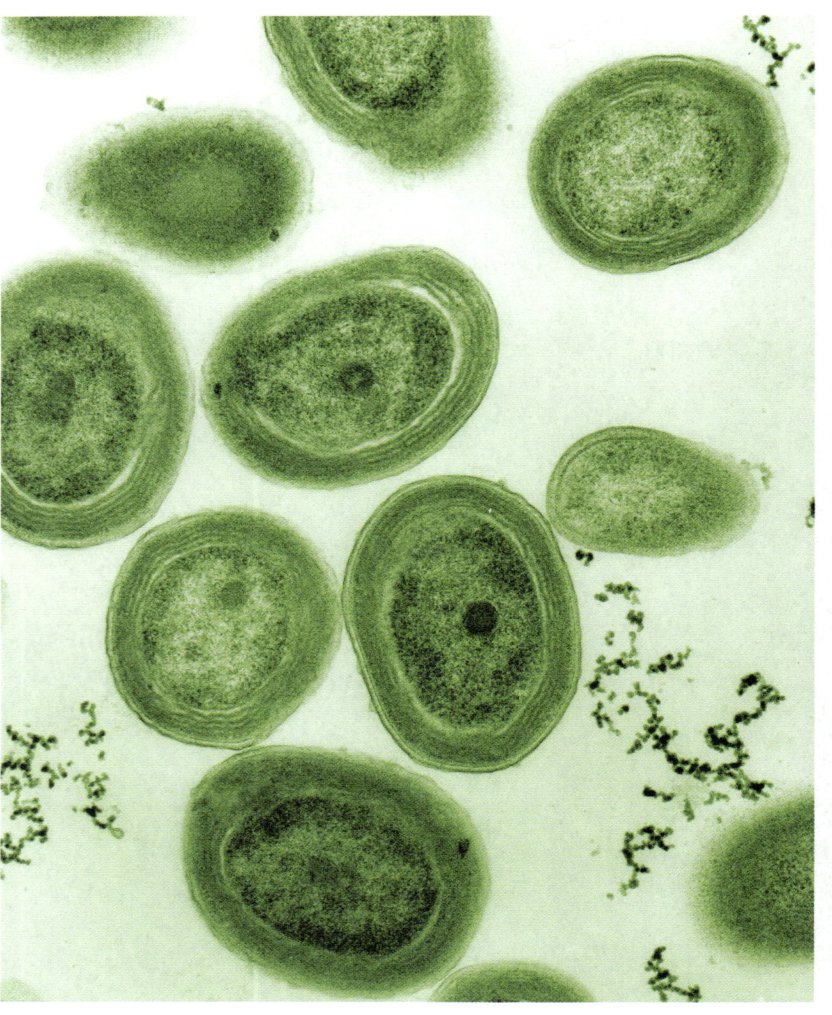

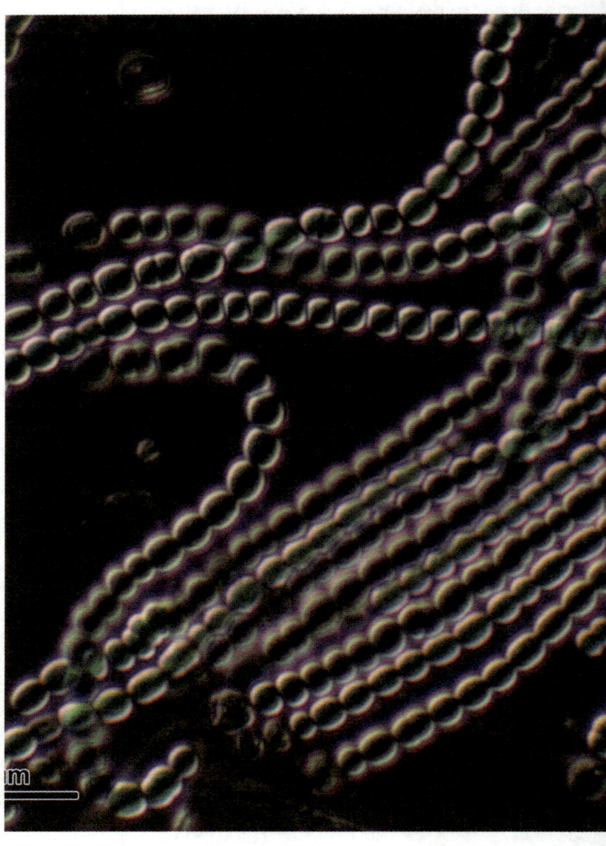

ORIGINS

Photosynthesis

OF LIGHT

The intricate dance of life and light within earth's ecosystems is captured through photosynthesis, a fundamental and ancient biological process that powers the biosphere. Although the exact origins of photosynthesis remain largely unknown—there is no direct evidence pointing to a specific beginning[1]—it is understood that this process emerged early in earth's history and has evolved through a complex, non-linear path.[2]

At the core of this process are cyano-bacteria, algae, and plants. These organisms range from microscopic to macroscopic organisms that harness light to sustain their existence and, by extension, support countless other life forms. Evidence of microbial life dates back about 3.8 billion years, with cyanobacteria emerging as earth's first photosynthesisers at least 2.4 billion years ago. The marine cyanobacterium *Prochlorococcus marinus*, for instance, plays a crucial role in oxygenating the earth and serving as a primary producer in oceanic ecosystems.

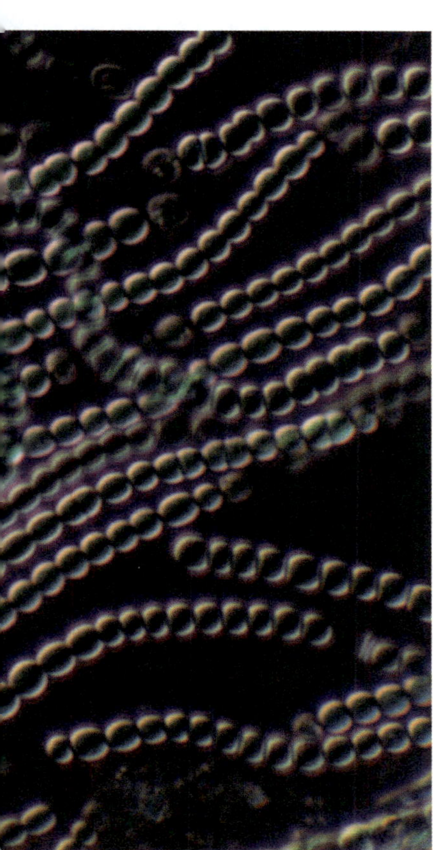

007
This transmission electron micros-copy (TEM) image, an analytical technique which is used to visualise the smallest structures in matter, captures *Prochlorococcus marinus* by adding green colouring. This vital marine cyanobacterium is the most abundant photosynthetic organism in our modern oceans. Despite their tiny cell sizes (0.0005 to 0.0007 millimetres), *Prochloro-coccus* is the smallest known photo-synthetic organism. They engage in oxygenic photosynthesis producing oxygen as a byproduct—which is key to ocean oxidation, a process that significantly altered the chemical composition of early earth's oceans and atmosphere. This oxygen pro-duction appears to have played as significant a role as light and nutrients in driving *Prochlorococcus* evolution.

008
Differential interference contrast (DIC) microscopy—an optical technique that enhances contrast in unstained, transparent samples—can capture images of cyanobacteria by magnifying it 2400 times. Cyanobacteria often live in colonial aggregates that can adopt various forms. These elongated, hair-like colonial structures are only one of many and diverse forms. Many cyanobacteria produce mobile filaments of cells called *hormogonia*, which detach from the main biomass, travel, and propagate to establish new colonies elsewhere.

Oceans act as critical hubs of life, revealing a micro-world of drifters such as cyanobacteria and diatoms, alongside diverse plankton populations. These organisms not only capture light but also contribute significantly to nitrogen fixation, enhancing soil fertility and supporting terrestrial ecosystems. The microscopic machinery of photosynthesis is housed within the chloroplasts of plant and algae cells. These chloroplasts, filled with chlorophyll, are the sites where the sun's energy is converted into life-sustaining oxygen and organic compounds. The diversity of structures that facilitate photosynthesis, from the gas-regulating *stomata* in leaves to the chloroplast-rich cells of submerged water plants, demonstrate the adaptability of life to harness light across varied environments. These photosynthetic organisms and the processes that define them demonstrate the fundamental role of light in sustaining life on earth.

009

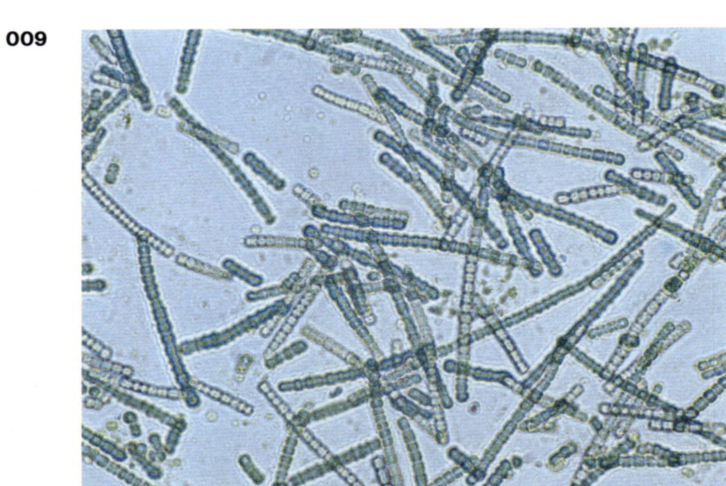

010

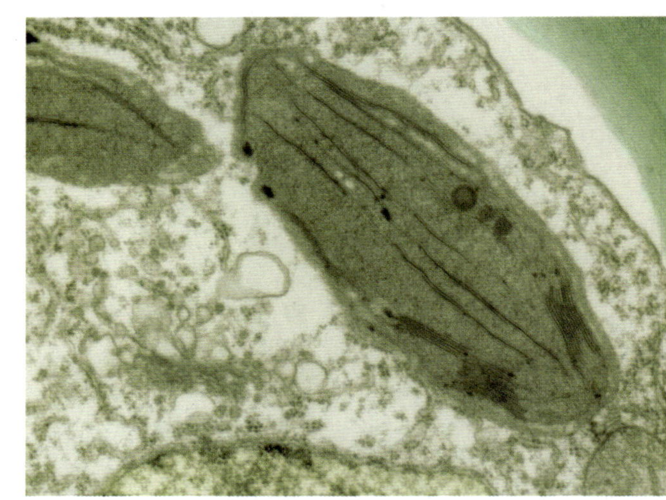

011

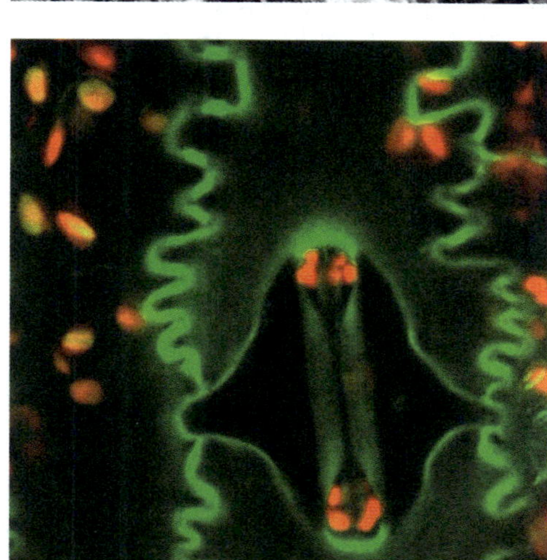

012

009

Cylindrospermum, a genus of filamentous cyanobacteria, is observed under magnification and often encountered in freshwater phytoplankton assemblages. This genus typically forms dense, slimy mats on damp soils or along shoreline vegetation. The cells are characteristically cylindrical or barrel shaped.

010

This chloroplast exists within a bean leaf, of which only 0.00045 millimetres is captured. Chloroplasts are specialised compartments rich in chlorophyll, found in certain plant and algae cells, where photosynthesis occurs. This process allows plants to convert light into energy. Chloroplasts are not only essential for photosynthesis but also exhibit a remarkable adaptability; they move within plant cells and can rearrange themselves depending on the intensity of light. In low light conditions, chloroplasts spread out to maximise their surface area and enhance light absorption. Conversely, in intense light, they align in vertical columns along the cell walls or position themselves to minimise direct light exposure and prevent damage.

011

As seen in this micrograph, the *stoma* (Greek for "mouth," plural *stomata*) is a vital structure located on a leaf's surface and stem that facilitates the exchange of gases like carbon dioxide and oxygen, essential for processes such as photosynthesis and respiration. *Stomata* dynamically adjust their openings in response to their environments including light intensity, humidity, and carbon dioxide levels. The orientation and disruption of *stomata* vary across different plant types. For instance, many plants have more *stomata* on the underside of leaves to reduce direct exposure to sunlight and minimise water loss through transpiration.

012

A *stoma* that is closed yet alive is seen in the mesophyll (middle cell layers) of a maize leaf. Highlighted in green is ferulic acid within the cell walls, and in red is the chlorophyll located within the chloroplasts. Since the degree to which *stomata* open is influenced by carbon dioxide levels, these structures are a focal point of scientific research into understanding plant responses to climate change.

013

The inner tissue of a thale cress leaf is stained to show chloroplasts in red and ferulic acid in blue. Thale cress is the first plant to have its entire genome sequenced, a pivotal model in molecular and plant biology. The sequencing allowed scientists to decode and map all its genes, providing insight into biological processes at a molecular level as well as gene functions, evolutionary biology, and various plant traits.

013

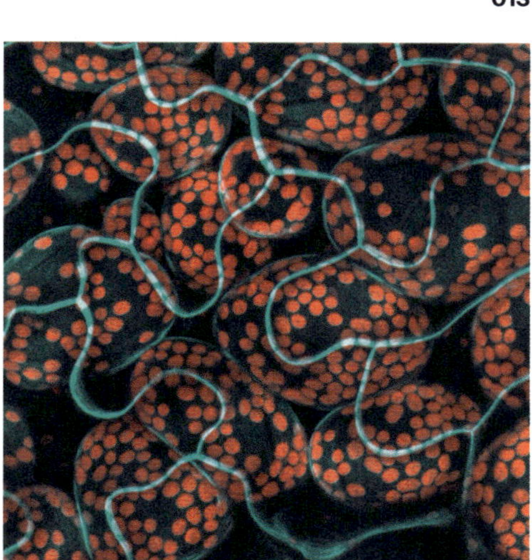

أصول الضوء – تركيب ضوئي

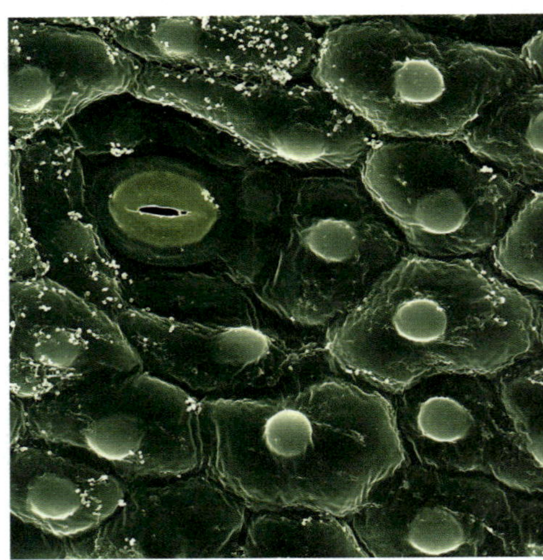

014
An open *stoma*, approximately 0.02 millimetres wide, on the lower surface of an orchid leaf and bordered by two guard cells. Unlike many parasitic plants, most orchids maintain the ability to photosynthesise. The guard cells are essential as they regulate the opening and closing of the *stoma* to control gas exchange and photosynthesis. This *stoma* was captured using scanning electron microscopy at 600 times magnification.

015
Chlorophyll absorbs light primarily in the blue and red wavelengths while it reflects green light, which is why plants appear green. As the weather cools in the colder seasons, chlorophyll pigments break down. The changing of colours of leaves such as red and orange, happen as other pigments begin to reflect light.

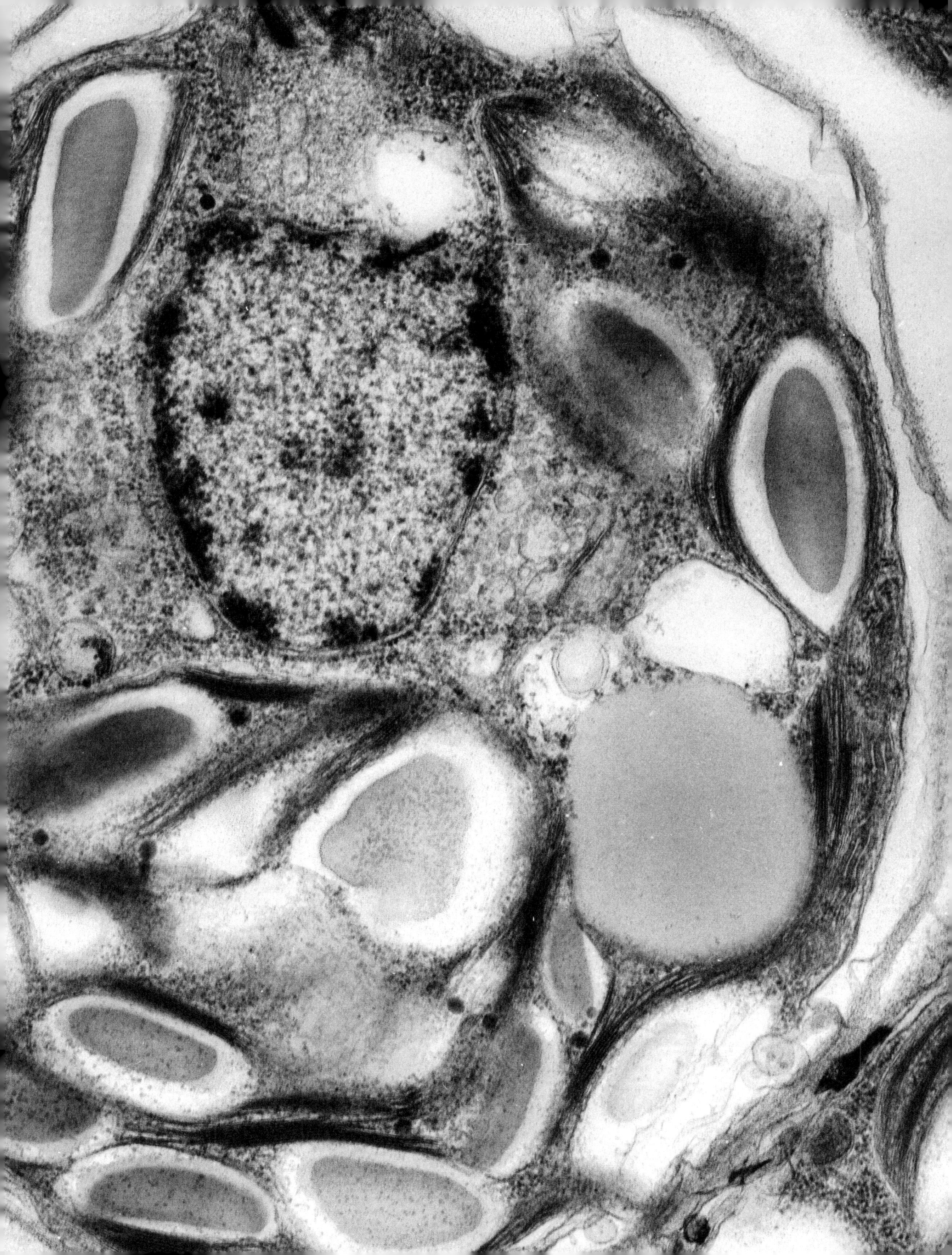

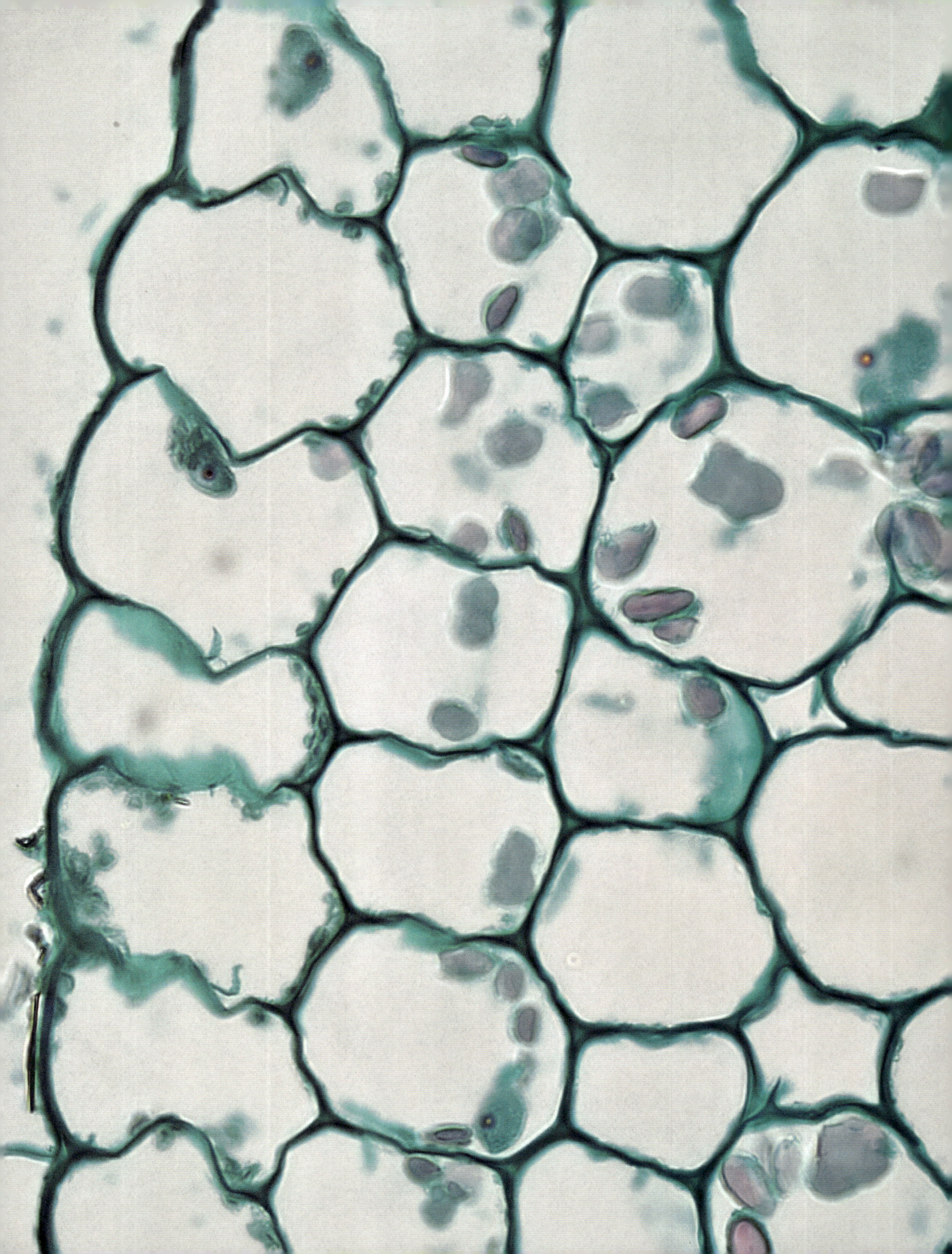

016

Chlamydomonas reinhardtii is a single-celled alga notable for its dual *flagella* (tails), which facilitate its movement. At its core lies the nucleus, surrounded by a distinctive cup-shaped chloroplast containing energy-storing granules. This alga also features an eyespot that detects light, guiding the organism toward or away from light sources, depending on the intensity and direction of the light. *Chlamydomonas* species are prevalent in soil and freshwater environments and are particularly significant for their roles in producing biopharmaceuticals and biofuels. They are also vital in scientific research on hydrogen production.

017

Submerged plants like *Elodea* are well-adapted to aquatic life and are one of the few aquatic plants that provide underwater habitat during winter months. They lack rigid internal structures, allowing them to float freely. Their skin is thin and green, equipped with tiny pores for gas exchange. Internally, a layer of tightly packed cells, rich in chloroplasts for photosynthesis, surrounds air-filled pockets that aid buoyancy. *Elodea* has a simple water transport system, sometimes featuring a central air space. Commonly found in lakes and ponds, they are popular in aquariums and as a tool in educational demonstrations of cellular processes.

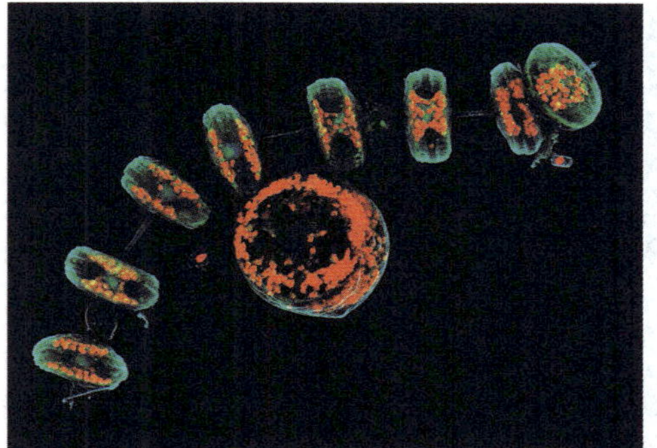

017

---

[1] Olson and Blankenship, "Thinking about the Evolution of Photosynthesis," 373.
[2] Blankenship, "Early Evolution of Photosynthesis," 438.

018

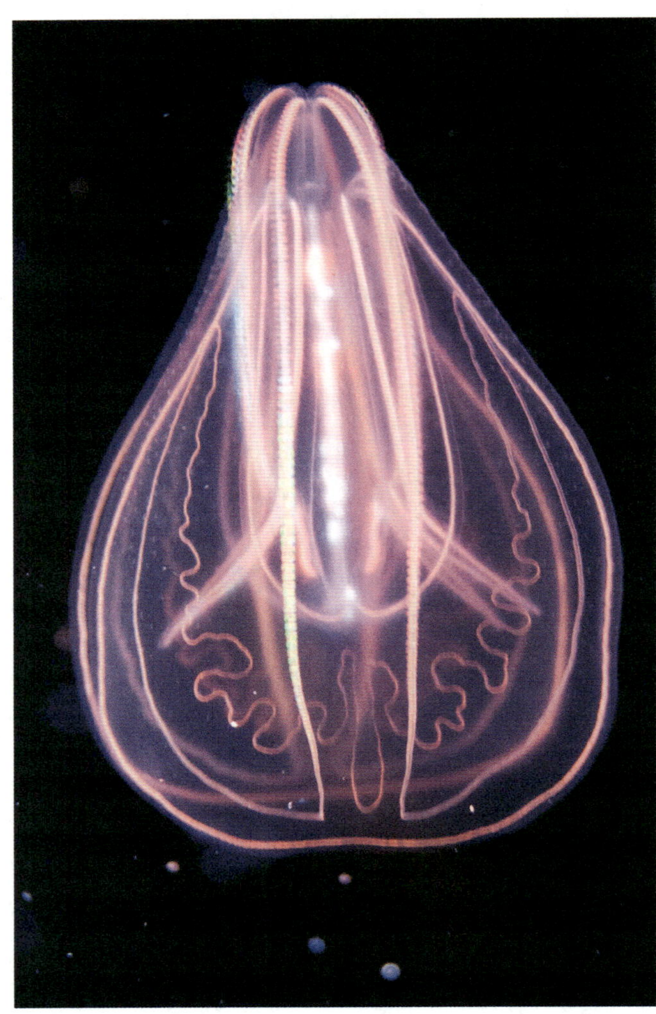

019

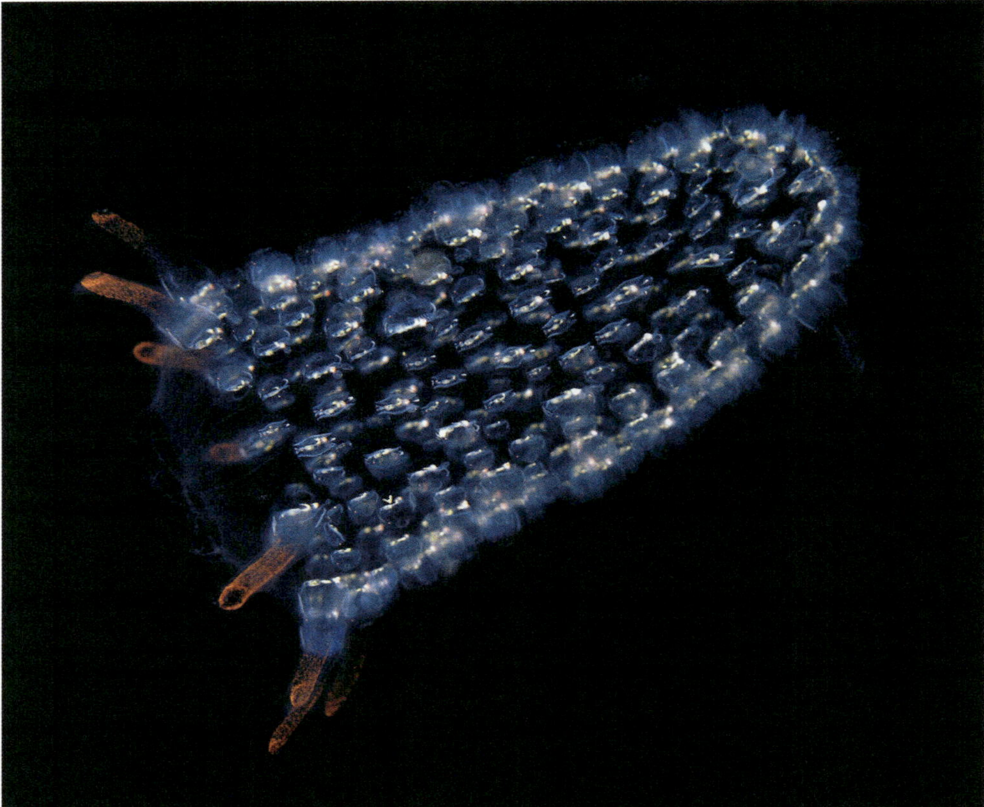

018

Ctenophores, known as comb jellies, use cilia groups, referred to as "combs," for swimming. They are the largest animals to use cilia for locomotion. These marine creatures vary in size, with adults ranging from a few millimetres to up to 1500 millimetres. Currently, there are only 186 recognised living species of ctenophores. They are ancient organisms, having emerged 500 million years ago, and are some of the earliest known metazoans, a group of multicellular animals.[3] Their bioluminescence originates from photoproteins activated by calcium. These photoproteins, found in cells called photocytes, are complex molecules made up of two chemicals, luciferin and luciferase. When calcium interacts with these molecules, they emit bright, brief flashes of light.

019

A *Pyrosome tunicate* encountered off Atauro Island, East Timor. The term *pyrosome* originates from the Greek *pyro* ("fire") and *soma* ("body"), which refer to the organism's striking bioluminescence.[4] *Pyrosomes* are part of the class *Thaliacea* and remain under-researched despite their ecological importance and wide distribution. *Pyrosomes* are colonial tunicates, meaning they can be made up of hundreds to thousands of individuals, known as zooids. They are one of the rare marine species that emit light in response to external light sources. These colonies are efficient planktonic grazers, capable of consuming significant amounts of phytoplankton.[5] Each individual zooid within a colony can detect light and produce a bioluminescent response. English biologist and anthropologist Thomas H. Huxley remarked in his 1849 diary while at sea: "I have just watched the moon set in all her glory, and looked at those lesser moons, the beautiful Pyrosoma, shining like white-hot cylinders in the water." [6]

020

Light bends off the comb-like rows of the ctenophore *Mertensia ovum*, creating vivid rainbow colours. This species deploys one of its two feeding tentacles while retracting the other. First identified as *Beroe ovum* by Danish zoologist Johan Christian Fabricius in 1780, *Mertensia ovum* is unique among ctenophores for thriving in the cold Arctic and adjacent polar seas, usually within surface waters down to fifty metres.

ORIGINS

Bioluminescence

OF LIGHT

Bioluminescence is the ability of organisms to emit light through a chemical reaction that produces light with minimal heat. Such organisms have been used to guide and illuminate in hazardous environments well before the advent of modern lighting. For example, Roman naturalist and philosopher Pliny the Elder once noted that the slime from the *Pelagia noctiluca* jellyfish could be applied to a walking stick, transforming it into a makeshift torch.

Similarly, in the late seventeenth-century, physician Georg Eberhard Rumpf observed Indigenous peoples in Indonesia using bioluminescent fungi to navigate forests in the dark. And before nineteenth-century mining operations and the invention of the safety lamp, miners used jars filled with fireflies as a light source instead of fire, to avoid the risk of igniting explosive gases. For many organisms, bioluminescence is a crucial evolutionary trait that helps them navigate, communicate, mate, and evade predators—a tool to survive and thrive in their environments.

020

021
Lobate Ctenophore.

022
Bolinopsis infundibulum is a predatory species that occasionally forms swarms. This organism captures its prey with its tentacles, using a feeding current generated by the movement of cilia. It primarily feeds on swimming organisms such as fish eggs, copepod larvae, veligers, rotifers, and other small zooplankton.

023
Tomopteris are nearly transparent marine creatures known for their predatory behaviour. These organisms have a unique defence mechanism: some species can release luminous particles to confuse predators when threatened. What sets *Tomopteris* apart is their yellow light emission, a rarity since most other bioluminescent marine animals produce light in different colours.

024
Copepods are a critical component of marine zooplankton communities, often making up more than 70 percent of the total abundance and biomass of these environments. Despite over a century of research into the bioluminescent capabilities of some copepod species, there remains a significant gap in understanding the structure and evolutionary development of their *luciferase* genes.[7] Their bioluminescence is generally thought to serve as an anti-predatory defence, but the specific functions and potential for communication through bioluminescence–possibly as a warning signal among copepods– have yet to be fully explored.

021

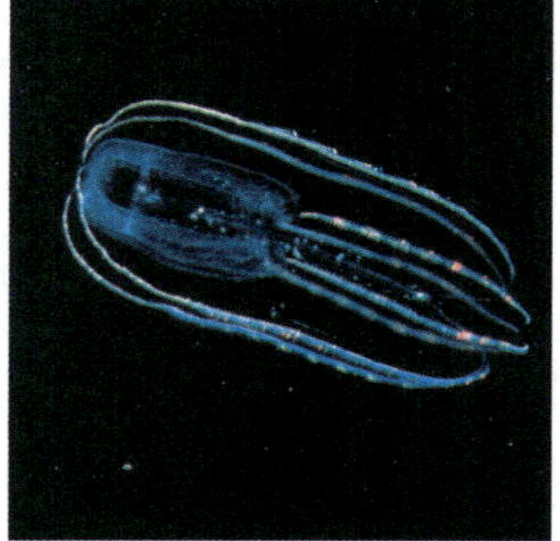

022

023

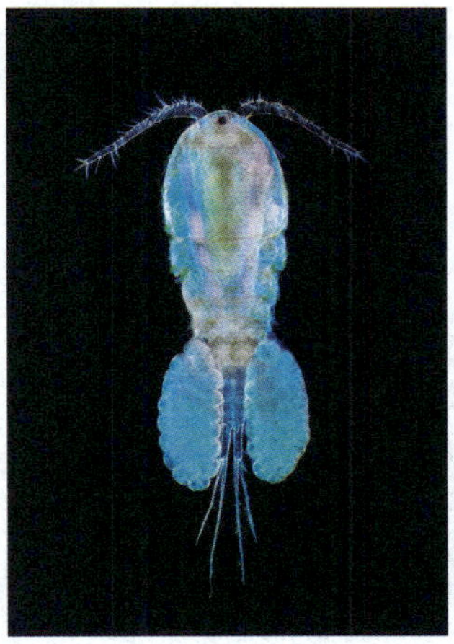

أركيولوجيا الضوء

025

Armillaria novae-zelandiae (Austral Honey Mushroom).

026

Knowledge of the biochemical processes behind the bioluminescence of the *Mycena nebula fungi* is limited. Various theories exist regarding the function of their glow: some suggest it might enhance spore dispersal by attracting insects, while others propose it could deter nocturnal fungivores or even attract predators of these fungivores, serving as a protective shield.

027

In Japanese folklore, the glow emitted by certain mushrooms at night is often thought to represent the spirits of the dead, misleading travellers off their paths. This phenomenon, occasionally witnessed by people encountering bioluminescent mushrooms or glowing mycelia in the dark, was sometimes attributed to *Yōkai*, meaning mysterious, supernatural creatures.[8] Similarly, Indigenous cultures of West Australia refer to luminescent fungi as *Chinga*, meaning spirit, and associate them with evil spirits and supernatural activities of ancestors.[9]

028

Omphalotus subilludens, commonly known as the Southern Jack O'lantern, is one of many bioluminescent fungi. It emits light from its gills due to the oxidation of the enzyme luciferase within its fruiting body. The light emitted by fungi can vary in colour from blue, white, to green, depending on the specific type of mushroom. The intensity of the light can also vary, sometimes visible from as far as forty metres away.[10] As an American journalist (name unknown) once wrote to his wife from a battlefield in New Guinea during World War II: "I'm writing to you tonight by the light of five mushrooms."[11]

025

026

027

028

029

029
Within this eight-second exposure, some fireflies flash five or six times. It is widely accepted that flashes by fireflies are primarily used to attract mates. It is an elaborate luminescent courtship ritual that involves recognising specific patterns such as flash frequency, response timing, and flight paths.

Firefly light differs in its colour, peak intensity, and kinetics of emission.[12]

030

030
Fireflies at the Tai Po Nature Reserve in Hong Kong.

031
Waawaatesi is the Ojibwe—an Indigenous people of North America—name for the firefly. With the world constantly getting lighter, these luminous insects face threats from light pollution, which interferes with their ability to see each other's signals and complicates their mating rituals. Common environmental issues such as habitat loss, pesticide use, and climate change also pose significant risks to their populations.

031

032

In August 2010, the Moderate Resolution Imaging Spectroradiometer (MODIS) on NASA's Terra satellite captured a significant phytoplankton bloom in the North Atlantic Ocean off the coast of Newfoundland, Canada. These blooms, visible from space, can emit a blue light that acts as a deterrent to predators. Phytoplankton blooms, which are dense clusters of microscopic algae, proliferate in the surface waters of oceans and lakes. While these blooms are ecologically vital, contributing to carbon fixation and supporting marine ecosystems and fisheries, others can be detrimental.[13] Known as harmful algal blooms (HABs), these occurrences pose increasing environmental challenges. They release toxins that can ascend the food chain, leading to fishery shutdowns and affecting the health of marine organisms and humans alike. Projections suggest that climate change will heighten the frequency and geographic spread of these blooms.[14] This could exacerbate the impact on aquatic ecosystems, fisheries, and coastal economies.[15]

033

A bloom stretched for over 500 kilometres long and 200 kilometres across near Hokkaido Island, Japan's second largest island. This area is where the cold Oyashio Current from the north meets the warmer Kuroshio Current from the south, creating water eddies that concentrate the phytoplankton.

032

034

034
At depths beyond 200 metres in the ocean, where 99 percent of sunlight is absorbed, marine biologists classify the environment as "deep" water. Beyond 1000 metres, the absence of light coupled with intense cold and extreme pressure, defines the abyssal zone.[16]

035
Despite considerable advances in technology and science over the last century, deep-sea research remains in its infancy. Previously, scientists thought the deep sea's lack of light significantly hindered the productivity of its organisms, such that until the 1970s they considered it isolated from surface waters as a site of primary productivity.

3 Mjoseth, "Sea Creatures Providing Clues on the Evolution of Vision," 13.

4 Lilly et al., "A Global Review of Pyrosomes," 813.

5 Sutherland and Thompson, "Pelagic Tunicate Grazing on Marine Microbes," 102.

6 Huxley, *T.H Huxley's Diary of the Voyage of H.M.S Rattlesnake*, 301.

7 Takenaka et al., "Evolution of Bioluminescence in Marine Planktonic Copepods," 1669.

8 Komatsu, *Introduction to Yokai Culture*, 128.

9 Willis, "A Bibliography of the 'Ghost Fungus,' *Pleurotus nidiformis (Berk.) Sacc*," 213.

10 Zahl, "The Secrets of Nature's Night Lights," 45.

11 Zahl, "Bizarre World of the Fungi," *National Geographic* (1965), cited in Sivinski, "Phototropism, Bioluminescence, and the Diptera," 288.

12 Johnson, *Bioluminescence*, 474; Buck, Buck, and Case, "Control of Flashing in Fireflies," 277; Seliger et al., "The Spectral Distribution of Firefly Light," 95.

13 Beman, Arrigo, and Matson, "Agricultural Runoff Fuels Large Phytoplankton Blooms," 211; Heisler et al., "Eutrophication and Harmful Algal Blooms," 3.

14 Barton et al., "Anthropogenic Climate Change Drives Shift and Shuffle," 2968; Barton et al., "On the Roles of Cell Size and Trophic Strategy," 263.

15 Fleming et al., "Review of Florida Red Tide and Human Health Effects," 233; Richlen et al., "The Catastrophic 2008-2009 Red Tide in the Arabian Gulf Region," 163; Hallegraeff and Bolch, "Unprecedented Toxic Algal Blooms Impact on Tasmanian Seafood Industry," 143.

16 Aversa et al.,"Under Water," 87.

036

037

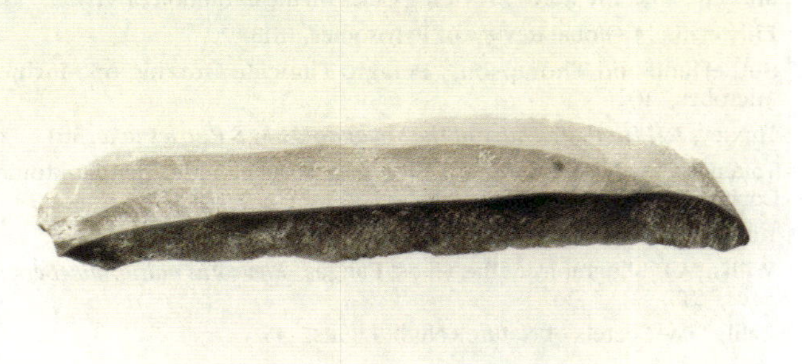

036
Neolithic representation of solar
symbols.

038
A flint shard found in Uadi Masauda,
Libya. Undated. 2.865 cm × 0.806 cm.

037
A flint shard found in Qasr-I
Abu Nasr, Iran. Sasanian period,
ca. 300-700 CE. 7.29 cm.

ORIGINS

Fire

OF LIGHT

Fire's profound role in human culture extends beyond mere survival, intertwining deeply with mythology, creativity, and societal development. It has been revered throughout history not only as a life-sustaining tool but as a symbol of renewal and transformation—as told by the myth of the Phoenix, which is reborn from its ashes every 500 years.

Fire has also played a central role in communal activities. It allowed early humans to extend their days, providing warmth and light for gatherings around campfires and hearths, where stories were shared, and knowledge was passed down through generations. Its ability to transform materials—turning clay into bricks and sand into glass—fundamentally altered our interactions with the natural world. And thus began the creation of other essential tools and crafts, from pottery to metal tools and weapons.

As French philosopher Gaston Bachelard noted, "If all that changes slowly may be explained by life, all that changes quickly is explained by fire."[17] Fire can alter landscapes through practices like burn agriculture, an act of dominating and reshaping ecosystems through which humans place themselves in a powerful position at the top of the food chain. Fire is not only a tool, but a shapeshifter, and a profound agent of both change and continuity.[18]

038

039

039
"It shines in Paradise. It burns in Hell. It is gentleness and torture. It is cookery and it is apocalypse. It is pleasure for the good child sitting prudently by the hearth; yet it punishes any disobedience when the child wishes to play too close to its flames. It is well-being and it is respect. It is a tutelary and a terrible divinity, both good and bad. It can contradict itself; thus it is one the principles of universal explanation."[19] – Gaston Bachelard

040

040
Hearths and campfires have acted
as social hubs, strengthened a
sense of community, and fostered
social bonds.

041

Painting in the Cave of Beasts, in the Western Desert of Egypt, which features Neolithic rock paintings with over 5000 figures. The flickering, dim light of fire transformed the appearance of cave walls, making them breathe and seem alive with moving shadows, enhancing the visual impact of the paintings.

042

Hands painted in the Cuevas de las Manos upon Rio Pinturas, near the town of Perito Moreno, Argentina. The illumination of dark caves marked an early chapter in early human creativity and expression, particularly during the Palaeolithic era, spanning from 30,000 to 10,000 BCE. Creating cave paintings required lighting; the simplest solution was a torch of burning wood. However, as torches burned out quickly, they evolved into more durable lamps fuelled by animal fat or tallow, with wicks made from materials like lichen, juniper, or grass.

043

Hearths have long provided a central gathering place for storytelling, which not only entertains but also reinforces group identity and offers protection by uniting individuals against external threats.

041

042

043

AROUND THE COUNCIL FIRE—THE YOUNG BRAVE'S SPEECH.—Drawn by E. A. Abbey, from a Sketch by Theo. R. Davis.—[See Page 394.]

Fire's applications extended to foraging across landscapes, maintaining social and domestic hearths for protection and cooking, and technological processes like pottery firing.

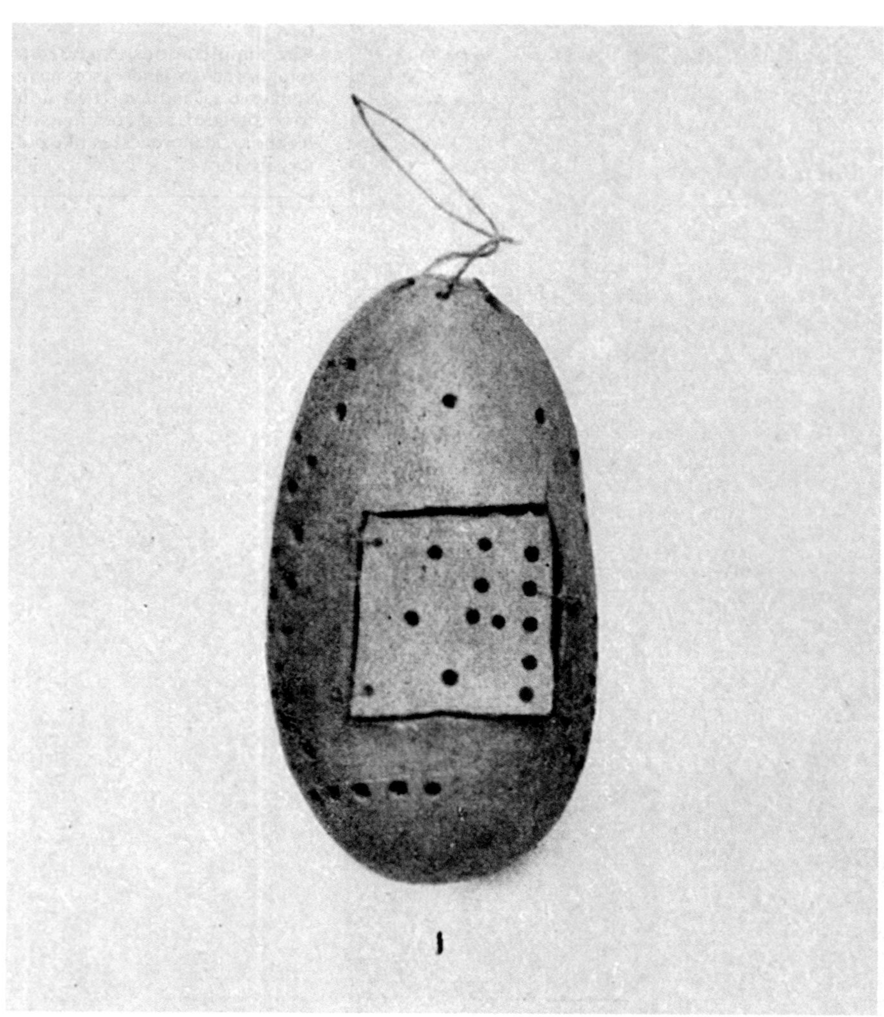

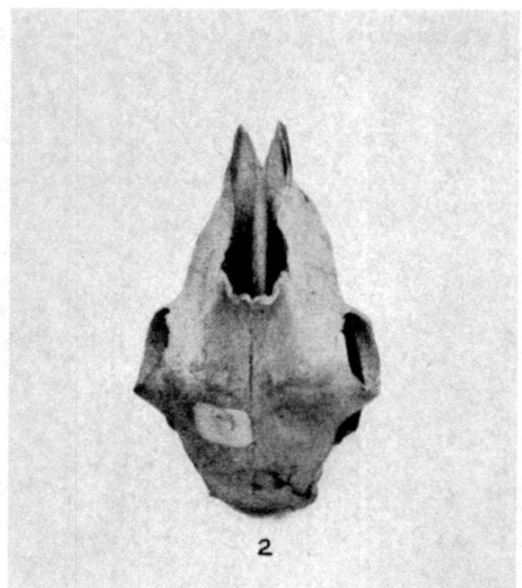

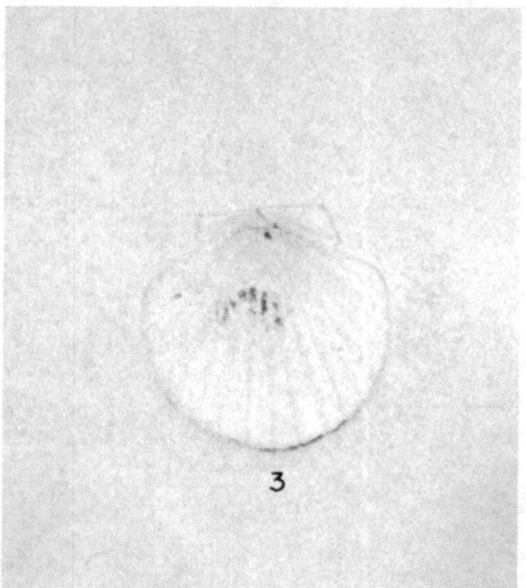

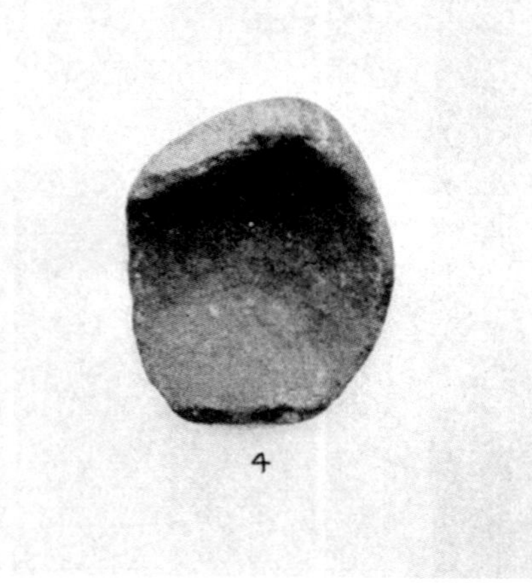

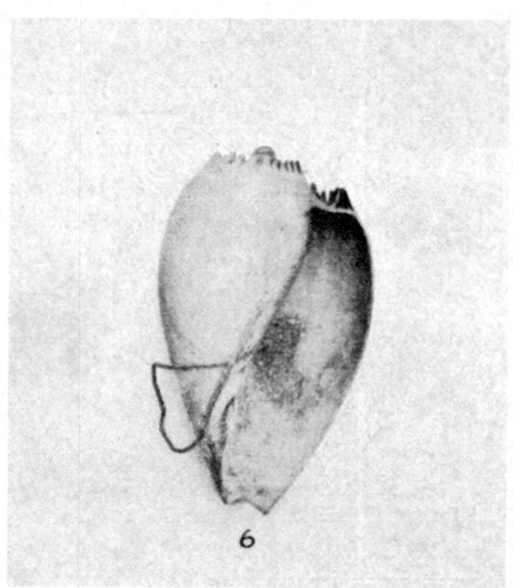

045

No. 1.

Firefly lamp. Perforated tree gourd in which fireflies are confined for light. Caribbean.

No. 2.

Lamp. Made from the skull of a sheep.

No. 3.

Lamp. Pecten shell with oil and wick of rush pith mounted on a forked branch. Japan.

No. 4.

Lamp. Unworked beach stone, with concavity, supplied with fibre wick and oil. Alaska.

No. 5.

Lamp. Hollowed beach stone with moss wick arranged along one edge. Alaska.

No. 6.

Lamp. Fusus shell suspended. Orkney Islands.

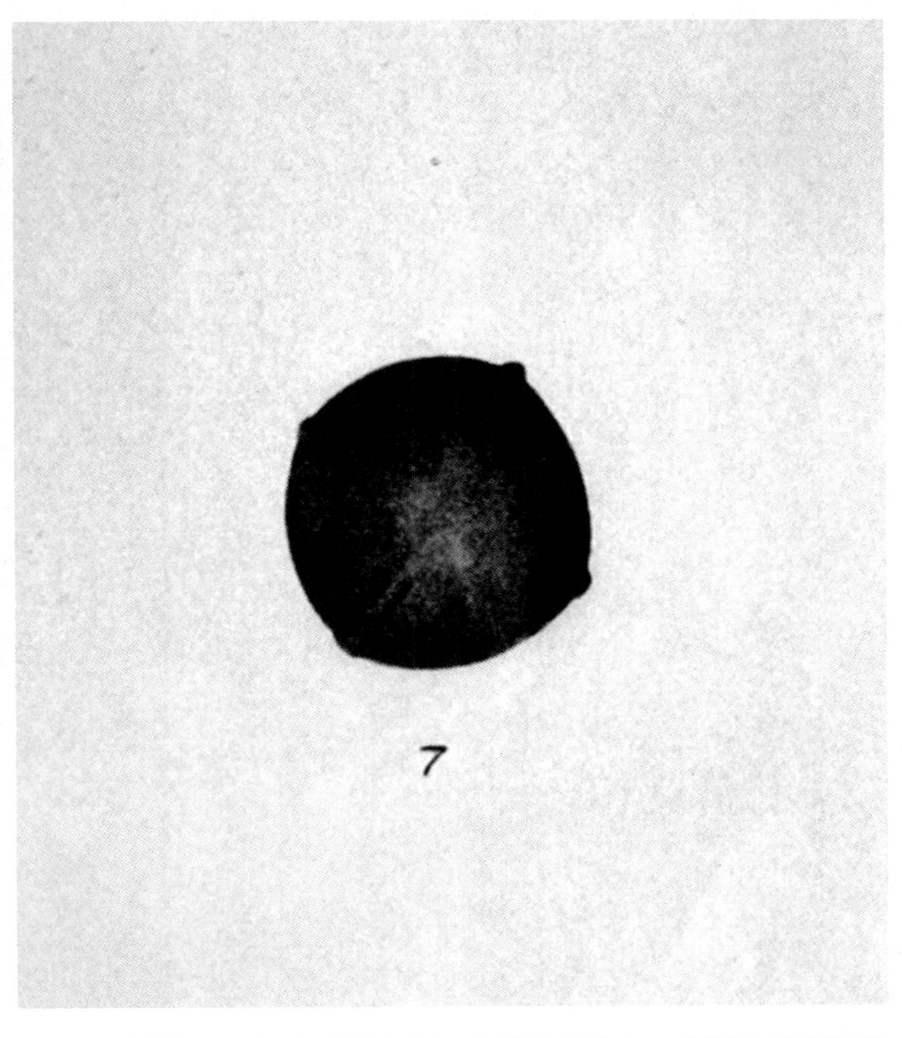

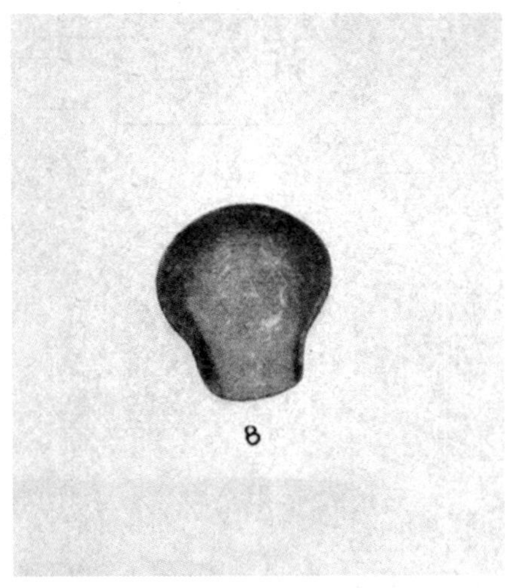

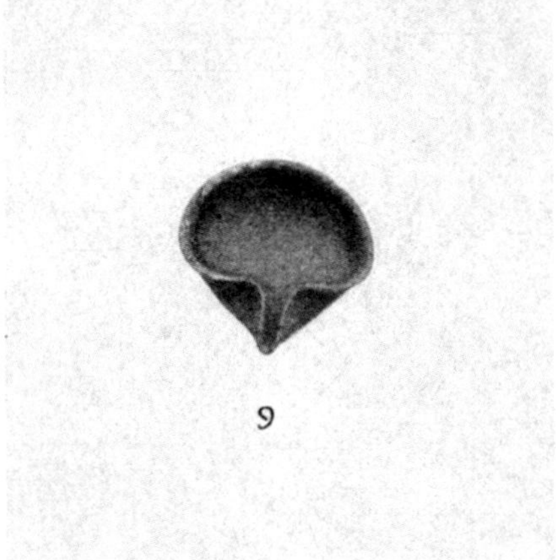

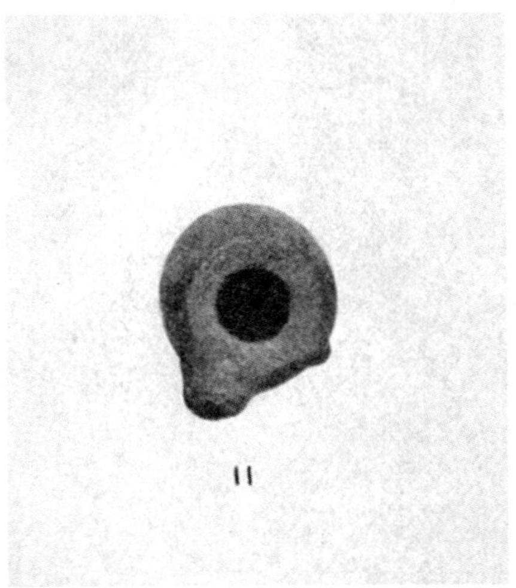

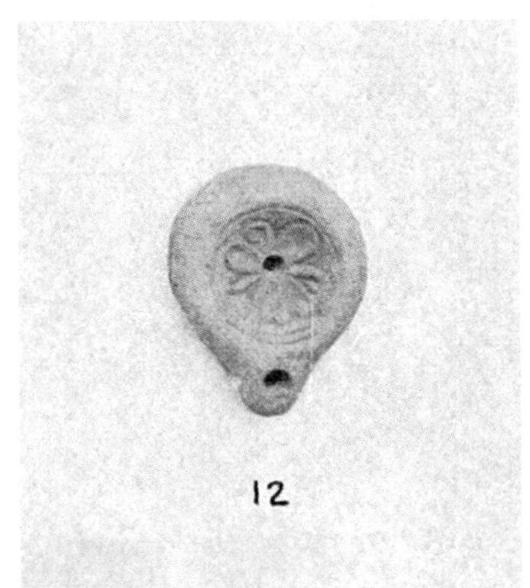

No. 7.

Lamp. Saucer with shallow grooves for wick. India.

No. 8.

Lamp. Terra-cotta saucer. India.

No. 9.

Lamp. Saucer with pinched-up spout for wick. Syria.

No. 10.

Lamp. Stone with pointed spout. India.

No. 11.

Lamp. Terra cotta. Reservoir almost closed over; spout for wick. Roman.

No. 12.

Lamp. Terra cotta. Reservoir closed over; spout for wick. Roman.

046

According to Charles Darwin, the mastery of fire is one of humanity's greatest discoveries, second only to language.[20]

047

Evidence suggests that fire has been present on earth for 400 million years.[21] Through this time it has deeply influenced the evolution of plants and terrestrial ecosystems, as well as played a role in regulating atmospheric oxygen.[22] Current insight into the historical role of fire primarily derives from charcoal found in the fossil record.[23]

048

Human culture is shaped by the ability to harness and control fire, which has impacted diets, social structures, and ritual practices. Approximately 1.7 million years ago, Homo erectus began to cook food and build a diet, making it easier to digest and unlocking nutritional benefits that were previously inaccessible.[24] The metamorphic effect of fire on both land and bodies is captured in this series titled *Heatwave* by Ibrahim Rashid.

047

048

[17] Bachelard, *The Psychoanalysis of Fire*, 7.

[18] Pyne, "Fire in the Mind," 2.

[19] Bachelard, *The Psychoanalysis of Fire*, 7.

[20] Darwin, *The Descent of Man in Relation to Sex*, 137.

[21] Scott, "The Pre-Quaternary History of Fire," 281; Belcher, Collinson, and Scott, "A 450 Million Year Record Fire," 352.

[22] Scott and Glasspool, "The Diversification of Paleozoic Fire Systems," 10861; Glasspool and Scott, "Phanerozoic Concentrations of Atmospheric Oxygen," 627; Glasspool et al., "The Impact of Fire on the Late Paleozoic Earth System," 1.

[23] Rimmer et al., "The Rise of Fire," 713.

[24] Wrangham et al., "The Raw and the Stolen," 586; Wrangham, "Control of Fire in the Paleolithic," S305.

049

049

An inscribed brick found in Nippur, an ancient Sumerian city about 200 kilometres south of modern Baghdad, Iraq. Stamped with ancient Sumerian script, it includes the (✳) symbol, a sun or star-shaped ideogram for divinity that often represents the god Anu, symbolising sky or heaven. Nippur served as the religious epicentre of Mesopotamia from 3000 to 2000 BCE. The inscription identifies it as from the time of Ur-Nammu, who ruled during the Ur III period of 2112 to 2095 BCE. Such bricks were used to memorialise rulers who undertook large architectural projects like restoring or rebuilding temples.

050

The Temple of Kom Ombo, part of the Aswan Governorate in Upper Egypt, was constructed during the Ptolemaic dynasty from 180 to 147 BCE. Decorating the temple's façade is a winged sun.

ORIGINS

Interpretations

OF LIGHT

"While myths never explain the facts which they attempt to elucidate, they incidentally throw light on the mental condition of the men who invented them; and, after all, the mind of man is not less worthy of investigation than the phenomena of nature, from which, indeed, it cannot be ultimately discriminated." [25] – James George Frazer

Myths and their fantastical elements often depict supernatural phenomena such as talking animals, human transfiguration, and gods and heroes wielding extraordinary powers. These narratives do not challenge the principles of reason but rather use the tangible elements of the world as constructs to convey deeper meanings and explore universal truths.

A common motif in many stories of diverse historical and geographical contexts is the influence of the sun. It is frequently revered as a symbol of creation and termination, and the cycle of day and night can be understood as a metaphor for enlightenment and visibility. Ancient cultures often personified the sun as a vigilant observer, akin to an all-seeing eye, reflected in the depictions of deities.

050

054

The Nebra Sky Disc, which dates to around 1600 BCE during the Middle Bronze Age, was buried after 200 years of use and found by treasure hunters in Mittelberg, Germany, in 1999. This artefact is a bronze disc that features symbols of the sun, moon, and stars, suggesting a mythical representation of the universe. It is believed that the central full circle symbolises either the sun or the full moon. It provides a glimpse into the astronomical understanding and artistic expression of the skies during the Nordic Bronze Age.

051

052

053

051

The Golden Sunbird, an iconic artefact from the ancient Shu civilisation, represents a critical part of the cultural heritage and modern identity of Chengdu, China. Discovered in the early twenty-first century during construction at the Jinsha archeological site, the gold leaf artefact weighs 20 grams and is 0.2 millimetres thick. It features a central sun pattern with twelve points and four birds circling it counterclockwise, symbolising the sun worship that was vital to the Shu people—the sun was believed to be carried across the sky by a giant bird. In ancient Chinese mythology, Wu or Jinwu, the three-legged crow, is described in the ancient text *Shan Hai Jing* as residing in and representing the sun.

052

A French pilgrim's badge with a human sun face, from the fifteenth century.

053

Discovered in Cwmystwyth, Wales, the Banc Ty'nddôl sun disc, which dates to 2450-2150 BCE, is Wales's earliest gold artefact. It was likely part of a funerary garment, symbolising the sun's life-giving power.

055

The Sun Chariot was discovered in 1902 in a former peat bog in Zealand, Denmark. Its creation dates to around 1400 BCE, during the Early Bronze Age, and features a horse pulling a disc, possibly symbolising the sun's movement across the sky. It is a significant find from the Scandinavian Bronze Age, when sun worship was central to religious practice.

055

056

The stele of Naram-Sin, dating from the Akkadian period of 2254 to 2218 BCE, was discovered in 1898 by French archeologist Jacques de Morgan at the Susa acropolis, in modern-day Iran. The artefact is unique for its depiction of a battle across three diagonal layers, rather than the typical horizontal registers common to the period. The top layer portrays Naram-Sin, grandson of Sargon, celebrated for unifying Mesopotamia around 2350 BCE. He is shown looking up toward representations of the sun and a star, thought to symbolise gods, and likely including the sun god Shamash. The stele was originally placed in Sippar, in modern-day Iraq, a city sacred to Shamash, the sun god.

057

In December 1790, during excavations for the Plaza Mayor in Mexico City, workers found a large boulder with intricate carvings, revealed to be an ancient Aztec monolith concealed by Christian conquistadors. This monument symbolised Aztec power and has evolved into a symbol of Mexican national identity. Known as the Sun Stone or Piedra del Sol, it illustrates the Aztec understanding of time as cyclical and details the interaction between gods and humans. While it functions as a calendar, it may also have had a ceremonial purpose—at the centre of the stone is the sun god Tonatiuh. Originally, the stone was painted in blue, red, green, and yellow.

058

A French pilgrim's badge in the form of a solar disc, from the fourteenth or fifteenth century.

059

A Babylonian kudurru ("boundary stone"), from the reign of King Melisipak, 1186-1172 BCE.

057

058

059

060

A scene from a sixteenth-century play depicting the life of Saint Euphrasia involves a figure with horns, dressed in a monastic robe, leading a nun from a building. The nun is touched by a hand that emerges from the sun, possibly symbolising divine intervention or guidance. This figure could be interpreted as the devil in disguise.

061

The emblem of the Majapahit dynasty, dating from 1293 to 1527 CE, incorporates a sun motif with seven points. This specific number of points is rare as it presents a greater challenge in carving compared to the more geometrically straightforward six or eight points.

060

061

062
The winged sun disc is an ancient motif common to several cultures across the Near East, including Egypt, Anatolia, Syria, Palestine, and Mesopotamia. Its frequent use demonstrates the transfer and borrowing of visual symbols, cultural meanings, and knowledge through art. This carved ivory plaque, dating from 800 to 700 BCE during the reign of Assurnasirpal II at Nimrud, the Assyrian capital in modern-day Iraq, features a bearded figure holding the stem of a lotus plant, with a protective winged sun disc hovering above. Such reliefs were common decorative elements in Assyrian royal furniture.

063
A woodblock with a representation of the rising red sun, created in 1824. In traditional Japanese landscape paintings, the new year is often symbolised by a vibrant red orb representing the rising sun. In Japanese, Japan is called "Nihon" or "Nippon," meaning "origin of the sun." Derived from the Chinese characters 日本, the name originates from the Chinese term "Yih-pen" ("sun-origin"), referring to Japan's geographical location East of China.[26]

064
The Stela of Aafenmut, dating from 924 to 889 BCE in Ancient Egypt, features a wooden panel crowned by the solar barque, symbolising the sun's journey across the sky. The sun god Ra, considered the primary force of nature, is portrayed as a falcon-headed mummy. The Egyptians closely observed the sun's daily and nightly cycles, representing its passage with symbols like the scarab and the solar disc. This cosmic view held particular significance in Ancient Egyptian civilisation, informing everything from the Nile's sedimentation cycles to its destructive heatwaves.[27]

062

063

064

065

065

The Ancient Greek sun god Helios is often shown with a radiant crown, embodying the view of the sun as an omniscient witness. This print, created by Flemish engraver Adriaen Collaert between 1580 and 1584, depicts Helios holding a salamander in one hand and a phoenix in the other, both symbolising fire and rebirth.

066

The universe is depicted as a celestial globe with Earth at its centre, encircled by concentric rings that denote the four elements, the known planets of mediaeval and Renaissance cosmology (including the Sun), and the zodiac constellations. Overseeing this is God, enveloped in celestial light and carried by seraphim. Adjacent to the world map (*mappamondo*), is the Garden of Paradise, marked by four rivers flowing from its base.

066

067
In *Persian Manuscript 373*, the sun is depicted as a four-armed figure seated cross-legged on a throne, flanked by two lions. Surrounding the deity's face are two *nimbi*, which are radiating halos typically used to signify sanctity or divine presence in artworks.

068
Louis XIV, King of France, is depicted as a faceless monk holding a torch, with the sun—his emblem—shining only from within his hood. Part of a series depicting the King and his court, this image reflects his early use of the sun as a personal symbol, representing Apollo, the god of peace, the arts, and the giver of life. Louis XIV not only styled himself as a peace-restoring warrior and patron of the arts but also dressed as the sun in a 1662 ballet, earning him the lasting nickname *le Roi-Soleil*. The Palace of Versailles in France further embodies this iconography, filled with sun-related allegorical motifs integrated with royal portraits and symbols.

068

069

Amaterasu, a key solar deity in the Shinto religion, is closely linked to Japan's imperial family and revered as a divine protector and ancestor. Her influence is profound in modern Japanese folklore and cultural traditions, where she embodies the sun and is often honoured at various shrines. These sites are known as Amateru or Amateru-mitama shrines, and they preserve many ancient solar rituals.

071

Irworobongdo is a traditional Korean folding screen showing a stylised landscape with a sun and moon above five peaks, historically positioned behind the royal throne of the Joseon dynasty. This screen is an interpretation of cosmic balance and royal authority. It is believed that the sun represents the king, and the moon symbolises the queen, together embodying the forces that govern the universe. When the king would sit before the screen, it represented his central role in the universe, both emanating from it and returning to him.

072

"The Surya (The Sun)
His bright rays bear him up aloft, the god who knoweth all that lives. The constellations pass away, like thieves, together with their beams, before the all-beholding sun. Swift and beautiful art thou, O Surya, maker of the light." [28]

A hymn from the *Rig Veda*, the first and oldest known Vedic Sanskrit text, which documents the foundation for Hindu beliefs.

070

070

In Greek mythology, Prometheus, a Titan associated with forethought and a deity of fire, is known for his act of defiance against the Olympian gods: he stole fire, symbolising knowledge and civilisation, and bestowed it upon humanity. One myth says he took the fire from the workshop of Hephaestus, another says it was from the hearth of the gods on Mount Olympus, and yet another suggests Prometheus lit his torch directly from the sun. His gift of fire to humans is seen as a double-edged sword: it brought technology and progress but also introduced the potential for damage and exploitation.

072

073
In this Hittite pendant dating from 1400 to 1200 BCE, a goddess with a sun-like headdress is seated and holding a child on her lap. The iconography suggests she may represent Arinna, the major sun goddess in Hittite mythology.

074
Tawa, the sun spirit and creator in the mythology of the Hopi, a Native American tribe, is believed to have crafted the so-called First World from the expanse of Topkella, or endless space.[29] This mural represents the sun disc mask and is adorned with eagle-wing feathers and a fringe of red horsehair. It is challenging to pinpoint a uniform set of beliefs for the Hopi since their mythology varies significantly across different regions, with varied renditions of myths having been developed over centuries.

075

Long winter months in Scandinavia are embraced with the notion of *hygge*.[30] The term is a concept that functions as a verb, a noun, and an adjective. It involves creating a warm and intimate atmosphere fostered by a comfortable and cosy setting. This practice is deeply embedded in the lighting culture of the region, which helps mitigate grey and dark seasons. Lights are typically dimmed to induce calm before bedtime, or light is emanated from windows after dark as a welcoming gesture and a way to enhance community bond.

075

LVX VENIT IN MVNDVN ET DILEXERVNT HOMINES MAGIS TENEBRAS QVAM LVCEM. IO. 3. 19

ANTRVM PLATONICVM.

HL. SPIEGEL FIGVRARI ET SCVLPI CVRAVIT. AC DOCTISS. ORNATISSQZ. D.PET. PAAW IN LVGDVN. ACAD. PROFESSORI MEDICO D.D.

076

077

076

Plato's *Allegory of the Cave* is a pivotal philosophical text that explores the themes of knowledge and ignorance. The story portrays prisoners who have been confined in a cave from birth, where their only experience of the world is through shadows cast on a cave wall by objects passing in front of a fire behind them. These shadows form their perceived reality. When one prisoner escapes and experiences the outside world, he realises that the shadows are mere representations of real objects that have been passing in front of the cave's mouth. This liberated prisoner gains true understanding and returns to inform the other prisoners, but faces difficulty convincing them, having only known shadowy illusions. The allegory argues that understanding the truth requires overcoming deceptive appearances and suggests that this enlightenment can be challenging to attain and communicate to those still in the dark.

077

Junichiro Tanizaki, in his seminal 1933 work *In Praise of Shadows*, critiques the intrusion of Western lighting techniques into Japanese spaces, arguing they disrupt the traditional aesthetic that favours subtlety and depth. Tanizaki cherishes how darkness magnifies the intimate quality of traditional Japanese rooms, which rely on the interplay of light and shadow, contrasting sharply with what he sees as the excessive ornamentation of Western interiors. He notes that darkness and shadows are essential elements of space, suggesting that both the presence of light and its absence are necessary to enhance human experience within a space.

078

A vivid biblical creation scene from the *Book of Genesis*, crafted during the Renaissance, a period marked by a renewed interest in humanism and naturalism. Part of a larger series in The Sistine Chapel, the fresco captures the divine act of creation, reflecting Christian theology that emphasises an orderly universe designed by God. It shows the formation of plants and the creation of celestial bodies like the Sun and Moon.

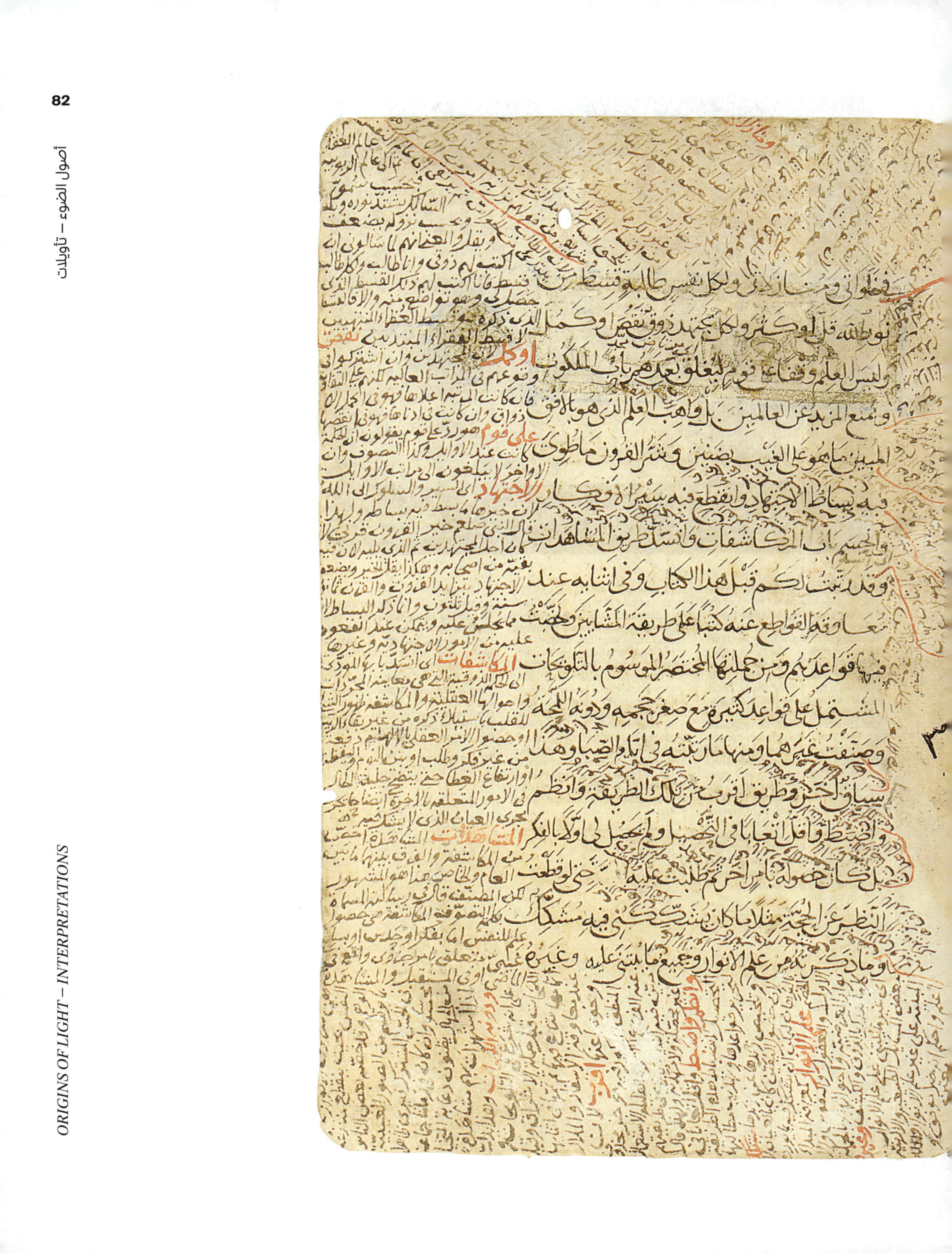

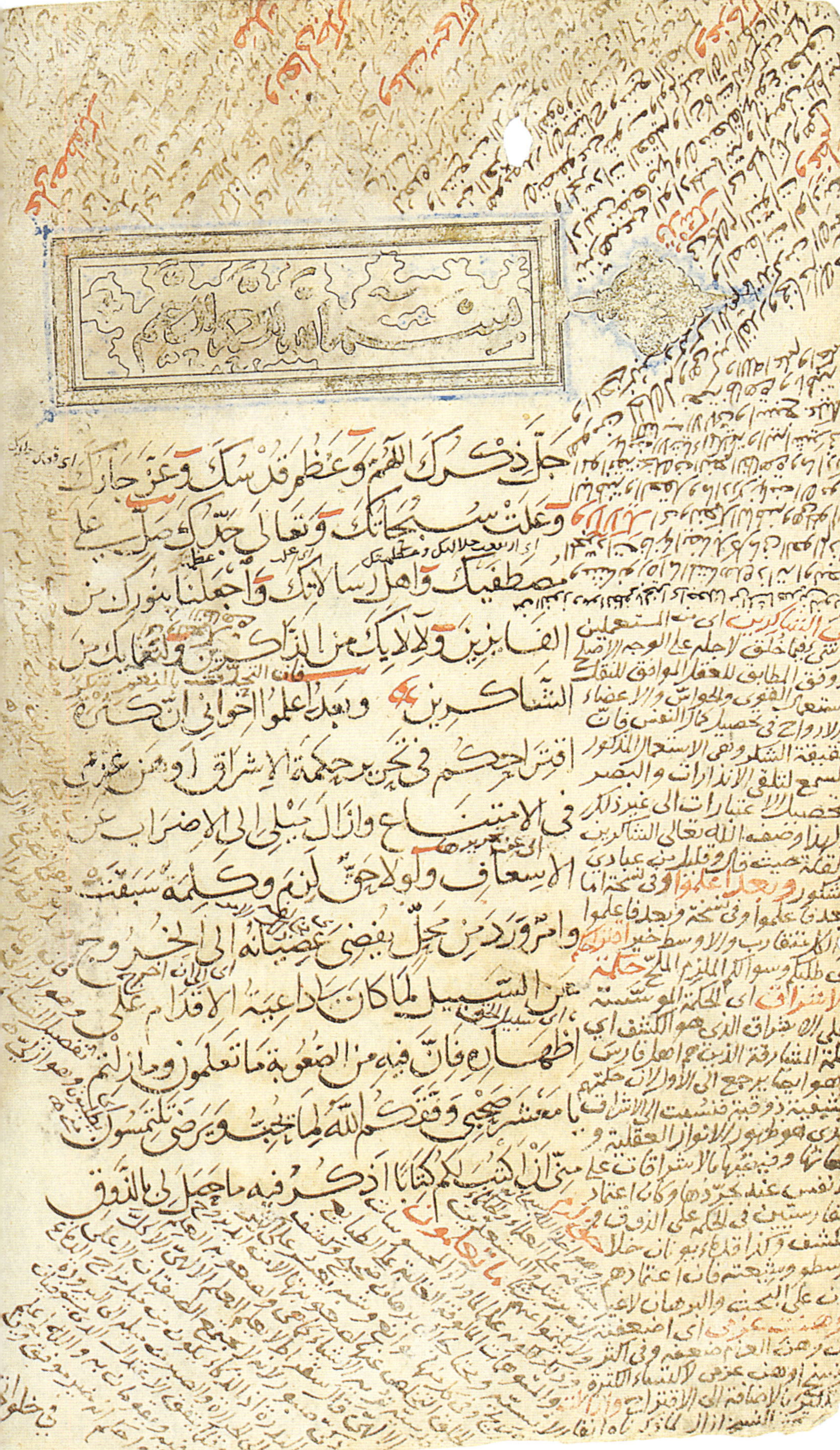

Persian philosopher Shihab al-Din al-Suhrawardi developed Illuminationism, a theory that positions light as the fundamental reality. He contends that light is self-evident and all-encompassing, and defines reality through degrees of light and darkness, without any causal relationships between them. Suhrawardi's metaphysical hierarchy, inspired by Neoplatonism, places light and its varying intensities at the core of existence, suggesting that direct experiences of light provide true knowledge, rather than discursive reasoning.[31] This philosophical framework emphasises the immediate and intuitive over the rational. He produced two key works, *Hayakal al-Nur (The Shape of Light)* and *Hikmat al-Ishraq (The Philosophy of Illumination)*. Suhrawardi views the world in modes of illumination, and summarised this ontological structure as follows:

"A thing either is light and luminosity in its own reality or is not light and luminosity in its own reality… Light is divided into light that is a state of something else (the accidental light) and light that is not a state of something else (the incorporeal or pure light). That which is not light in its own reality is divided into that which is independent of a locus (the dusky substance) and that which is a state of something else (the dark state)."[32] – Suhrawardi

[25] Frazer, *Myths of the Origin of Fire*, 1.

[26] Garbuny, "Japan: Regeneration," 499.

[27] Javadi, "How the World Views Solar Deities," 7.

[28] Laughlin, "The Surya (The Sun)," 11.

[29] Courlander, *The Fourth World of the Hopis*, 17.

[30] Schulte-Römer, "Research in the Dark," 216.

[31] Marcotte, "Suhrawardi," *Stanford Encyclopedia of Philosophy*, revised April 4, 2012
https://plato.stanford.edu/Archives/Spr2013/entries/suhrawardi/.

[32] Suhrawardi, cited by Morkoç, "In Between the Mind and the Heart."

SURVEYING LIGHT

*TRAVELLING OBELISKS, ANCIENT SUNDIALS,
OBSERVATORIES, AND THE SPEED OF LIGHT:
PART 2 TRAVELS THROUGH TIME AND SPACE
TO EXPLORE EARLY DISCOVERIES IN OPTICS.*

رصد الضوء

080
In Egypt's Valley of the Kings, a team from the University of Basel unearthed one of the earliest sundials recorded in Egypt, dating from 1300 to 1200 BCE. The flat limestone slab has black semicircular lines divided into twelve segments, and the central hole used to hold a bolt to cast shadows marking the hours.

081
A Roman hemispherical sundial, over 2000 years old, at the Side Archeological Museum in Turkey. The device is shaped like a quarter sphere with a gnomon whose shadow marks the time differently across the seasons. It was gifted by Marcus Novius Tubula, a politician who served in the Tribune of the Plebs, the first office of the Roman state open to commoners, which throughout the Republic's history protected the interests of the plebeian class. Tubula's name is etched in Latin on the base of the sundial, and an adjacent inscription on the curved edge records that he commissioned the public work as a commemoration of his electoral victory in his hometown.[37] Like obelisks, this marker of time not only served a purpose but also symbolised power and prestige.

080

SURVEYING

Orientations

LIGHT

|

"He opened the gates on both sides [of the ecliptic],
A lock he made strong on the left and the right,
In the midst thereof he places the zenith."[33]

The ordering of the heavens
and the stars from solar god Marduk.
The Creation Tablets.

081

The words *ishraq* إشراق and *mashriq* مشرق originate from the shared root *sh-rq*, which "sharq" شرق identifies as the geographic East. *Ishraq* إشراق translates to "Enlightenment," while *mashriq* مشرق refers to "the rising," or the first light emitted by the sun at dawn. Persian philosopher and doctor Ibn Sina (also known as Avicenna) was the first to use *mashriq* مشرق in a philosophical context. He referred to it as *al-hikmat al-mashriqiyya*, which means "Eastern Philosophy." [34] Here, cardinal East is synonymous with revival and renewal due to the sunrise, and it holds particular importance in religious contexts where structures and rituals are oriented to capture early morning light. In contrast, cardinal West is typically associated with the afterlife, shadows, and the setting sun. [35]

Orientation has always been and remains crucial to religious rituals, even in political and social contexts—such as the direction in which a priest or a worshipper stands or sits. [36] The creation of instruments such as obelisks, sundials, and astrolabes therefore enabled early civilisations not only to measure time and to situate themselves on earth, but also to link the earthly with the divine.

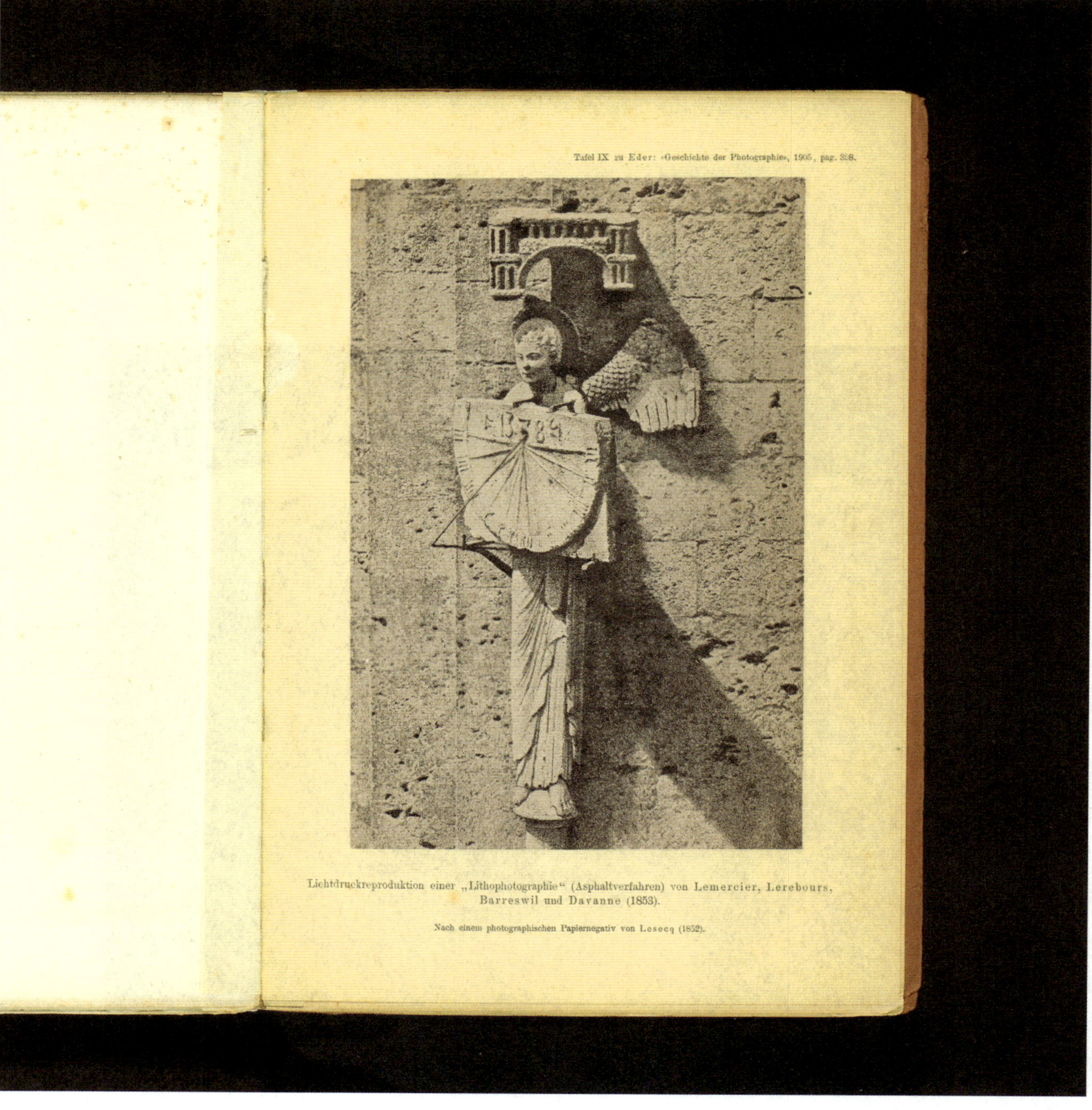

Tafel IX zu Eder: «Geschichte der Photographie», 1905, pag. 308.

Lichtdruckreproduktion einer „Lithophotographie" (Asphaltverfahren) von Lemercier, Lerebours, Barreswil und Davanne (1853).

Nach einem photographischen Papiernegativ von Lesecq (1852).

084

082
The Chartres Cathedral sundial, created between 1900 and 1905, in France.

____

083
The Lateran Obelisk as depicted circa 1600, behind the Basilica di San Giovanni in Laterano, in Rome.

____

084
Cleopatra's Needle was repositioned in Central Park, New York, in 1882. Originating circa 3500 BCE, obelisks were primarily erected in honour of sun deities, but they often commemorated pharaohs or marked sacred spaces. Beyond religious significance, they functioned as timekeepers, casting shadows that marked the ground as the sun moved to help estimate the passage of time over a day. After the decline of Egyptian and Ptolemaic rule, the Romans relocated many obelisks to Rome, installing them in prestigious locations as symbols of religious devotion and imperial conquest. They became known for their grand scale, rarity, and extensive recorded histories—their hieroglyphic inscriptions have been studied over centuries.

____

085

085
Obelisks were called _tekhenu_ by the ancient Egyptians, meaning "to pierce the sky."[38] The later term obelisk comes from the Greek _obeliskos_, meaning "a pointed tool." More and more obelisks were relocated to Europe after the arrival of French and British forces in Egypt in the early nineteenth century. Dubbed the Cleopatra's Needles, displaced obelisks were positioned at significant sites of important cities and recognised as landmarks.

____

DISEMBARKING THE OBE[LISK]

Copyright, 1881, by HARROUN & BIERSTADT, New Yo[rk]

Plate XX

086

"His Majesty has ordered the commissioning of multitudinous works for the making of very great obelisks and great and wondrous statues in the name of His Majesty. He made great barges for transporting them, and ships crews to match them (for) ferrying them from the quarry while the officials and transport-men hastened and his eldest son was before them doing what is beneficial for His Majesty." [39]

Inscriptions on an Aswan rock stela.

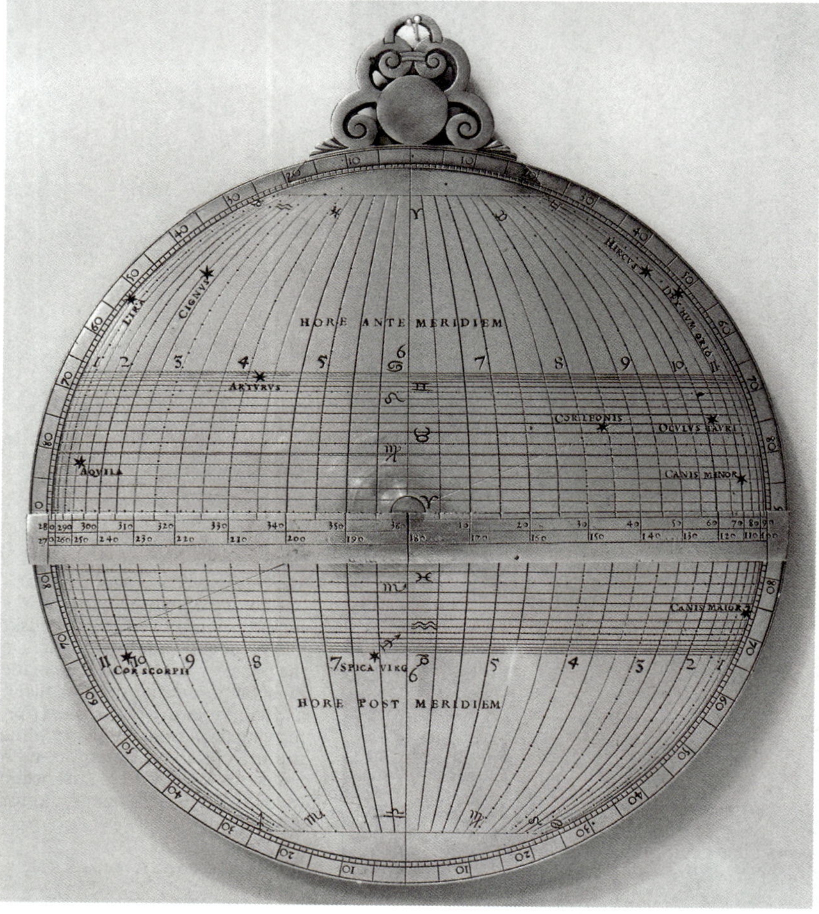

087

"From the small hole (in the alidade) the sight becomes clear (and) the secret of the sun becomes obvious like the daylight."[40] – Abū 'l-Hasan Yamin al-Din Khusrau, known as Amīr Khusrau, in *Ayina-I Iskandarī (Alexandrine Mirror)*.

088

Astrolabes were widely used across the Islamic world by the late ninth century, from Spain to India, and later adopted in Christian Europe. Astrolabes are crucial navigational and astronomical tools that model the movement of stars around the celestial pole. The device consists of a solid base known as the mater, which contains two plates covered by a circular star chart or rete (referred to as *ankabut* in Islamic regions) and is equipped with a sighting vane, or alidade, on the reverse side, all fastened together by a central pin. This early example from North Africa, dating to the ninth century, is distinguished by its rete that marks stars identified in Babylonian-Hellenistic catalogues and by pre-Islamic Bedouin names. These names were crucial for navigation, providing practical alternatives to the classical constellations predominantly used in Islamic astronomy.[41]

088

089

A solid walnut astrolabe-quadrant, created in the Ottoman Empire in 1840-1841, that is portable and versatile, with details like prayer times. It depicts a two-dimensional celestial sphere, simplified to a quadrant format, with a moveable bead on a plumb line that allows for recording observations.

090

A mediaeval quadrant found in Buckinghamshire, England.

089

090

091

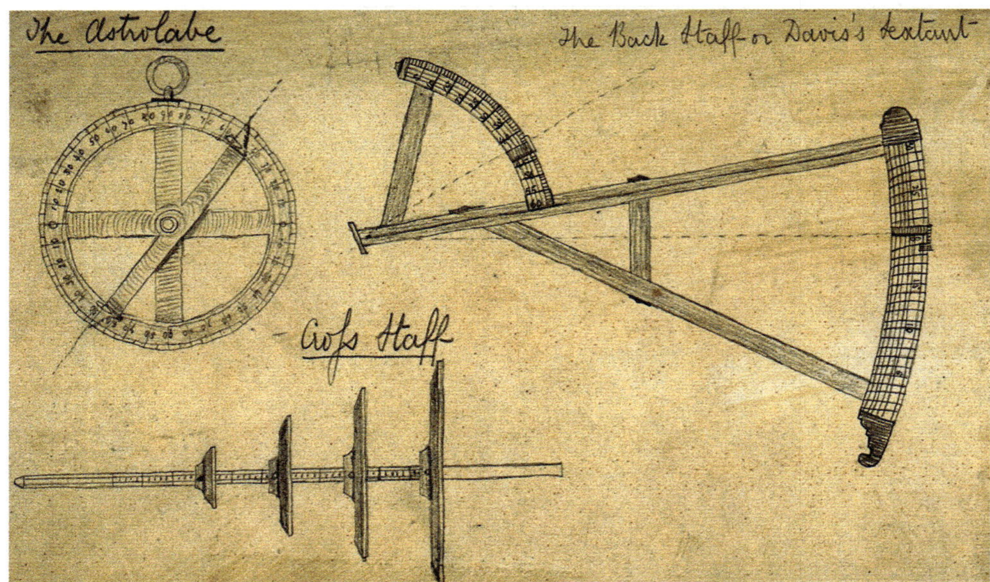

091

An astrolabe, a cross-staff, and a back-staff (Davis's sextant), as illustrated in 1624 by English mathematician and geometer Edmund Gunter. These tools of discovery were essential for early navigators to determine latitude and map their routes across uncharted waters.

092

An astrolabe depicted in *Kitab-i viladat-i Iskandar (The Book of the Birth of Iskandar* or *Iskandar Horoscope)*, a 1411 manuscript featuring the horoscope of Timurid prince Iskandar Sultan. Authored by his court astrologer, the document is among the most exquisite Middle Eastern mediaeval horoscopes.

093

The mariner's sextant is crafted to precisely measure the altitude of celestial bodies from the unstable environment of a ship's deck.[42] The first known sextant was created around 1757 by John Bird, a renowned maker of scientific instruments.

092

094

American Lieutenant Commander Ray Schoppe, measuring horizontal sextant angle during inshore ship hydrographic operations.

095

Taking sextant angles for positioning.

096

Seated woman with enormous wig dressed by a French hair dresser. Her husband, a naval officer, is holding a sextant to his eye, measuring the altitude of her hair.

أركيولوجيا الضوء

093

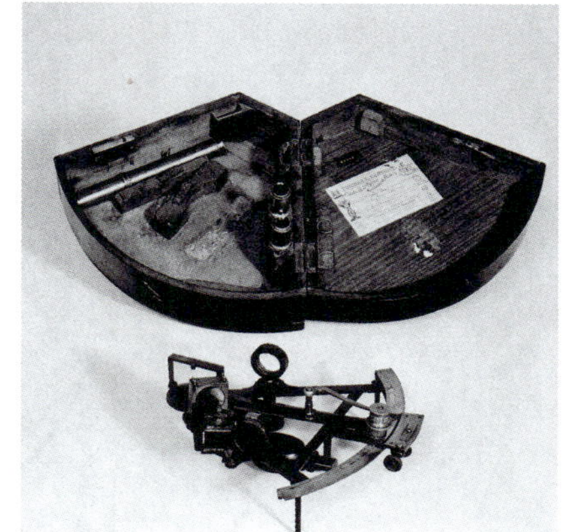

094

095

096

097

097

Astronomers manipulating a huge armillary sphere and tools for measuring longitude and latitude. As shown in the miniature of the manuscript *Sehinsahname (The Story of the King of Kings)*, an epic poem by the Persian poet Ala ad-din Mansur-Shirazi.

098

In 1853, British archeologist Austen Henry Layard uncovered a 3000-year-old lens during his excavation of the palace of Assyrian king Ashurbanipal in Nimrud, in modern-day Iraq. This artefact, often referred to as the Nimrud lens or the Layard lens, has a plano-convex shape measuring 35 × 41 millimetres in diameter and 6 millimetres in thickness. While it is possible that this lens served as a basic magnifying glass, its exact purpose remains unknown.

099

The Antikythera Mechanism is an ancient Greek device discovered in 1901 that demonstrates an early attempt to mechanise mathematical and scientific predictions. The calculator merges Babylonian astronomical cycles with Greek geometric knowledge to compute the positions and phases of the Sun, Moon, eclipse timings, and the Olympiad cycle.[43] Though only one-third of the original artefact is intact, including thirty corroded bronze gear wheels, its intricate mechanical components still offer critical insights down to the millimetre scale. The thousands of tiny inscriptions within the object were unread for over 2000 years[44]—it remains somewhat of a mystery for modern scholars.

100

Derived from the Latin *armilla*, meaning "ring" or "bracelet," the term armillary sphere refers to a three-dimensional model of the celestial sphere that displays elements like the equator, tropics, polar circles, and the ecliptic. Composed of a series of concentric rings centred around a small sphere representing Earth, the armillary sphere is often credited to Eratosthenes of Cyrene (276-195 BCE), a Greek astronomer, mathematician, and the head of the famed Alexandria Library. Before the era of telescopes and satellite technology, this device allowed for the study of planetary movements based solely on observations made with the naked eye.

101

The Prague Orloj, constructed in 1410 in the Old Town Hall of Prague, is one of the most renowned astronomical clocks, both a historic and symbolic artefact of European Renaissance and heritage. The clock displays Old Bohemian time, marking the new day at sunset; Babylonian time, running from sunrise to sunset; Central European time with a sun-shaped hand; and Star time, indicating the apparent motion of the stars due to Earth's rotation.[45] It has additional features such as a calendar dial that marks the days, months, and years, and a zodiacal ring tracing the Sun and Moon's path through the sky. At the core of its mechanical operation is the astrolabe.

098

099

100

101

---

[33] King, *History of Sumer and Akkad*, 78.

[34] De Macedo, "Between Philosophy and Mysticism."

[35] King, "A Survey of Medieval Islamic Shadow Schemes for Simple Time-Reckoning," 194.

[36] Frothingham, "Ancient Orientation Unveiled," 55.

[37] Romey, "Ancient Sundial Find Celebrated Roman Election Win," November 8, 2017, https://www.nationalgeographic.com/history/article/ancient-rome-election-victory-sundial-archaeology.

[38] Curry, "Egypt's Eternal City," 30.

[39] Brand, "The Lost Obelisks and Colossi of Seti I," 104.

[40] Abbasi and Sarma, "An Astrolabe by Muhammad Muqīm of Lahore Dated 1047 AH (1637-38 CE)," 41.

[41] "Planispheric Astrolabe," The Khalili Collections, https://www.khalilicollections.org/collections/islamic-art/khalili-collection-hajj-and-the-arts-of-pilgrimage-planispheric-astrolabe-sci430/.

[42] Cotter, "The Mariner's Sextant and the Royal Society," 23.

[43] Freeth et al., "Calendars With Olympiad Display and Eclipse Prediction on the Antikythera Mechanism," 614.

[44] Mardon et al., *Decoding the Antikythera Mechanism*, 42.

[45] Santora, "One of the World's Oldest Clocks Stops Ticking, Briefly," *The New York Times*, January 18, 2018, https://www.nytimes.com/2018/01/18/world/europe/prague-astronomical-clock-orloj.html.

102

103

Observations

LIGHT

|

102
The Zorats Karer site, also known as Karahundj (Carahunge), has been used continuously from the prehistoric to the mediaeval periods. It has a prehistoric mausoleum and more than 200 large stone monoliths, eighty of which have smoothly drilled holes near the top.[47] It has been compared to England's Stonehenge due to its links to astronomy. It was first explored in 1935 by Georgian ethnographer Stepan Lisitsian; in the 1950s, Armenian philologist Marus Hasratyan discovered burial chambers dating from 1100 to 800 BCE; and in 1984, Soviet archeologist Onnik Khnkikyan suggested the megalithic stones were an ancient observatory and that the holes were primitive telescopes for observing the stars. Several of the holes align with the sunrise and sunset during the summer solstice.

"It is true that the infinite distances between ourselves and objects have been overcome by the microscope and the telescope; but we were first conscious of these distances only at the very same moment in which they were overcome... coming closer to things often only shows us how far away they still are from us."[46]

Georg Simmel

103
Archeologists suspect that Stonehenge was constructed between 3100 and 1600 BCE, based on radiocarbon dating that suggests it was erected over millennia. It was initially likely used for solstice rituals, with "a distinctive idea of time, which revolved around the cyclical movements of sun, moon, and stars across the heavens, as indicators of the passing seasons."[48]

104
Professor Adolphus Hall of the United States Naval Observatory looking through a twenty-six-inch telescope on August 18, 1924.

104

The Observatory at Delhi.

105

106

105

Built within the eighteenth-century planned city of Jaipur, India, the Jantar Mantar observatory houses the most significant and best-preserved collection of pre-telescopic masonry astronomical instruments in the country. It showcases the height of Zij astronomy, with instruments that emerged from an exchange of ideas among Indian, Central Asian, West Asian, and European cultures.

106

Jantar Mantar houses the Brihat Samrat Yantra, the world's largest equinoctial sundial, which marks a critical moment in Indian history when astronomical and astrological sciences were first integrated and made accessible to the public through such grand structures. Continually studied by astronomers, architects, and historians, the observatory is crucial for understanding the evolution of astronomy and architectural science.[49]

107

Taqī al-Dīn (1526-1585), known as al-Rāsid ("the observer"), was an Ottoman astronomer from Damascus who made significant contributions in mathematics, optics, mechanics, and engineering. With the support and funding of Sultan Murād, Taqī al-Dīn established the Dār al-Rasad al-Jadīd (the New Observatory) in 1579, which became the first of its kind in Istanbul and rivalled Tycho Brahe's Uraniborg Observatory established in 1576.[50] Consisting of two buildings on the city's higher grounds of Tophane, Dār al-Rasad al-Jadīd also housed a significant library on astronomy and mathematics. Taqī al-Dīn not only reproduced instruments from previous Islamic observatories but also invented new ones for the facility. The observatory, staffed by sixteen people (eight observers, four clerks, and four assistants), was one of the largest in the Islamic world.

108

Excavated in 1970, the Maragheh Observatory was established in 1259 on the Rasad Dāghi hill, under the patronage of Hūlāgū, grandson of Genghis Khan. This observatory, directed by the Persian scholar Nasīr al-Dīn Tūsī, played a pivotal role in mediaeval astronomy, contributing to a significant phase of scientific advancements in the Islamic world during the mid-thirteenth century. It not only inspired the construction of later observatories up to the seventeenth century but also significantly influenced the astronomical revolution of the sixteenth century. The observatory housed advanced equipment, a library containing around 400,000 volumes, and a staff of prominent astronomers from across the Islamic world.[51]

107

108

"To observe," from the Latin *ob-servare*, means "to adapt." Ancient civilisations constructed enigmatic structures that not only served to mark the passage of time but also connected the realms of science and spirituality. Such observatories tracked celestial movements, assisting with navigation and agriculture, while also reinforcing social cohesion by tying community and religious events to astronomical phenomena. From the Babylonians, known for their precise eclipse and planetary predictions, to the Mayan peoples who intertwined their astronomical observations with a deeply animistic worldview, each culture wove their insights on light into their societal fabric. These historical practices had a common goal to derive meaning from the sky—a pursuit that continues to inform our understanding of both the universe and our own intrinsic affinity of looking upward.

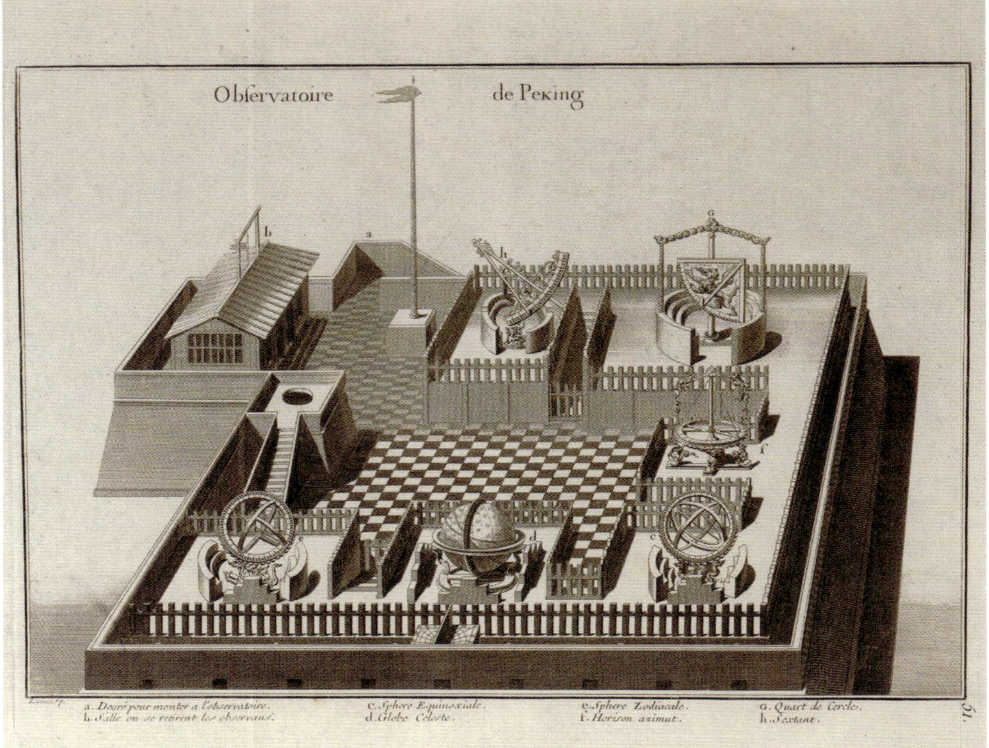

109

The Beijing Ancient Observatory is the world's only fully preserved observatory from the seventeenth century. This historic site celebrates the rich legacy of astronomical study in traditional China. The observatory's instruments show the merging of Chinese and European scientific practices during the seventeenth and eighteenth centuries, a pivotal era of cultural and scientific exchange.

110

In 1576, King Frederick II of Denmark commissioned Tycho Brahe to build an elaborate residence and observatory known as Uraniborg, on the island of Ven, Sweden. It was inspired by the divine proportion principles outlined in Palladio's *Four Books of Architecture*, published in 1570. Brahe designed Uraniborg to be both a living space and a centre for astronomical study. It was coined the "castle of heavens," hosting a vibrant community in which artisans crafted astronomical instruments, scholars accessed a rich library, and alchemists experimented in laboratories.[52] The complex also included a paper mill, a printing press, kitchen gardens, fish tanks, orchards, an irrigation system, and a flour mill. Over two decades, Brahe meticulously recorded planetary positions from here, contributing significantly to the field of astronomy. His work was later detailed in *Astronomiae Instauratae Mechanica*, published in Wandsbeck in 1598.

111

The twenty-eight-inch refracting telescope at the Greenwich Observatory, the largest refracting telescope in the United Kingdom, was commissioned in 1885 by the Astronomer Royal, William Christie. Constructed by the Grubb Telescope Company in Dublin, it was installed in 1893.

112

The Rundetaarn Observatory, located atop Copenhagen's Round Tower, was initiated by King Christian IV of Denmark in 1929 and is the oldest functioning observatory in Europe. It enabled University of Copenhagen's astronomers to study the stars, free from the city's lights and smoke. For centuries, it served as the hub of Danish astronomy, crucial for meteorological observations and geographical surveying. From the year it opened the observatory housed a refracting telescope capable of magnifying between 80 and 450 times.

113

The N'Dalla Tando Observatory, supported by a baobab tree, in Angola, Africa.

113

46 Simmel, *The Philosophy of Money*, 481.

47 Vann, "Unraveling the Mystery of the 'Armenian Stonehenge,'" *Smithsonian Magazine*, July 27, 2017, https://www.smithsonianmag.com/travel/unraveling-mystery-armenian-stonehenge-180964207/.

48 Fagan, *From Black Land to Fifth Sun*, 146

49 Archeological Survey of India, "Nomination of The Jantar Mantar, Jaipur (for inclusion on World Heritage List)," 30.

50 Ayduz, "Taqi al-Din Ibn Ma'ruf: A Bio-Bibliographical Essay," June 26, 2008, https://muslimheritage.com/taqi-al-din-bio-essay/.

51 Maragheh Observatory, Iran," UNESCO Portal to the Heritage of Astronomy, https://web.astronomicalheritage.net/index.php/show-entity?identity=29&idsubentity=1.

52 Luminet, "Science, Art and Geometrical Imagination," 255.

114

115

114
Ptolemy, an influential figure in mathematics, geography, and astronomy flourished in Alexandria, Egypt, during Marcus Aurelius's reign of 161–180 CE.[54] Little is known of Ptolemy's personal life, but his scholarly contributions are well known, such as the *Almagest* and *Optics*. The latter work, likely written in the 160s and preserved through a Latin translation of an Arabic version, delves into theories of light, vision, and the mechanics of seeing. More specifically, the book explores visual phenomena including perspective, clarity, and the physical and psychological aspects of perception—colour perception and the effects of ageing on vision for instance. Ptolemy distinguished himself by integrating physical instruments like rulers and mirrors to further explore visual theories, thereby broadening the understanding beyond the theoretical diagrams of his predecessors like Euclid.

115
"Empedocles says there are two suns. First there is the archetypal (*archetypos*) sun. This is fire in one hemisphere of the cosmos; it fills the hemisphere and is always positioned opposite its own reflection (*antaugeia*). Second there is the visible sun. This is a reflection (*antaugeia*) in the other hemisphere: the hemisphere that consists of air mixed with heat. The reflection is produced as a result of light bouncing off the circular earth onto the crystalline sun while it—the reflection—is dragged round with the motion of the fiery hemisphere. In short, the sun is a reflection (*antaugeia*) of the fire around the earth."[55] – Aetius

116
Ptolemy's work and models, based on spheres and perfect circles, positioned Earth at the universe's centre, around which celestial bodies revolve. This was detailed in *Almagest*, originally titled the *Great Composition*, which became a foundational text in mediaeval astronomy.

SURVEYING

Optics

LIGHT

|

*"And of the organs they first contrived the eyes to give light, and the principle
according to which they were inserted was as follows: So much of fire as would
not burn, but gave a gentle light, they formed into a substance akin to the light of
every-day life; and the pure fire which is within us and related thereto they made
to flow through the eyes in a stream smooth and dense, compressing the whole
eye, and especially the center part, so that it kept out everything of a coarser
nature, and allowed to pass only this pure element. When the light of day
surrounds the stream of vision, then like falls upon like, and they coalesce,
and one body is formed by natural affinity in the line of vision, wherever
the light that falls from within meets with an external object. And the whole
stream of vision, being similarly affected in virtue of similarity, diffuses
the motions of what it touches or what touches it over the whole body,
until they reach the soul, causing that perception which we call sight."* [53]

Plato

116

117

Between 300 and 400 BCE, atomists, including Plato, proposed that vision was an outcome of material contact between the object and the eye—a form of "visual fire." This view is reflective of the extramission theory of vision, where the eyes emit light rays that make contact with objects and reveal them to the viewer. Aristotle, while dismissing the idea of a visual fire, concurred with earlier thinkers on the need for a material intermediary between the eye and the object. He proposed that the medium facilitating sight is defined by its transparency—a characteristic present in air and water. However, this transparency can only be activated in the presence of light. Without light, substances merely possess the potential for transparency, which light actualises. Therefore, when light is present, a medium capable of transparency enables the object to become visible to the observer.

This line of thinking gradually evolved into modern optics, where the understanding of light moved from a subjective experience to a quantifiable science. Over time, contributions from mathematics and physics have dissected light's properties, framing it as a medium governed by predictable laws. Advancements in optics have been instrumental in expanding the understanding of light's behaviour—how it travels, reflects, and refracts. These studies have not only demystified the mechanics of seeing but also enhanced the ability to manipulate light, leading to innovations in technology and communication.

117
Introducing Ptolemy's *Optics*, Euclid outlines a model of vision which incorporates physics and mathematics. This model proposes that visual rays, emanating from the eyes, spread outward, maintaining an orderly and angular arrangement.[56] This geometric framework for understanding optical perception is built on three foundational concepts: discreteness, alignment, and angularity. According to Euclid:

1 - Visual rays extend from the eye, traversing a vast space.
2 - The visual field forms a cone, originating at the eye (the apex) and expanding to the boundaries of what can be seen (the base).
3 - Objects are visible when they intercept these visual rays, and invisible when they do not.[57]

118

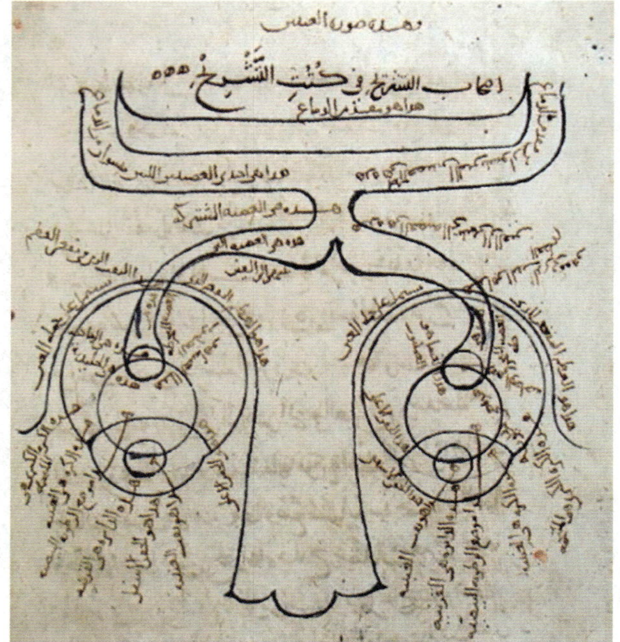

119

120

118

"It is fitting then to acknowledge the utmost gratitude to all those who have contributed even a little to truth not to speak of all those who have contributed much. If they had not lived, it would have been impossible for us, despite all our zeal, during the whole of our lifetime, to assemble these principles of truth which form the basis of the final inferences of our research. The assembling of all these elements has been affected century by century, in past ages down to our own time... It is fitting then for us not to be ashamed to acknowledge truth and to assimilate it from whatever source it comes to us, even if it is brought to us by former generations and foreign peoples." [58] – Al-Kindi

119

Ibn al-Haytham, more commonly known as Alhazen, was a pivotal Arab-Islamic scholar whose work during the mediaeval period significantly advanced the field of optics. He departed from the widely held extramission theory of optics, proposing instead that vision occurs through light rays entering the eye from external objects.[59] His work, *Kitab al-Manazir* كتاب المناظر (*Book of Optics*) expands into this theory, marking a crucial turning point in the understanding of how we see. Alhazen's contributions were made during the golden age of Islamic medicine, a period from the ninth to the twelfth century that saw significant advancements in medical science across the Near East.[60]

120

"If what the eye gives off is material, then how does it happen that it is not used up when the viewed object is as far from the viewer as, for example, the sky? Even if the material is extra-fine, the distance is so great that it will more than use up all the material that a living being might possess... Furthermore, if what is emitted is so fine that it can stretch out to a great distance without using up the supply of the creature that sent it, how could it fail to be easily damaged by any stray object? Obviously, it wouldn't require a very strong wind to divert it from its straight line." [61] – Alexander Aphrodisias.

121

Ptolemy holding an armillary sphere, with Earth at the universe's centre.

122

"I know that I am mortal by nature and ephemeral, but when I trace at my pleasure the windings to and fro of the heavenly bodies, I no longer touch earth with my feet. I stand in the presence of Zeus himself and take my fill of ambrosia." [62] – Ptolemy

LA LUNETTE DE HOLLANDE
apliquée à l'Astronomie,
en 1609.
Voyez l'explication fin du Tome IV.

123

Copernicus delayed publishing his revolutionary heliocentric model and theory until 1543, just before his death, due to concerns about both scientific critiques, potential censoring, and the Church's disapproval. Initially, the theory attracted some scholars who validated the work but some faced accusations of heresy.[63] The adoption of Copernicus' views gained momentum when Galileo Galilei began to validate the theory. He was influenced by the telescope's invention in 1609, which transformed it from a novelty into a powerful scientific tool.[64]

In 1632, Galileo published *Dialogo sopra I due massimi sistemi del mondo (Dialogue Concerning the Two Chief World Systems)*, using a dialogue format to subtly advocate for the Copernican system over the Ptolemaic. This approach allowed him to appear impartial while clearly favouring the heliocentric model, asserting Earth's orbit around the Sun. His stance led to his trial for heresy in 1633, resulting in lifelong house arrest and marking a significant tension between emerging scientific knowledge and established Church doctrines. The conflict highlighted a broader struggle for intellectual freedom in scientific discourse.[65] The book was subsequently banned.

124

"Of all discoveries and opinions, none may have exerted a greater effect on the human spirit than the doctrine of Copernicus. The world has scarcely become known as round and complete in itself when it was asked to waive the tremendous privilege of being the centre of the universe."[66] – Johann Wolfgang von Goethe

---

125

"We revolve around the Sun like any other planet."[67] – Nicolaus Copernicus

---

124

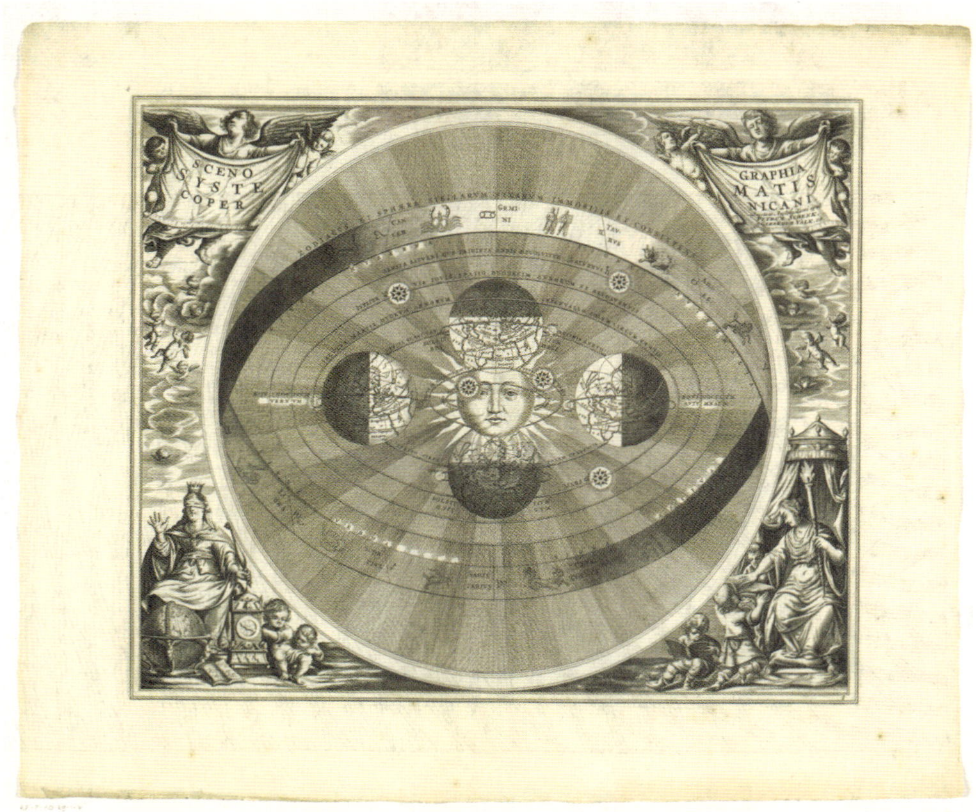

125

126

British polymath Thomas Young is celebrated for a pivotal experiment, presented in a Royal Society lecture in 1803, through which he demonstrated how a beam of light, when split by a card, created a diffraction pattern. This pattern was crucially dependent on the interference of the two light beams. He noted: "It will not be denied by the most prejudiced that the fringes are produced by the interference of two portions of light."[68] This experiment fundamentally supported the wave theory of light.

127

"This most beautiful system of the sun, planets and comets, could only proceed from the counsel and dominion of an intelligent and powerful Being... This Being governs all things, not as the soul of the world, but as Lord over all; and on account of his dominion he is wont, to be called Lord God or Universal Ruler."[69] – Isaac Newton

Newton's *Principia* establishes how particles behave under forces, predicting their trajectories and emphasising a universe governed by divine order.

128

Thomas Young's sketch of the two-slit diffraction of light.

129

In 1676, Danish astronomer Ole Roemer made the first measurement of the speed of light by observing the moons of Jupiter, specifically Io. Previously, scientists believed the light's speed was immeasurable or infinite. Roemer noted that Io's eclipses by Jupiter occurred later than expected when Earth was moving away from Jupiter in its orbit, suggesting that light took time to travel from Jupiter to Earth. By quantifying this delay, Roemer was able to calculate the speed of light.[70]

126

127

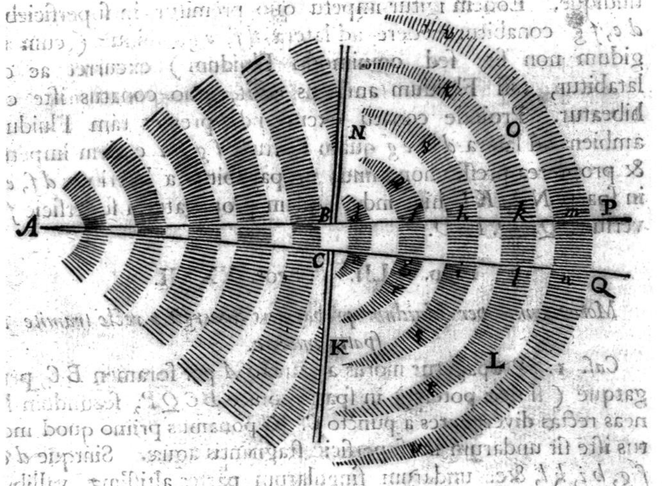

128

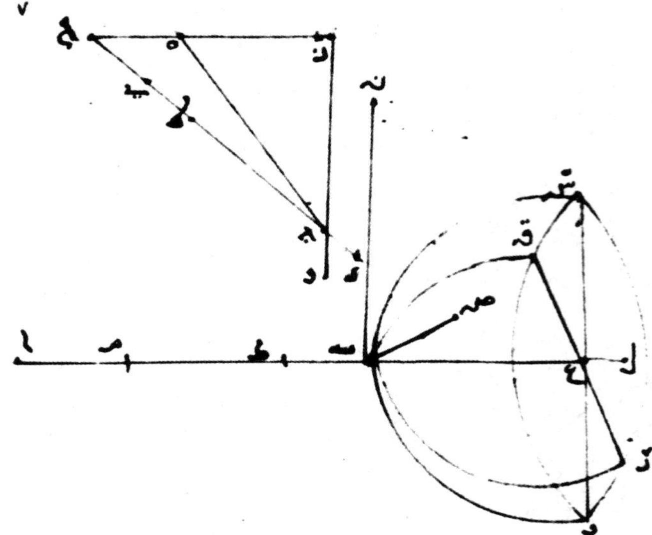

كأنه إن ماسته عليها سطح مستو وغيره فلأن هذا السطح يقطع سطح ب ن ص
على نقطة ب فلا بد من أن يقطع أحد خطي ب ن ثم فليكن ذلك
الخط ب ص والفصل المشترك بين هذا السطح وبين سطح قطع ق ر
خط ب ث فلأن هذا السطح يمر بنقطتين ب ع على نقطة ت ب خط
ب ث على قطع ق ب د على نقطة ت ب وكذلك خط ب ص وهذا محال
فلا يمر بسيط ت ب على نقطة ت ب سطح مستو وغير سطح ب ن ص ⊙

[53] Allen, "Philosophy for Understanding Theology," 31.

[54] Webster, "Ptolemy's Optics, Double-Vision, and the Technological after Image," 191.

[55] Kingsley, "Empedocles' Sun," 316.

[56] Burton, "The Optics of Euclid," 93.

[57] Siebert, "Transformation of Euclid's Optics in Late Antiquity," 93.

[58] Lindberg, *Theories of Vision From Al-Kindi to Kepler*, 18.

[59] Lindberg, 44.

[60] Daneshfard, "Ibn al-Haytham (965-1039 AD)," 227.

[61] Thibodeau, "Ancient Optics," 132.

[62] Ptolemy, Almagest, quoted in Sobel, *The Planets*, 31.

[63] Riebeek, "Planetary Motion," NASA Earth Observatory, https://earthobservatory.nasa.gov/features/OrbitsHistory.

[64] Gingerich, "Galileo, the Impact of the Telescope, and the Birth of Modern Astronomy," 136.

[65] Zewail, "Micrographia of the Twenty-First Century," 1193.

[66] Riebeek, "Planetary Motion."

[67] Riebeek, "Planetary Motion."

[68] Young, "The Bakerian Lecture," 1.

[69] Riebeek, "Planetary Motion."

[70] Tyson, *Cosmic Horizons*, 144.

[71] Zghal et al., "The First Steps for Learning Optics," 3.

[72] Rashed, "A Pioneer in Anaclastics," 466.

Supremum Orbita Cœlum
Cœlum Chrystallinum
Firmamentum
Saturnus
Jupiter
Mars
Sol
Venus
Mercurius
Luna
Fig. I.
Terra
Fig. VI.
Fig. III.
Sol
Leo
Cauda Leonis
Cor Leonis
Orbita Saturni
Virgo
Spica Virginis
Libra
Orbita Jovis
Scorpius
Cor Scorpii
Sagittarius
Aphelium
Capricor
Cancer
Perihelium
Orbita Martis
Orbita Terræ
Orbita Veneris
Orbita Mercurii
Aphelium
Apogæum
Semidiametri Terræ pro Planetarum distantys.
5000   100000   200000   300000
5   10   15   20   25
30

CAPTURING LIGHT

THE CAMERA OBSCURA, MAGIC LANTERN, STREETLIGHTS, SOLAR ENERGY, AND SPACE TRAFFIC: PART 3 RECORDS EARLY INNOVATIONS AND THE IMPACTS OF LIGHT ON ENVIRONMENTS.

إلتقاط الضوء

131

MI CARDANI
MEDIOLANENSIS,
MEDICI.

DE SVBTILITATE
LIBRI XXI.

Nunc demum ab ipfo autore recogniti, atque perfecti.

IN VIRTVTE. ET FORTVNA.

LVGDVNI,
Apud Gulielmum Rouillium,
M. D. LVIIII.

132

131
In 1550, Milanese astrologer and physician Gerolamo Cardano made a significant advancement in the technology of the camera obscura by suggesting the insertion of a convex lens into the aperture. This dramatically improved image clarity and brightness.[76]

132
Dutch scientist Reinerus Gemma Frisius is thought to have been the first to publish an illustration of a camera obscura in 1544.[77]

133
"Portable camera obscura. To make views by means of the camera obscura, it should be light and portable, and should not occupy too large a space. [This figure] represents a simple and convenient form of the apparatus. It consists of a wooden tripod, supporting a board of the same material, and surrounded by a curtain which forms a small tent, in which the artist places himself. In the centre of the tent is a small table resting on a tripod, on which is produced the image. At the top of the apparatus, in a brass tube open at the side, is a glass prism, which produces the effect both of the inclined mirror and of the lens in the camera obscura described above."[78] – Adolphe Ganot and Edmund Atkinson

CAPTURING

Images

LIGHT

|

"What determines me, at the most profound level, in the visible, is the gaze that is outside. It is through the gaze that I enter light and it is from the gaze that I receive its effects. Hence it comes about that the gaze is the instrument through which light is embodied and through which—if you will allow me to use a word, as I often do, in a fragmented form—I am photo-graphed." [73]

Jacques Lacan

134

135

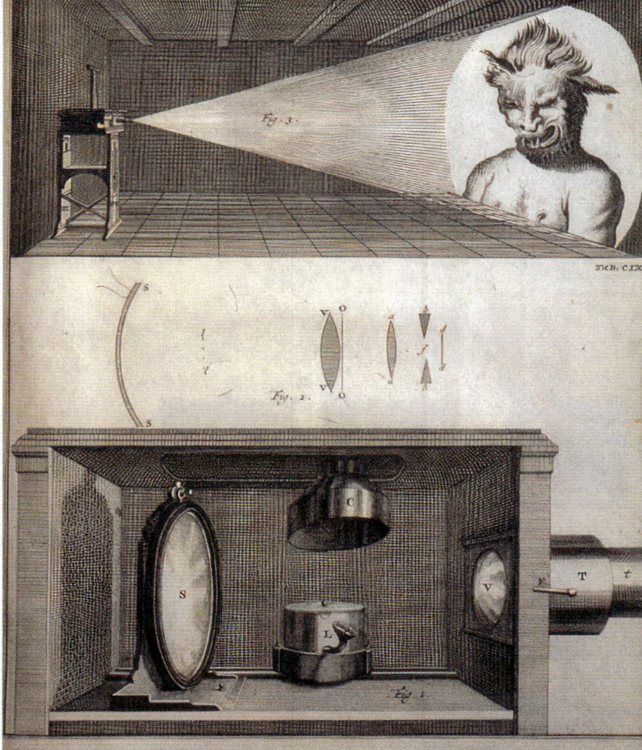

136

The term "photography" derives from the Greek φωτός (phōtós), which means "light writing." Just as a small window lets in the morning light or the aperture of a camera gives way to images, a preface allows us to experience a kind of light.[74] This light is a condition and matter of presentation, casting future significance on what has already been written. It is created to be left behind, a writing of light, a form of language.

The relationship between memory, thought, and photography is defined by how well these elements can be repeated, reproduced, cited, and inscribed. Seeing historical photographs can be investigative and a model for understanding and reading about history. Capturing light suggests that it can be a medium that transmits information across great distances by technical means. According to American scientist Benjamin Franklin, it transforms an event in history into a "mass article," allowing the event to be experienced repeatedly, wherever it is viewed and heard.[75]

LA DIOPTRIQUE

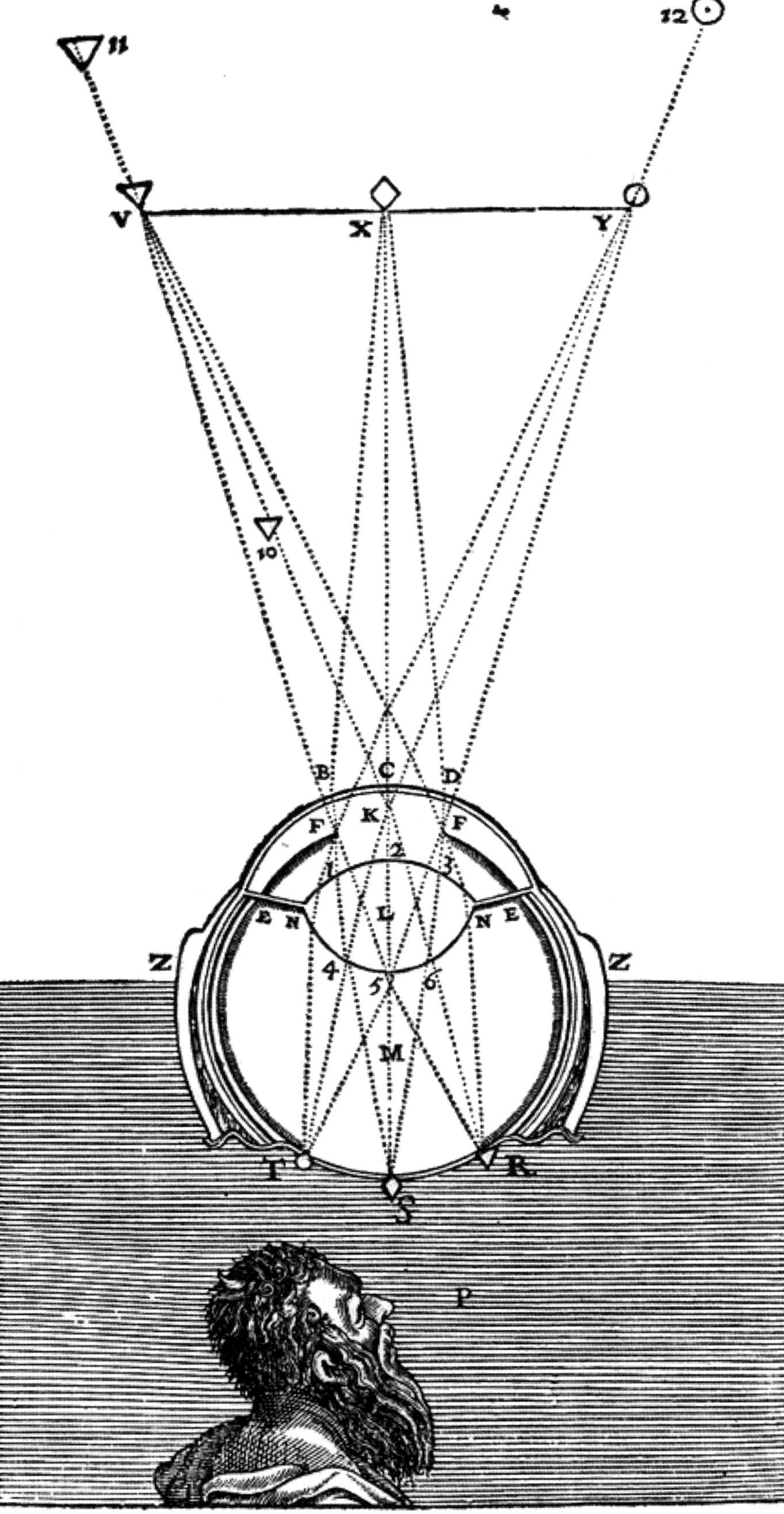

134
Painted glass for a magic lantern.

135
A magic lantern show in modern day Beijing, China.

136
The magic lantern, an early form of optical projection, is known to be the ancestor of cinema. First developed around the 1660s, likely by Dutch physicist Christiaan Huygens, this device pioneered the realm of projected storytelling and visual entertainment. It allowed for the dissemination of visual information and narratives across all ages, races, the literate and the illiterate. The magic lantern was not only a tool for education and entertainment but also, in some cases, a means to manipulate or mystify less discerning audiences.

137
"From the Sun and the colours illuminated by the Sun, species flow...until for whatever reason, they fall on an opaque medium, where they paint their source: and vision is produced, when the opaque screen of the eye is painted this way... For, there are certain passions of light...illuminating and altering the screens [of the eye] through which colours, that is to say light, are not only poured upon but are also imprinted."[79] – Johannes Kepler

---

137

138

139

138

Escaped American slave Wilson Chinn, who had been branded with the initials of his owner, was photographed by Charles Paxson in the 1860s and featured in *Harper's Weekly* in 1864. The use of photography to document and disseminate images like Chinn's branded face was revolutionary, turning evidence of the horror of slavery into a broader call for change, and marking an early example of photography as a medium for significant societal impact and reform.[80] It became a pivotal tool for the abolitionist movement, helping to sway public opinion by bringing the inhumanity of slavery into the public eye.

139

Aerial photography was pioneered by French photographer Gaspard-Félix Tournachon, known as Nadar, in 1858. While his initial photographs over Paris no longer exist, the earliest available aerial image is of Boston, offering a bird's-eye view of the city. This method became critically important during wartime for reconnaissance, aiding in the strategic mapping of enemy movements and fortifications.

140

In 1872 at the Paris Observatory, French astronomers Paul and Prosper Henry began to map space, cataloguing nearly fifty thousand stars over twelve years. Confronted by the dense star clusters of the Milky Way, they shifted to using a photographic telescope in 1884, to capture a precise visual record of the sky. By 1885, the Henry brothers had perfected a powerful photographic telescope that could capture images of distant, faint stars invisible to the naked eye, producing some of the most profound images of space to date.[81]

AGRANDISSEMENT 2 FOIS
PHOTOGRAPHIE D'UNE PORTION DE LA CARTE DU CIEL

142

143

144

145

146

142
A photo reproduction of a drawing based on a photo of a solar eclipse.

143
Spots of the moon.

144
Sunspots on the surface of the sun.

145
Solar eclipse from Caroline Island, United States, in 1883.

146
American chemist John W. Draper was the first to capture a clear image of the moon using the daguerreotype process. On March 16, 1840, Draper noted in his lab journal that he directed moonlight onto a chemically treated plate through a convex lens, producing a haloed crescent image reminiscent of the lunar phases. Despite his pioneering work in astronomical photography during the winter of 1839-1840, Draper's lunar images initially received little acclaim and were thought to be lost for many years.

147
Twelve microscope images of solidified sulphur.

148
Sixteen microscope images of sulphur.

147

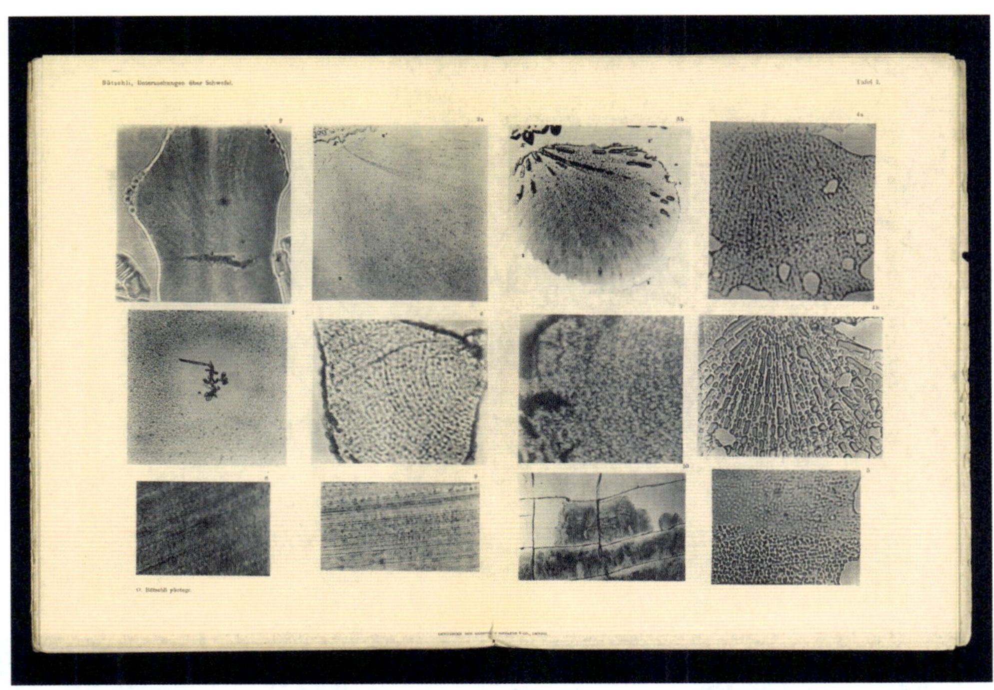

148

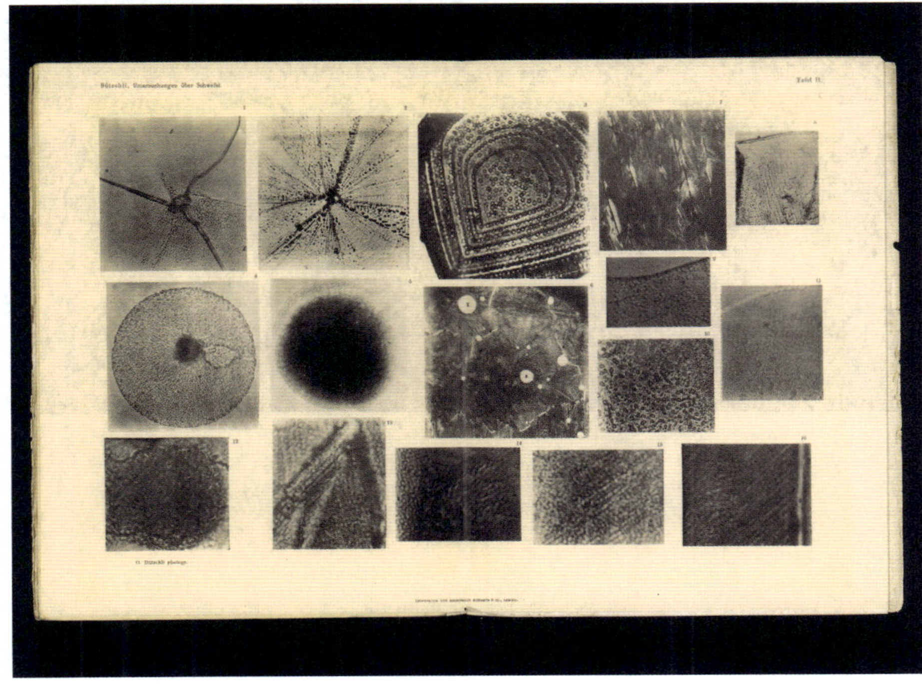

صور — القبض الضوء

149

In 1872, English photographer Eadweard Muybridge was commissioned by Leland Stanford, a Governor of California and railroad magnate, to photograph a horse in full gallop to determine if all four hooves left the ground simultaneously. This inquiry led to the development of stop-action photography, employing an array of twenty-four cameras activated by the horse tripping wires as it passed. Muybridge's pioneering work produced a sequence of images capturing the horse's movement in a way that was previously unseen by the naked eye, visually breaking down the stages of the gallop.[82]

150

Eadweard Muybridge, *Animal Locomotion*, 1879, printed 1881.

151

French photographer Louis-Jacques-Mandé Daguerre revolutionised visual documentation through his 1839 invention of the daguerreotype process. It captures sharp images on a silvered copper plate, offering clarity and detail that had not been previously achievable through earlier methods.[83] Daguerre's work opened new possibilities for capturing the intricacies of the world, making photography accessible and practical for widespread use. His contributions not only advanced the scientific community's ability to study and document, but also transformed the arts, forever changing how people perceived and interacted with images.

149

150

الگيولوجيّة الضوء

152

152
The journey into photography began with French inventor Joseph Nicéphore Niépce, who in 1827 captured the first enduring image using a camera. This initial photograph, known as View from the *Window at Le Gras*, required an eight-hour exposure and was taken from an upstairs window of Niépce's home, capturing the view of the surrounding buildings. Photography was introduced to the public in both France and England in 1830, captivating audiences.[84]

Niépce's groundbreaking technique called heliography, derived from the Greek *helios* for "*sun*" and *graphein* for "writing," involved using light-sensitive bitumen coated on pewter plates.[88] His inventive process included placing translucent engravings on these plates and then exposing them to sunlight through a camera obscura. The sunlight solidified the exposed bitumen, while the areas shielded by the engravings remained soft. These soft parts were then removed with a mixture of lavender oil and turpentine, leaving a permanent image.

153
William Henry Fox Talbot,
The Open Door, 1844.

154
In his 1604 work *Ad Vitellionem Paralipomena*, German astronomer and mathematician Johannes Kepler advanced the field of optics by introducing the concept of the *pictura*, a term he used to describe an image that is projected onto a screen within a camera obscura. He distinguished this *pictura* from the traditional concept of an *imago*. Kepler analogised the human eye to a camera obscura, explaining that the pupil functions like the device's aperture, the eye's tunics act as a lens, and the retina serves as the screen where a real, inverted image is formed and received. This explanation marked a pivotal shift in understanding vision, positing the retina as the receiver of images, akin to how a screen captures pictures in a camera obscura.[85]

153

154

155
A photograph of a tartan ribbon taken by Scottish physicist James Clerk Maxwell in 1861, considered the first durable colour photographic image. A few months after, English photographer Thomas Sutton published a brief explanation of how he reproduced the process:

"A bow made of ribbon, striped with various colours, was pinned upon a background of black velvet, and copied by photography by means of a portrait lens of full aperture, having various coloured fluids placed immediately in front of it and through which the light from the object had to pass before it reached the lens. The experiments were made out-of-doors in good light, and the results were as follows."[86]
– Thomas Sutton

155

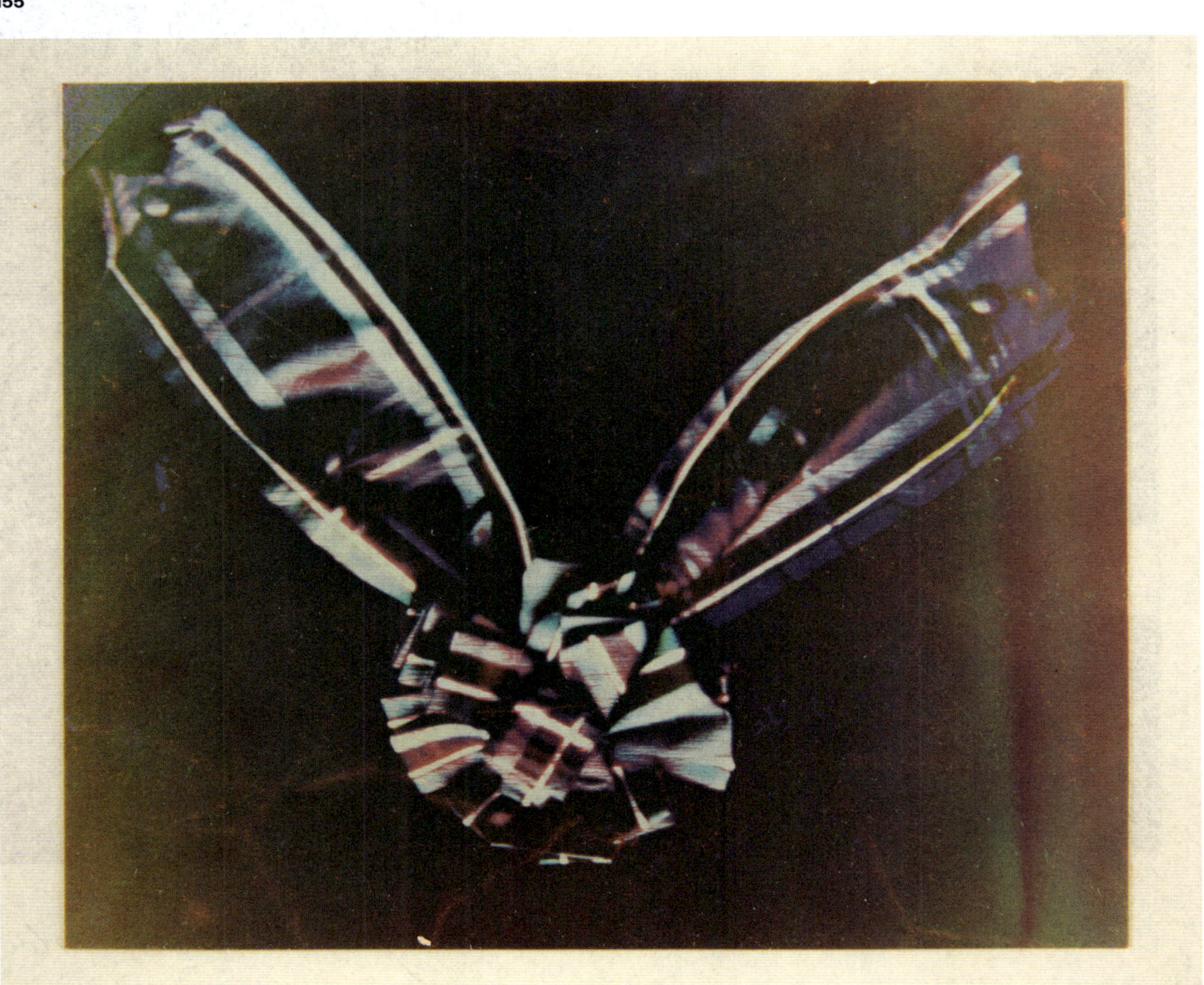

Robertson inv.t
Fantasmagorie de Robertson da

la Cour des Capucines en 1797.

156
The term "phantasmagoria" originated in late-eighteenth-century France, where it was used to describe spectral lantern shows created and coined by Belgian inventor Étienne-Gaspard Robertson.[87] These shows, known for their ghostly themes, became highly influential in early-nineteenth-century popular entertainment.

[73] Friedlander, "La Jetée," 76.

[74] Cadava, "Words of Light," xviii.

[75] Benjamin, "The Arcades Project," 107.

[76] Snyder, "Picturing Vision," 512.

[77] Harry Ransom Center, "The Niépce Heliograph," https://www.hrc.utexas.edu/niepce-heliograph/#top/.

[78] Ganot, Natural Philosophy for General Readers and Young Persons, 385.

[79] Kepler, *Ad Vitellionem*, 41-42.

[80] Gage, "Icons of Cruelty," *The New York Times*, August 5, 2013, https://archive.nytimes.com/opinionator.blogs.nytimes.com/2013/08/05/icons-of-cruelty/.

[81] "Paul Henry: A Section of the Constellation Cygnus (August 13, 1885)," The Metropolitan Museum of Art, https://www.metmuseum.org/art/collection/search/283255.

[82] "Eadweard Muybridge: Attitudes of Animals in Motion," The Metropolitan Museum of Art, https://www.metmuseum.org/art/collection/search/700109.

[83] "On This Day: Louis-Jacques-Mandé Daguerre Is Born," *JSTOR* (blog), November 18, 2011, https://about.jstor.org/blog/louis-jacques-mande-daguerre/.

[84] Harry Ransom Center, "The Niépce Heliograph," https://www.hrc.utexas.edu/niepce-heliograph/#top/.

[85] Shapiro, "Images: Real and Virtual, Projected and Perceived, from Kepler to Dechales," 270.

[86] Sutton, *Photographic Notes*, 169-170.

[87] Spence "The Phantasmagoria," 3.

[88] Harry Ransom Center, "The Niépce Heliograph," www.hrc.utexas.edu/niepce-heliograph/#top/.

أركيولوجيا الضوء

ARCHEOLOGY OF LIGHT

158

157

In 1752, American scientist and founding father Benjamin Franklin conducted a groundbreaking experiment to demonstrate the electrical nature of lightning. By flying a kite during a thunderstorm and attaching a metal key to its string, Franklin captured electrical charges from the storm clouds.[90] This experiment, which could have been dangerous, successfully established a connection between static electricity and lightning, marking a significant milestone in the understanding of electricity.

158

"I say, if these things are so, may not the knowledge of this power of points be of use to mankind, in preserving houses, churches, ships from the stroke of lightning, by directing us to fix on the highest parts of those edifices, upright rods of iron made sharp as a needle, and gilt to prevent rusting, and from the foot of those rods a wire down the outside of the building into the ground, or down round one of the shrouds of a ship and down her sides till it reaches the water? Would not these pointed rods probably draw the electrical fire silently out of a cloud before it came nigh enough to strike, and thereby secure us from that sudden and terrible mischief?"[91]
– Benjamin Franklin

157

CAPTURING

Electricity

LIGHT

|

"A fear haunted the latter half of the eighteenth century: the fear of darkened spaces, of the pall of gloom which prevents the full visibility of things, men and truths... It was the dream that each individual, whatever position he occupied, might be able to see the whole of society, that men's hearts should communicate, their vision be unobstructed by obstacles, and that opinion of all reign over each."[89]

Michel Foucault

159
Pseudodoxia Epidemica, also known as *Vulgar Errors*, is a seminal 1646 work by English author Sir Thomas Browne, in which he confronts and dispels many widespread misconceptions and superstitions of his time. It is also the first documented use of the word "electricity."[92] The text was influential in its approach because Browne employed a methodical examination of topics organised from the most elemental aspects of the world to the more complex, following a Renaissance conceptual framework. He used a mixture of empirical observation and scholarly inquiry to categorise errors ranging from natural phenomena to human and cosmic misunderstandings. The book had several editions and was translated into multiple languages, reflecting its significance in the shift toward empirical methods during the seventeenth-century Scientific Revolution.

160

In an ion gauge, which creates a low-pressure vacuum, photons and photoelectrons can be accurately measured for experiments. A vacuum can be described as an area devoid of any particles, essentially a space without matter.

161

In 1886, German physicist Heinrich Hertz developed the spark gap oscillator, meaning the first radio transmitter, which confirmed the existence of radio waves and thereby supported electromagnetic theory. The device not only generated and detected electromagnetic waves but also highlighted their similarities to light—both phenomena are forms of electromagnetic radiation. The interconnection between light and electromagnetic waves was further explored by Albert Einstein in his study of the photoelectric effect, where he revealed light's particle nature and introduced the concept of photons. This work earned Einstein the Nobel Prize and played a crucial role in the advent of quantum physics, and continues to have applications in modern technologies like solar panels.

162

In 1879, American inventor Thomas Edison developed an innovative carbon filament light bulb, introducing a practical and commercially viable option for electric lighting. This bulb featured a carbonised cotton thread filament that was able to glow for up to 14.5 hours.[93] Edison's pursuit for a more durable filament led to the adoption of bamboo, which extended the bulb's life up to 1200 hours, setting a new standard for the next decade.[94] These advancements were part of Edison's broader efforts to develop a comprehensive electric lighting system that mimicked the existing gas lighting networks, further solidifying his impact on modern electric lighting.

163

Edison's famous horseshoe paper-filament lamp of 1870, shown in *The Story of Great Inventions*.

164

British chemist Sir Humphry Davy invented the safety lantern in 1815, improving protection for miners by using a mesh screen to encase the flame. Later on, he added an ignition that could be regulated, preventing methane gas explosions in coal mines. This innovation not only saved countless lives but also influenced industry safety protocols.

165

In the 1870s, English physicist Joseph Swan invented an early electric light bulb using a carbonised paper filament enclosed in an evacuated glass bulb. This design offered a practical and durable source of light. Demonstrated in Newcastle, England, it significantly advanced the development of electric lighting, laying the groundwork for the widespread adoption of electric light and altering the course of lighting history. Swan's contributions are foundational, predating and influencing the work of other inventors like Thomas Edison.

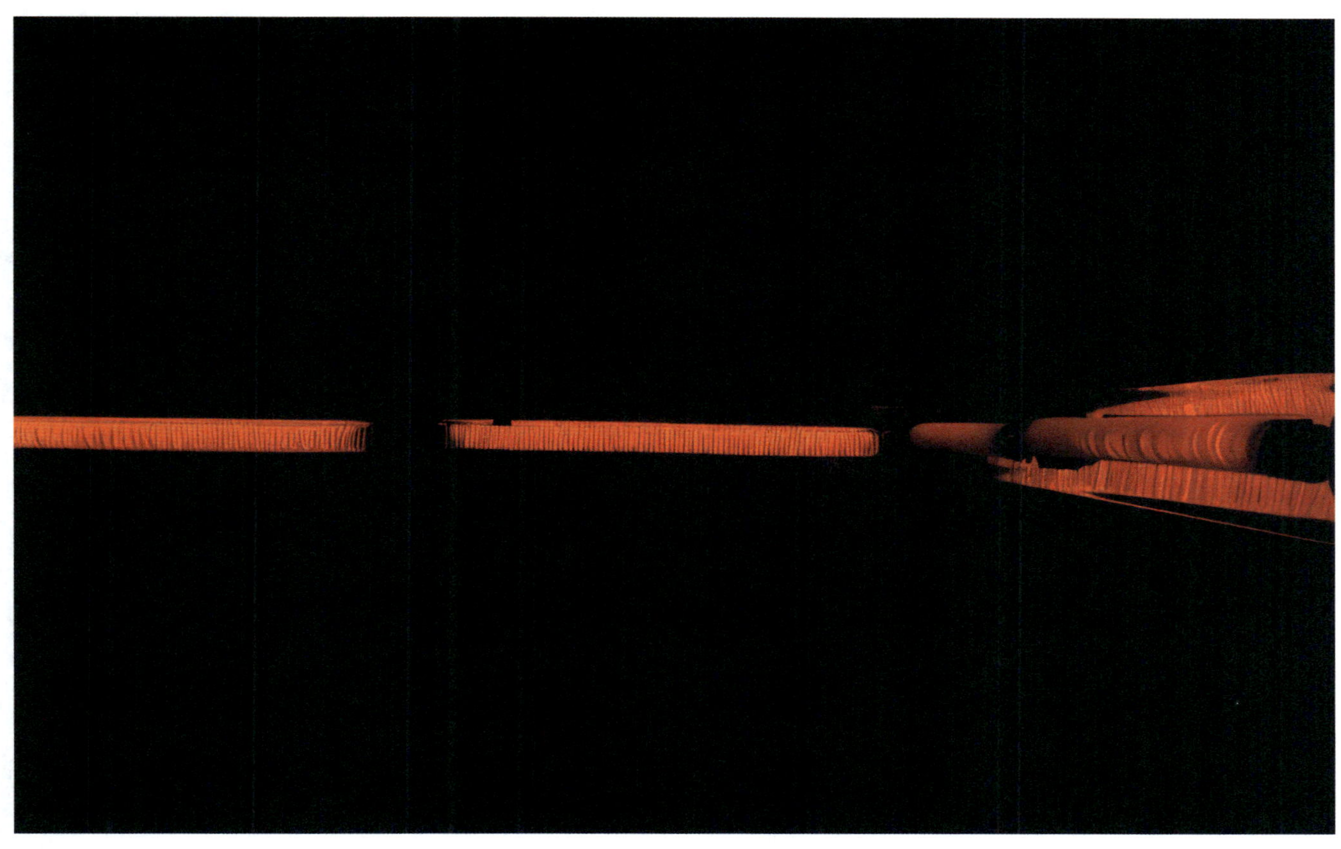

161

163

162

164

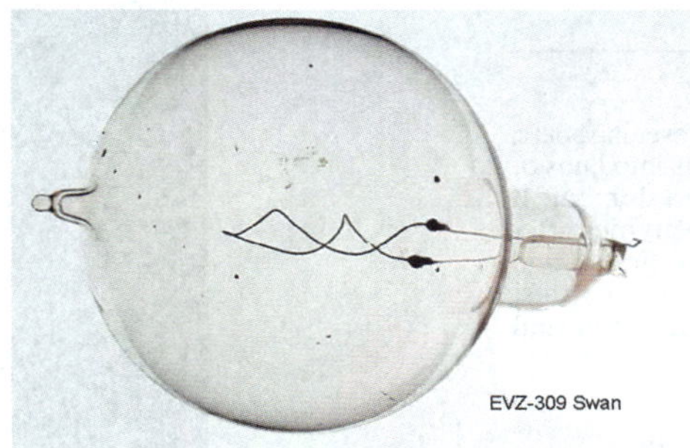

165

166

166
Thomas Rowlandson's 1809 caricature
A Peep at the Gas-lights in Pall Mall
humorously depicts Londoners'
mixed reactions to the introduction
of gas street lighting. The drawing
captures the marvel, scepticism,
and concerns surrounding the then
innovative technology, contrasting
its promise of brightness against
fears of change and its impact on
traditional practices. As gas lighting
illuminated the streets, it sparked
debates on progress versus tradition,
safety, and the transformation of
urban nightlife.

167
Illumination extended evening hours,
revolutionising streets into hubs of
enjoyment and entertainment. It
facilitated outdoor activities after
sunset, enriching public life and
communal interaction in cities,
thereby reshaping the nocturnal
urban landscape.

167

Le Général d'Alton poursuivi par les Reverberes Patriotiques.

G. 26346

168

169

168

In 1667, Louis XIV established public lighting in Paris, which coincided with the creation of the city's police department, intertwining absolute monarchy with the maintenance of public order and surveillance.[95] Strict lighting schedules and instructions for lamplighters were implemented, which were centrally managed by the police as a way to facilitate urban control and state rationalisation through city planning. The role of street lighting extended beyond practical illumination to symbolise the power of the monarchy. By the late eighteenth century, street lanterns evolved into symbols of revolutionary fervour, representing a shift in societal structure and political power. The term *lanterner*, originally meaning "to loiter," took on a more sinister connotation after the French Revolution, referring to acts of hanging. This changed societal perceptions of streetlights, blending their practical utility with significant political symbolism.[96]

169

In 1878, the gas lighting on Victoria Embankment was replaced with the innovative Jablochkoff candle arc lighting system, powered by Gramme AC generators and steam engines. This early experimentation was a stark contrast between gas and electric lighting. The Embankment lighting was ultimately reverted back to gas in 1884 because electricity costs were not competitive enough at the time.

التقاط الضوء – كهرباء

170
Elanto's store with store manager
Paavo Aaltonen in Helsinki 1958.

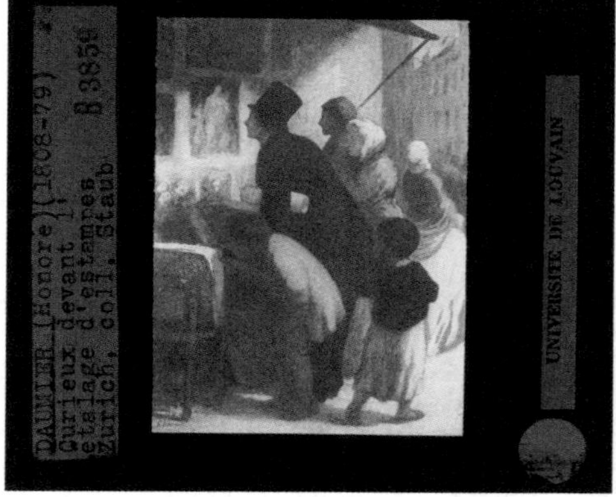

171
Curious people in front of a shop
window, illustrated by French painter
Honoré Daumier. The illuminated
window at nighttime not only draws
attention but also transforms the
street into a stage for interaction and
observation. The advancements in
lighting began to alter the dynamics of
urban life, making the public domain
more accessible and engaging for
evening activities, fostering a new
culture of nighttime social gathering
and spectacle.

172
"The passer-by is indisposed by a
brand which uses and abuses his
eyes, obliging them to submit to
work they had not consented to." [97]
– Désiré Hémet

173

173
The world's first neon sign illuminated a Parisian boulevard in 1912,
marking the beginning of a new
era in advertising. Developed over
a century ago in Paris, neon signs
are more than just advertising tools,
they capture a pre-World War I era
in Europe, which can be characterised by a sense of progressive
innocence. They extended shopping
and working hours, furthering the
advancement of capitalism. Today,
neon signs are often either discarded
objects or treasured pieces.

174
"Our markets, our commercial
thoroughfares, our supermarkets
mimic a rediscovered, prodigiously
fertile, natural environment. They
are for us like the biblical Promised
Land of Canaan, where instead
of milk and honey, the neon
flows over ketchup and plastic."[98]
– Jean Baudrillard

In *The Consumer Society*, Baudrillard
was writing not long before the
end of the thirty-year post-World
War II boom.

Society's fear of dark spaces was emblematic
of a broader fear of the unknown and uncon-
trolled, which electricity sought to illuminate
and manage. Electricity's impact on society
began with its ability to colonise the dark
corners of cities. Street lighting did more than
extend the functional hours of urban centres, it
symbolically and physically claimed the night
for human activity. This illumination was not
just a conquest over the natural cycle but also
a way to impose order and facilitate surveillance, integrating marginalised areas into the
centre and extending the reach of established
social hierarchies into the night. As electricity
became more commonplace, it facilitated the
spread of communication technologies—from
the telegraph and radio to the internet—each
leap in technological capability brought with
it a corresponding shift in how societies functioned, interacted, and governed.

The accessibility of electric light and power also
highlighted and sometimes exacerbated social
divisions, with electrified areas symbolising
progress and power, while those left in the dark
were further marginalised. This integration
of electrical technology into daily life also
transformed domestic spaces and influenced
economic structures, pushing the boundaries
of when and how commerce and industry ope-
rated. The introduction of neon lighting, for
example, changed the face of advertising and
consumer culture, making it a vivid symbol of
both commercial opportunity and, as French
philosopher Jean Baudrillard would critique, of
a society increasingly dominated by spectacle
and superficiality. Electricity's ability to "light
up" the world has been as much about power
and control as it has been about connectivity
and progress.

1. The Chandelier in the Concert Room.—2. Chandelier (Brush System) in the Tropical Section.—3. The Time o' Day.—4. The Concert Room, The Edison Company's Exhibit.—5. The Siemens Chandelier Over the Fountain.—6. The Balloon for Photographing.—7. The First Telegraph Instrument, 1816.—8. The Five-Needle Instrument.—9. The Single Current Sounder.

THE CRYSTAL PALACE ELECTRICAL EXHIBITION

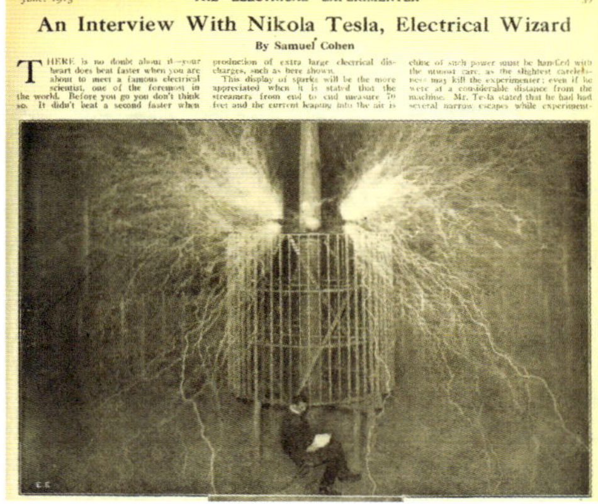

June. 1915   THE ELECTRICAL EXPERIMENTER

An Interview With Nikola Tesla, Electrical Wizard

By Samuel Cohen

THERE is no doubt about it—your heart does beat faster when you are about to meet a famous electrical scientist, one of the foremost in the world. Before you go you don't think so. It didn't beat a second faster when

production of extra large electrical discharges, such as here shown.

This display of sparks will be the more appreciated when it is stated that the streamers from end to end measure 70 feet and the current leaping into the air is

chine of such power must be handled with the utmost care, as the slightest carelessness may kill the experimenter; even if he were at a considerable distance from the machine. Mr. Tesla stated that he had had several narrow escapes while experiment-

176

The 1882 Electrical Exhibition at Crystal Palace in Sydenham, England, was set to surpass nearly all previous displays of electrical appliances. It highlighted the rapid advancements in electrical science over the prior years and showcased an extensive array of new inventions, such as the first telegraph instrument, electric chandeliers, and complex machinery. Visitors were able to engage with extensive and varied uses of electricity, from trams and sewing machines to pianos and cannons. This exhibition presented electricity's potential to revolutionise society, exceeding that of the impact of the steam power.[99]

177

"The largest sparks ever produced by Man. Mr. Tesla is seen sitting. Seventy feet across spark streamers. Lower photo: Mr. Tesla and his marvellous wireless light."[100] – Samuel Cohen, *The Electrical Experimenter*.

178

The Electrical Experimenter, launched in May 1913 and edited by Hugo Gernsback, was an American science magazine focused on innovations in radio and electrical science. It featured a mix of scientific articles and early science fiction, reflecting Gernsback's interest in fostering imaginative approaches to technology. It was published monthly until July 1920, after which it evolved into *Science and Invention*.

179

"While there have been many novel applications made recently of the electric flashlight, probably one of the most useful for literary people, such as reporters, etc., is that shown in the illustration, and embodying a complete miniature electric flashlight with battery, adaptable to a pencil. A simple switch on the same enables the user to utilise the light whenever desired."[101]

180

180
A 1-watt power LED.

181
Thousands of factory workers assembling and testing fibre optic systems.

182
Historically, people used light to transmit critical information (like the outcome of a battle) by way of tools like mirrors, fire beacons, or smoke signals.[102] Although optical fibres were already in use during the 1960s for applications like gastroscopes, they were not initially considered seriously for broader communication purposes. It was not until the development of low-loss fibres that their potential was fully recognised. Since then, nearly two billion kilometres of fibre have been produced—enough to span the distance from Earth to Jupiter, significantly advancing global communication infrastructure.[103]

183
The term "laser" stands for Light Amplification by Stimulated Emission of Radiation. This revolutionary technology was first demonstrated on May 16, 1960, by American physicist Theodore Harold Maiman at Hughes Research Laboratories, United States.[104] During a press conference on July 7, 1960, Maiman highlighted several promising applications for his invention, including the first true amplification of light, its use as a research tool to probe matter, and the potential for high-power beams in space communications. He also envisioned lasers increasing the number of communication channels and concentrating light for uses in industry, chemistry, and medicine. However, Maiman was cautious about discussing the potential military uses of lasers, acknowledging the possibility but preferring to focus on their constructive applications.[105]

181

182

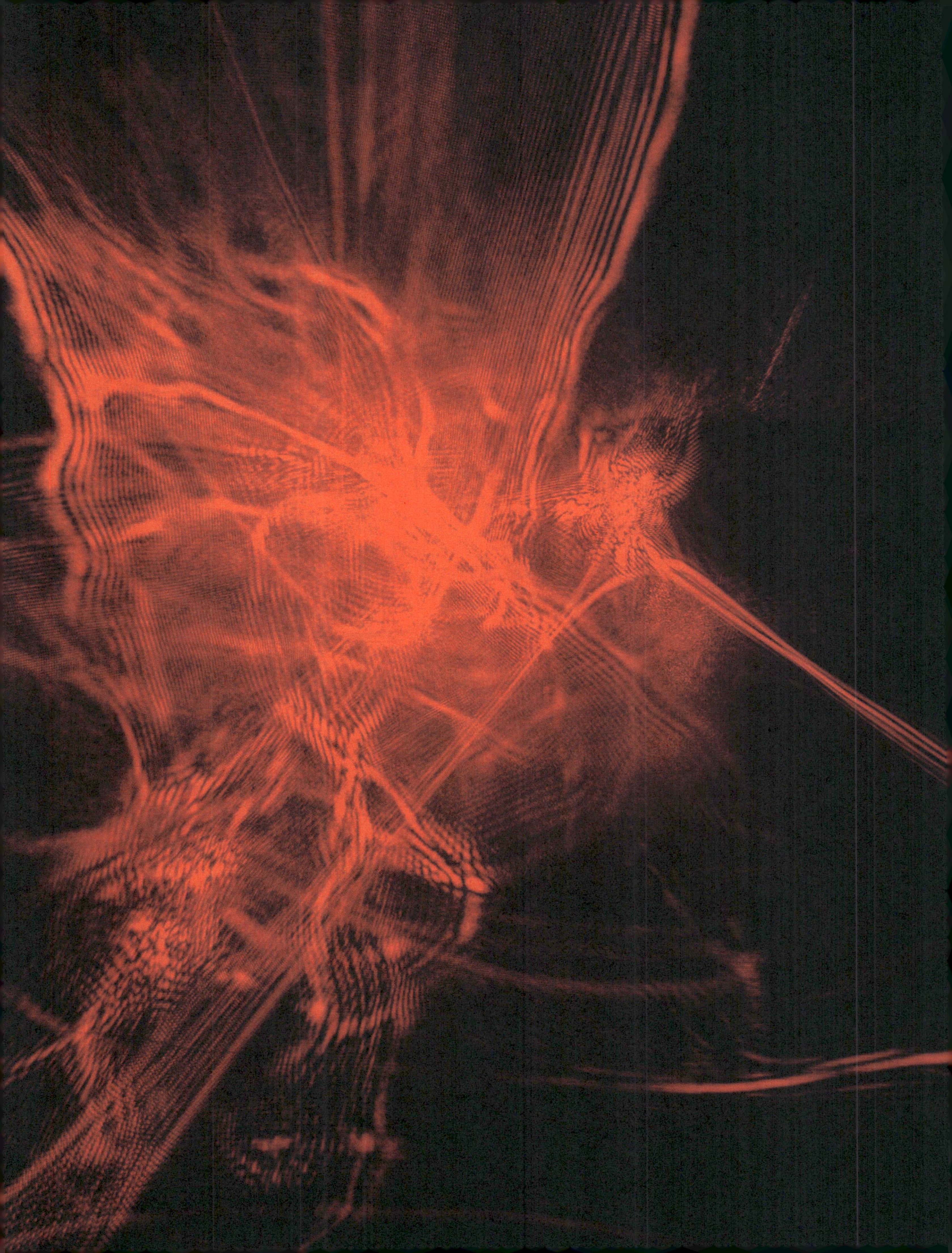

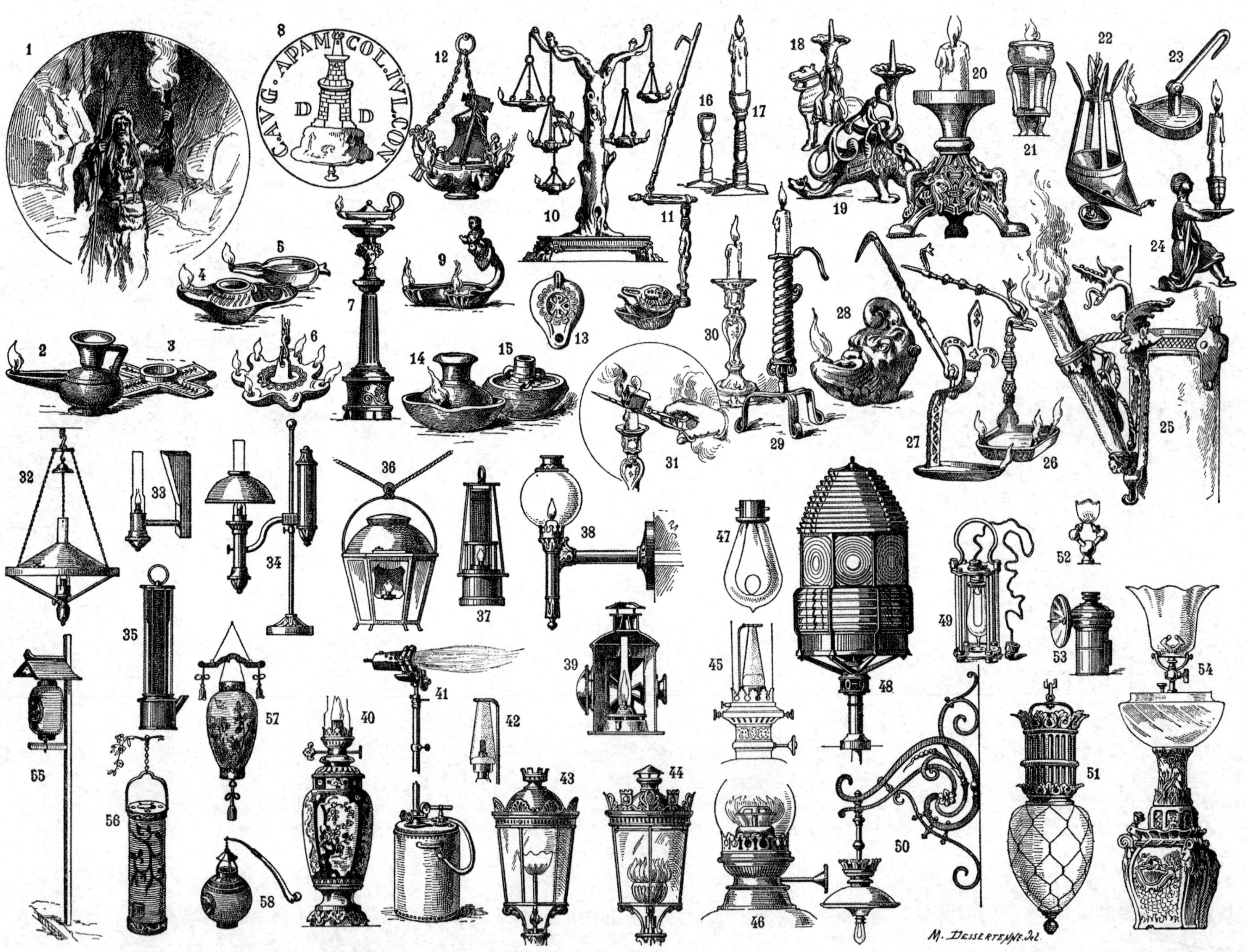

184
Maurice Dessertenne, Eclairage, ca. 1900, from *Nouveau Larousse Illustré*, tome 4, "E-G."[106]

No. 1. Antiquity	No. 2. Antiquity	No. 3. Antiquity	No. 4. Antiquity	No. 5. Antiquity	No. 6. Antiquity
Prehistory	Egyptian	Egyptian	Assyrian	Assyrian	Roman
No. 7. Antiquity	**No. 8. Antiquity**	**No. 9. Antiquity**	**No. 10. Antiquity**	**No. 11. Antiquity**	**No. 12. Antiquity**
Roman	Roman	Roman	Roman	Roman	Roman
No. 13. Antiquity	**No. 14. Antiquity**	**No. 15. Antiquity**	**No. 16. Antiquity**	**No. 17. Antiquity**	**No. 18. Antiquity**
Roman	Carthaginian	Carthaginian	Merovingian period	Merovingian period	Firefly lamp
No. 19. Middle age and modern times	**No. 20. Middle age and modern times**	**No. 21. Middle age and modern times**	**No. 22. Middle age and modern times**	**No. 23. Middle age and modern times**	**No. 24. Middle age and modern times**
11th century	11th century	12th century	13th century	14th century	14th century
No. 25. Middle age and modern times	**No. 26. Middle age and modern times**	**No. 27. Middle age and modern times**	**No. 28. Middle age and modern times**	**No. 29. Middle age and modern times**	**No. 30. Middle age and modern times**
15th century	15th century	15th century	16th century	17th century	18th century
No. 31. Middle age and modern times	**No. 32. Contemporary period**	**No. 33. Contemporary period**	**No. 34. Contemporary period**	**No. 35. Contemporary period**	**No. 36. Contemporary period**
18th century	Argand lamp (original)	Argand lamp (Antoine Quinquet's improved)	Argand lamp (Antoine Quinquet's improved)	Stephenson (Geordie) lamp (mines)	Street light
No. 37. Contemporary period	**No. 38. Contemporary period**	**No. 39. Contemporary period**	**No. 40. Contemporary period**	**No. 41. Contemporary period**	**No. 42. Contemporary period**
Davy lamp	Air-fed wick lamp (theatre)	Railway lamp	Carcel lamp	Gasifier	Auer (gas) lamp with gas mantle
No. 43. Contemporary period	**No. 44. Contemporary period**	**No. 45. Contemporary period**	**No. 46. Contemporary period**	**No. 47. Contemporary period**	**No. 48. Contemporary period**
Gas street lighting (regular burner)	Gas street lighting (high intensity burner)	Auer (petrol) lamp	Petrol lamp (air-fed)	Incandescent (electricity)	Lighthouse (electricity)
No. 49. Contemporary period	**No. 50. Contemporary period**	**No. 51. Contemporary period**	**No. 52. Contemporary period**	**No. 53. Contemporary period**	**No. 54. Contemporary period**
Mine lamp (electricity)	Incandescent (electricity)	Arc light (electricity)	Acetylene lamp (burner)	Acetylene lamp (bicycle)	Acetylene lamp (lamp)
No. 55. Contemporary period	**No. 56. Contemporary period**	**No. 57. Contemporary period**	**No. 58. Contemporary period**		
Street light	Transportation (rickshaw)	Lantern for funerals	Portable lantern		

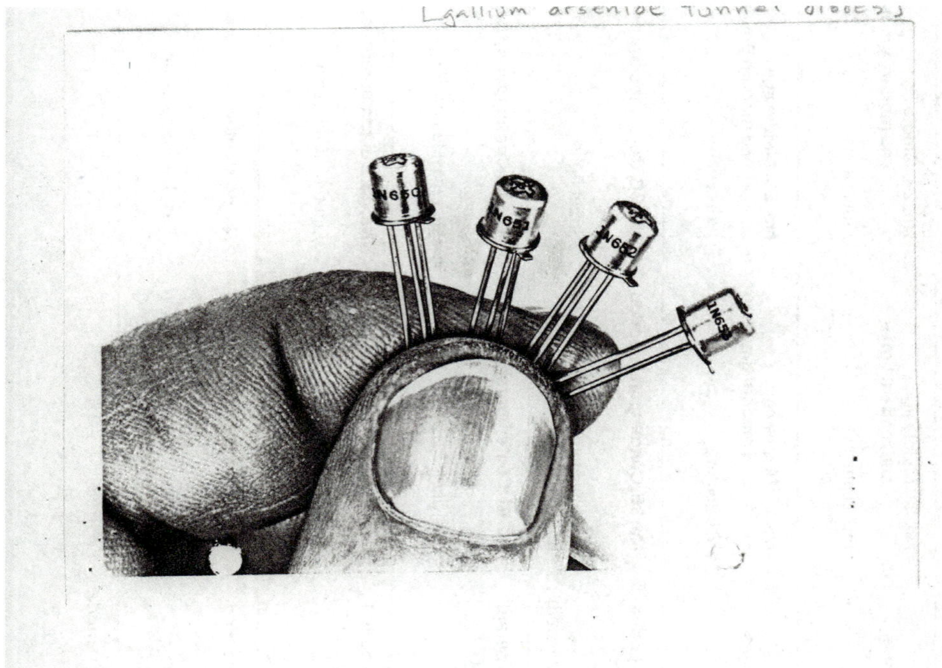

185
The 1N650 series of GaAs tunnel diodes. American electrical engineer and inventor James Robert Biard, held 73 U.S. patents, including the first infrared LED. Initially used in traffic lights to better manage pedestrian and vehicular movement, light-emitting diodes (LEDs) eventually expanded into household appliances. LEDs emit visible light, which is now ubiquitous in everything from light bulbs and device screens to lasers. They offer numerous benefits over traditional incandescent sources: they consume less power, last longer, are more durable, more compact, and can switch on and off more quickly.

ciency of emission was poor. The MIT Lincoln Laboratories first reported the efficient generation of incoherent infrared radiation from gallium arsenide p-n junction diodes. A coherent source would yield greater directionability, power density, and spectrum narrowing of the emitted beam. The ability to obtain coherent electroluminescent emission from a p-n junction diode would greatly simplify certain electronic equipment problems.

A gallium arsenide infrared-source diode, the SNX-100, is shown in Fig. 2-11. The SNX-100 may be applied in such applications as a source for equipment in secured optical communication links, transmission of TV signals, light source for tape or card reader on computers, and source in infrared radar equipment.

Fig. 2-11. A gallium arsenide infrared-source diode.

Courtesy Texas Instruments, Inc.

The diode is designed to operate as a forward-biased diode to emit light of a relatively narrow spectral width in the near infrared. The output can be modulated linearly with the forward bias current. The device has been successfully modulated at frequencies from dc through 900 mc.

36

This device produces noncoherent light, but semiconductor junction diodes which emit coherent infrared radiation have been produced as well. These devices consist of gallium arsenide p-n junction diodes which, when biased in the forward injection region, generate coherent infrared radiation of approximately 8400Å and a spectral width of 15Å.

In the p-n junction LASER a population inversion is produced in a thin layer of semiconductor in the immediate vicinity of the junction by the injection of electrons and holes from the strongly n- and p-type adjoining regions. When biased above the threshold for coherent light emission, a guided wave is established in the plane of the junction, propagating in a direction normal to the reflecting faces of the resonator cavity. This can be represented in other terms as a dielectric slab corresponding to the region of population inversion within which the electrical conductivity is negative, and which is embedded between semi-infinite regions of dielectric having positive conductivities.

A LASER of this type does not require pumping from a light source by an auxiliary process. Instead, the excitation is achieved directly by injection of electrons (and holes) into the plane of the junction region. This narrow plane (less than one ten-thousandth of an inch thick) is in the middle of a tiny diode of gallium arsenide. A directional and coherent beam of infrared light is emitted from the junction-plane edges at two carefully polished and precisely parallel sides of the device. This light has a wavelength of about 8400 angstrom units. The crystal used in this diode LASER is the shape of a cube, each edge measuring about one-third of a millimeter.

Current drive is used for this type system rather than an optical pump. To achieve LASER action, intense electric currents, as high as 20,000 amperes per square centimeter, are applied to the crystal. The device is cooled to liquid-nitrogen or liquid-helium temperatures. Also, to keep the device from overheating, the current is applied in pulses a few microseconds long and at a low duty cycle which is a short on-time and long off-time. Refinements in semiconductor materials and different designs may permit the continuous-wave operation needed for some applications. It should also be possible to build substantially larger and more powerful devices than the present developmental models.

Gas LASERS

Gas-phase LASERS date from 1961 as continuous-wave light sources or oscillators. Various gas mixtures are placed in

37

186
SNX-100, the first commercial LED product, taken in the early 1960s by the Semiconductor Components Division at Texas Instruments.

89 Foucault, *Power/Knowledge*, 152.

90 Rahman, "Basics of Electricity," 27.

91 Franklin, *Experiments and Observations on Electricity*, 62.

92 Fulton, *A Bibliography of the Honourable Robert Boyle*, 85.

93 Blakemore, "Thomas Edison Didn't Invent the Light Bulb—But Here's What He Did Do," *National Geographic*, April 13, 2022, https://www.nationalgeographic.com/history/article/thomas-edison-light-bulb-history.

94 Matulka and Wood, "The History of the Light Bulb," United States Department of Energy, November 22, 2013, https://www.energy.gov/articles/history-light-bulb.

95 Phillips, *Enlightened Nightscapes*, 11.

96 Jean Baudrillard, *The Consumer Society*, 26.

97 Hémet, *Practical Treatise on Advertising*, cited in De Miranda, *Being and Neonness*, 17.

98 Jean Baudrillard, *The Consumer Society*, 26.

99 "Electrical Appliances Exhibited at the 1882 Electrical Exhibition, Including Chandeliers and the First Telegraph Instrument. Wood Engraving, 1882," Wellcome Collection, https://wellcomecollection.org/works/pvwzyswy.

100 Cohen, "An Interview with Nikola Tesla, Electrical Wizard," The Electrical Experimenter (June 1915): 39.

101 "A Flashlight for the Pencil," *The Electrical Experimenter* (July 1915): 92.

102 Agrawal, "Optical Communication: Its History and Recent Progress," 178.

103 Ballato and Dragic, "Glass," 413.

104 Bernatskyi, and Khaskin, "The History of the Creation of Lasers," 127.

105 Gernsback, "An Electric Thermometer Sign," *The Electrical Experimenter* (June 1915): 46.

106 Maurice Dessertenne, "Eclairage," Wikipedia, https://commons.wikimedia.org/wiki/File:Eclairage.jpg.

أركيولوجيا الضوء

ARCHEOLOGY OF LIGHT

187

CAPTURING

Energy

LIGHT

|

"Everything in the universe may be described in terms of energy. Galaxies, stars, molecules, and atoms may be regarded as organizations of energy. Living organisms may be looked upon as engines which operate by means of energy derived directly or indirectly from the sun. The civilizations or cultures of mankind, also, may be regarded as a form or organization of energy. [107]

Leslie White

187
In 1861, French innovator and mathematician Auguste Mouchot filed a patent for a solar machine, one of the earliest attempts to harness solar energy for mechanical use.[108] In 1878, during the Universal Exposition in Paris, Mouchot showcased what was then considered the world's largest machine capable of producing solar steam. This exhibit featured his solar machine powering a printing press in the Tuileries Garden, which impressively produced 500 copies per hour of the newspaper *Le Soleil*. By 1897, American inventor Frank Shuman had already patented a safety glass for skylights before he turned his focus to solar energy. He then established the Sun Shine Power Company, which patented a full-scale solar engine in 1912. A year later, his experiments culminated in building the world's first solar power station in Maadi, Egypt. This facility used solar power to operate a 60-70 horsepower engine that pumped 6000 gallons of water per minute from the Nile to irrigate cotton fields.[109]

188

188
The first electricity generated wind turbine was installed at the Vienna International Electrical Exhibition in 1883 by Austrian Josef Friedländer.

189

190

CAPTURING LIGHT – ENERGY

189
Moto (Senegal) PV Power Plant with bifacial solar cells. In the 1970s, the oil crisis changed the heavy global reliance on imported oil, prompting significant economic and energy policy shifts. United States President Jimmy Carter installed solar panels on the White House in 1978, promoting solar energy as a cleaner alternative to conventional fossil fuels and "resolving" the energy crisis.[110] The crisis also led to innovations in energy conservation, such as extending daylight saving time to reduce energy consumption, echoing measures from World War II under different circumstances. These initiatives were part of broader strategies aimed at reducing dependence on oil and exploring sustainable solutions, thereby laying the groundwork for the ongoing shift from "alternative energies" to what is now broadly recognised as "renewable energy sources."[111]

190
The Topaz Solar Farm, United States. It is a 550-megawatt facility that produces enough electricity to power 180,000 homes.[112]

191
"Years Ago Man Endeavored to Make Practical Use of the Energy Contained in the Sun's Rays—Even Tesla, the Electrical Wizard, Has Patented a Sun Motor, While the Shuman-Boy's Engine and Sun Boiler Has Developed 100 H. P. There Is Great Promise Held Forth to Future Engineers Who May Work on This Problem."[113] – Hugo Gernsback

THE ELECTRICAL EXPERIMENTER

H. GERNSBACK EDITOR
H. W. SECOR ASSOCIATE EDITOR

Vol. III. Whole No. 35 — MARCH, 1916 — Number 11

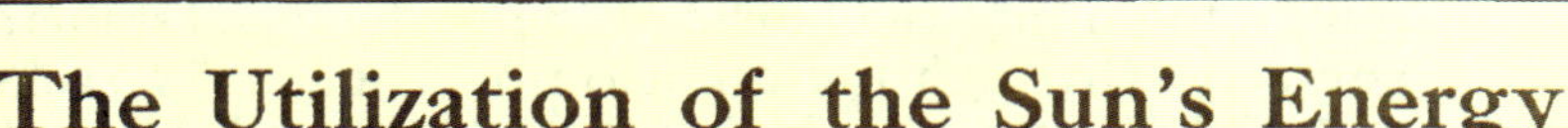

The Utilization of the Sun's Energy

Years Ago Man Endeavored to Make Practical Use of the Energy Contained in the Sun's Rays—Even Tesla, the Electrical Wizard, Has Patented a Sun Motor, While the Shuman-Boy's Engine and Sun Boiler Has Developed 100 H. P. There Is Great Promise Held Forth to Future Engineers Who May Work on This Problem.

IT has been given to astrophysicists to measure the heat generated by the sun and calculate the force emanating from it. We know that the surface of our luminary gives out a heat estimated to be about 6,000° centigrade, and that its light equals that of 27,000,000,000 candlepower a quarter of a mile away. The heat which the

were lacking, our planet, with all its thousandfold life, its thick forests and fruitful plains, would turn into a dead, rigid ball of rock, for the average annual temperature, which is now one of 13° centigrade of warmth for Europe, would, without the heat of the sun, sink to 73° centigrade of frost, it is calculated.

the untaught son of nature brightens his hut, the twigs with which he stokes his fire, what are they but pieces of trees that grew in the sunlight? The gas of the city dweller, the coals with which he heats his house and from which the gas has been sucked, what are they but transformed sunbeams? The coal in the grate is the

Energy embodies many meanings and roles, permeating every aspect of our universe, from the cosmic to the microscopic. At the heart of energy is photosynthesis, the earliest method of capturing solar energy, which has fuelled our ecosystems and sustained our human societies. It has supported life on earth and driven early agricultural practices, organising communities around the cultivation of energy-rich crops. Ancient cultures did not simply harness energy, they integrated it into the fabric of their societies through the creation of material objects, rituals, ideas, and symbols—energy as a manifestation of cultural identity.

Today, our engagement with energy is bound to a critical shift toward sustainability. The transition from fossil fuels to renewable sources like solar is not just a technological shift but a necessary adaptation to global ecological challenges. Energy security, involving the complex dynamics of production, distribution, and consumption, has become a currency crucial for national independence. And yet past and current consumption patterns, particularly in capitalist cities, are highly influenced by social status and exceed reasonable needs. The relationship with energy extends beyond utility to encompass ethical and ecological dimensions, forcing society to rethink how to ensure both human and non-human life survives and flourishes in coexistence with earth.

192
An organic solar cell.

193
The Roll-Out Solar Array (ROSA) represents a breakthrough in solar panel technology, featuring a design that allows it to unroll in space like a tape measure. This innovative approach offers a more space-efficient alternative compared to the traditional, bulkier rigid solar panels.

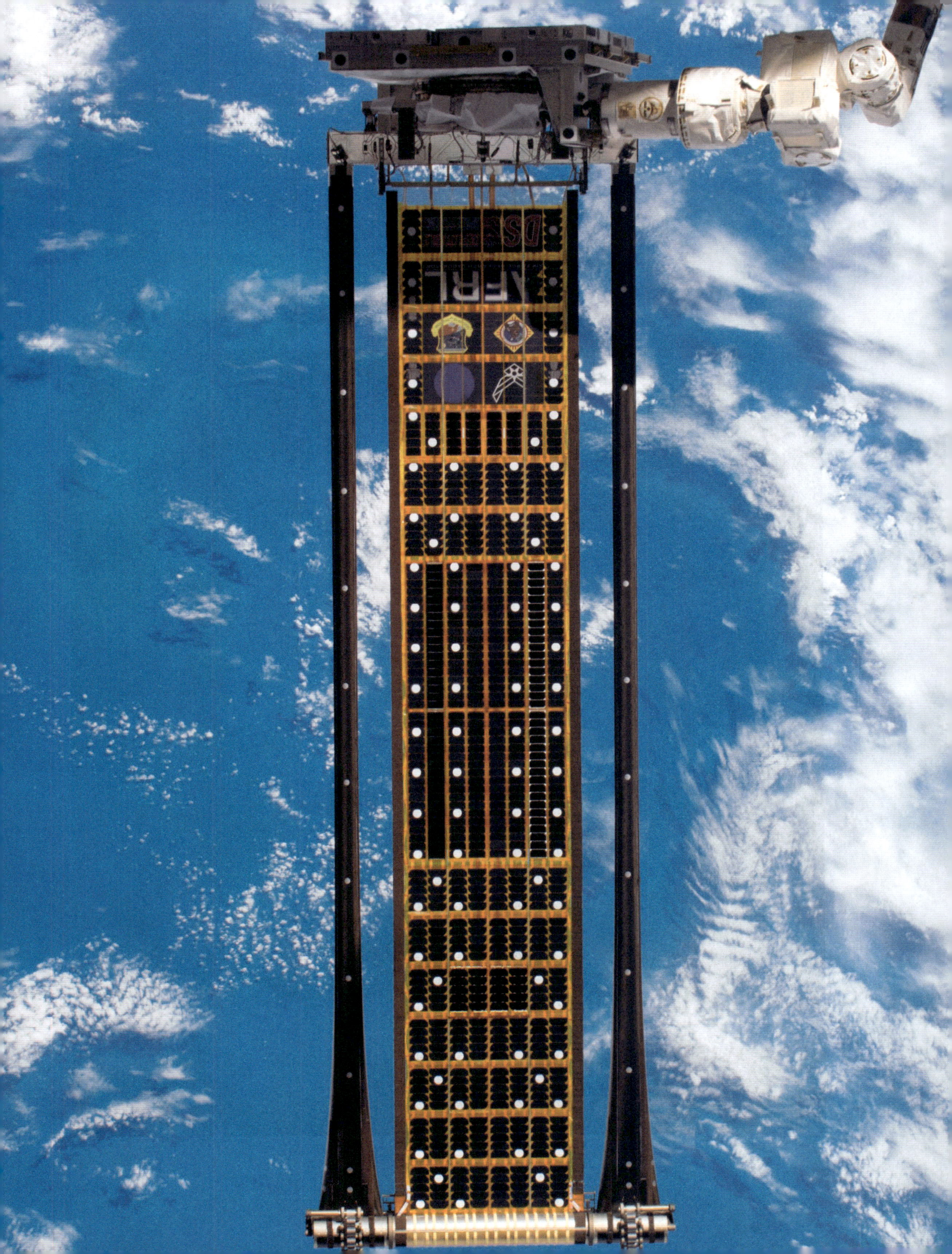

196

197

196
Ivanpah Solar Energy Plant, United States. It is a 392-megawatt facility that produces enough electricity to power 140,000 homes.[115]

197
Solar Photovoltaic Panels on top of the mountains in Colorado, United States.

198

198
The Crescent Dunes Solar Energy Project near Tonopah, United States. It is a 110-megawatt facility.

194
An intense "energy flash" was produced on January 1, 1963 when a projectile travelling at speeds of up to 17,000 miles per hour collided with a solid target at NASA's Ames Research Center Hypervelocity Ballistic Range. This experiment was designed to mimic the effects of orbital debris striking a spacecraft in orbit.[114]

195
The Crescent Dunes Solar Energy Project taken through the window of a commercial airliner between Chicago and San Francisco, United States.

199

200

201

199

American astronomer Nancy Grace Roman was a trailblazer during the mid-twentieth century, particularly during the formative years of NASA, which she joined in 1959.[116] In 1961, Roman became the first woman to hold an executive position at NASA as the Chief of Astronomy and Relativity in the Office of Space Science. Between 1966 and 1972, she was instrumental in launching four Orbiting Astronomical Observatories that set the stage for future advancements in space-based astrophysics. She also championed the International Ultraviolet Explorer—a 1970s collaboration between NASA, the European Space Agency, and the United Kingdom—and the Cosmic Background Explorer, which significantly contributed to our understanding of the universe's origins. Perhaps her most significant contribution was to the development of the Hubble Space Telescope. Ed Weiler, Hubble chief scientist until 1998, referred to Roman as "the mother of the Hubble Space Telescope".[117]

200

The Hubble Space Telescope, 1986.

201

Early construction of the frame of the Hubble Telescope, which was completed in 1985.

202

203

204

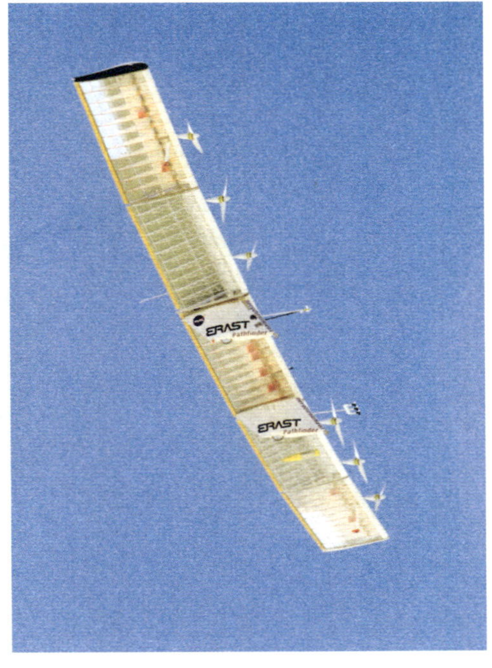

202
The Hubble Space Telescope captured by a crew member on the Space Shuttle Atlantis, 2009.

203
NASA's compact rover with deployed solar panels prepares for a lunar mission. It is approximately the size of a carry-on suitcase.

204
Pathfinder, NASA's solar-powered, unmanned aircraft, was involved in conducting a series of missions over Kauai, Hawaii. These missions were designed to demonstrate the aircraft's capabilities in scientific research by gathering data on forest and coastal ecosystems. During these flights, Pathfinder was equipped with two innovative instruments: the Digital Array Scanned Interferometer (DASI) for high spectral resolution, and the Airborne Real-Time Imaging System (ARTIS) for high spatial resolution.

205
Pathfinder during a test flight over California, 1996.

206
Six satellites, each roughly the size of a cereal box and equipped with solar panels, are part of an ambitious project to study the Sun. They function collectively as a large radio receiver, capable of detecting solar radio bursts from the Sun's outer atmosphere. By monitoring and locating these bursts, the mission aims to provide crucial data that could help forecast space weather events.

207
Close up of the Solar Wind Panel, Apollo 12 mission in 1969.

206

207

208
The Crab Nebula is the residue of a massive supernova. It was documented nearly a millennium ago in 1054, by observers in China and Japan.

209
Observations by NASA's Fermi Gamma-ray Space Telescope have revealed images showing the emission of radiation from supernova remnants, which is a billion times more energetic than visible light. These findings help astronomers advance their understanding of cosmic rays, some of the most high-energy particles in the universe. Supernovae, the explosive deaths of massive stars at the end of their evolutionary cycles, release enormous amounts of energy across various wavelengths. This explosion can briefly cause the deceased star to shine brighter than the entire galaxy it resides in.

208

209

210

211

212

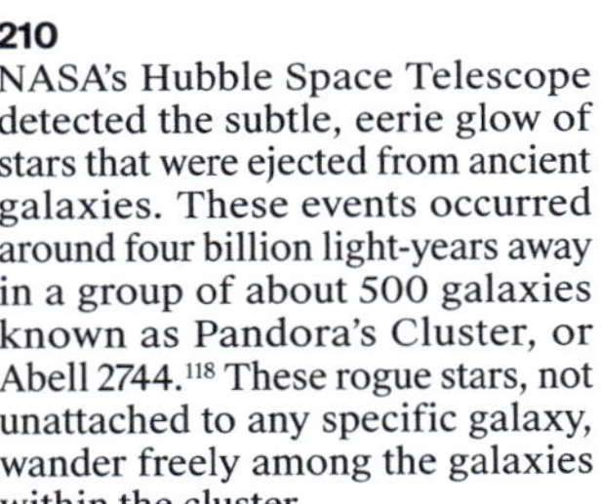

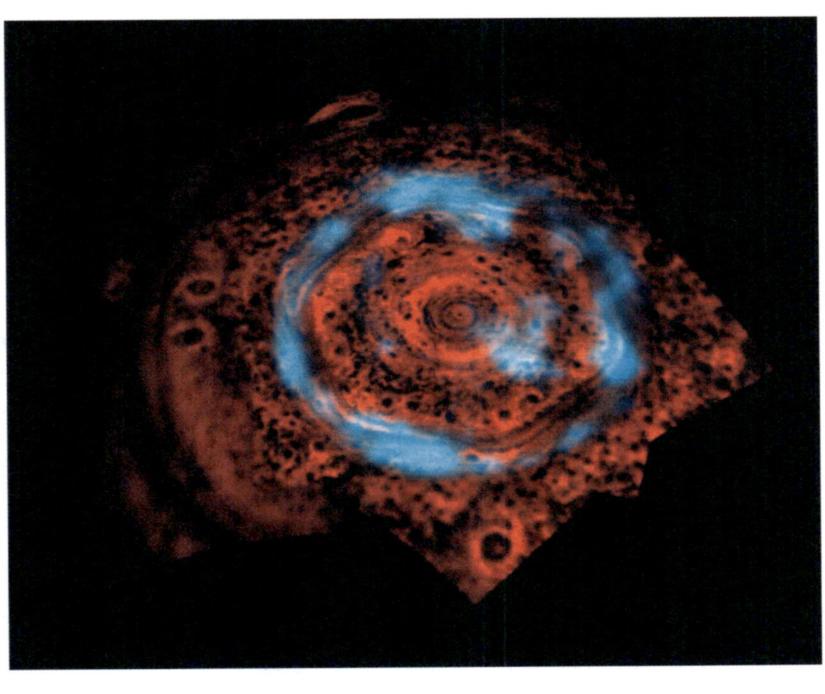

210
NASA's Hubble Space Telescope detected the subtle, eerie glow of stars that were ejected from ancient galaxies. These events occurred around four billion light-years away in a group of about 500 galaxies known as Pandora's Cluster, or Abell 2744.[118] These rogue stars, not unattached to any specific galaxy, wander freely among the galaxies within the cluster.

211
Using a 35 mm camera lens, the southern lights, or the Aurora Australis, was recorded from the Discovery shuttle in 1997.

212
Saturn polar aurora captured in 2008.

[107] White, "Energy and the Evolution of Culture," 335.

[108] Silvi, "Italian Contribution to CSP With Flat or Almost Flat Reflectors," 2.

[109] Gernsback, Electric Light from Windmills," *The Electrical Experimenter* (June 1915): 46.

[110] Starowicz, "Photovoltaic Cell," 174.

[111] Matulka and Wood, "The History of the Light Bulb," United States Department of Energy, November 22, 2013, https://www.energy.gov/articles/history-light-bulb.

[112] Allen, "Topaz Solar Farm, California," NASA Earth Observatory, March 5, 2015, https://earthobservatory.nasa.gov/images/85403/topaz-solar-farm-california.

[113] Gernsback, "The Utilization of the Sun's Energy," *The Electrical Experimenter* (March 1916): 605. https://library.si.edu/digital-library/book/electricalexperi03gern.

[114] "Impact!," NASA, March 23, 2008, https://www.nasa.gov/image-article/impact/.

[115] "Ivanpah Solar Energy Plant, California," NASA Jet Propulsion Laboratory, December 5, 2013, https://www.jpl.nasa.gov/images/pia17746-ivanpah-solar-energy-plant-california.

[116] "The Mother of Hubble," European Space Agency, https://esahubble.org/about/history/the-mother-of-hubble/.

[117] "Nancy Grace Roman," NASA, https://science.nasa.gov/people/nancy-grace-roman-for-hubble/.

[118] "Hubble Sees 'Ghost Light' From Dead Galaxies," NASA Image and Video Library, https://images.nasa.gov/details/GSFC_20171208_Archive_e000914.

|

*"On a cloudless night, looking upwards, you experience
a sudden flipped vertigo, the sensation that your feet might
latch off from the earth and that you might plummet upwards into space.
Star-gazing gives us access to orders of events, and scales of time
and space, which are beyond our capacity to imagine: it is unsurprising
that dreams of humility and reverence have been directed towards the moon
and the stars for as long as human culture has recorded itself.
Our disenchantment of the night through artificial lighting may appear,
if it is noticed at all, as a regrettable but eventually trivial side-effect
of contemporary life. That winter hour, though, up on the summit ridge
with the stars falling plainly far above, it seemed to me that
our estrangement from the dark was a great and serious loss."[119]*

Robert Macfarlane

213

The Andromeda Galaxy, our nearest giant spiral galaxy, is believed to have formed from a significant merger less than three billion years ago. This finding stems from a computational study conducted with high-capacity computers and led by the Galaxies, Stars, Physics, and Instrumentation Laboratory (GEPI) at the Observatoire de Paris.[121] The large nebula that is now known as Andromeda was first documented by astronomer Abd al-Rahman al-Sufi, and described in his *Book of the Fixed Stars* from 964.[122] This significant mediaeval astronomical treatise expanded on Ptolemy's *Almagest*, incorporating al-Sufi's personal observations. Over time, the *Book of the Fixed Stars* has been preserved and copied, with thirty-five manuscripts currently held in various archives worldwide. Andromeda was identified as a galaxy in 1923 and is often considered the Milky Way's twin, providing astronomers a detailed view of its structure, and raising questions that continue to pique the interest of astrophysicists.

214

An image with a 333-second exposure contains at least nineteen streaks from the second batch of Starlink satellites. These were visible to the naked eye.

214

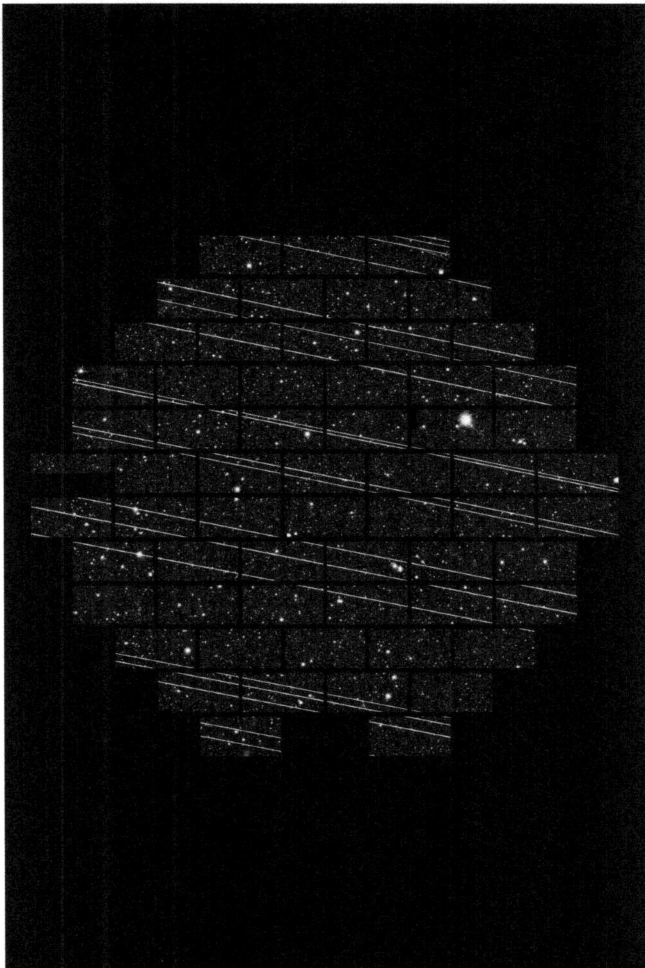

215

Gazing at the stars is a reminder of the vast distances to the planets and the Sun, the innumerable cosmic bodies that move at immeasurable distances, and the origins that created such an extraordinary system. The act transcends earthly confines and allows the imagination to escape the pace of daily life, and for a moment feel a loss of time. One feels boundlessly small, and yet infinitely connected to something vast. However, excessive light in urban environments has obscured many dark skies.[120]

Many Indigenous cultures have foundational nocturnal practices organised around dark skies. For instance, Indigenous Australians view the stars as essential guides for understanding the natural world, embedded in millennia of tradition that informs everything from seasonal changes to medicinal plant usage. Light pollution also affects wildlife by disrupting the nocturnal rhythms that are the basis of feeding and breeding cycles for many species.

The city of Flagstaff, Arizona, United States, was the world's first international Dark Sky City, implementing measures to mitigate light pollution in place since 1958. These were introduced because it is the location at the Lowell Observatory, where Pluto and dark matter were first observed. Despite these efforts, the increasing glow of artificial lighting around the world continues to mask stars, severing ties with a heritage that extends beyond the planet. As the stars fade from view, humanity becomes increasingly disconnected from the vastness of space, losing a sense of perspective and significance of its place in the universe. Perhaps by losing sight of the stars, there is a loss of the innate ability to wonder and be curious about the unknown and the otherworldly.

215
The NGC 5353/4 galaxy group, captured with a telescope at Lowell Observatory on May 25, 2019.[123] The diagonal streaks visible across the image are trails of reflected light from over twenty-five of the sixty Starlink satellites that were launched as they moved through the telescope's viewing range. It is important to note that the concentration of these satellites appears particularly high shortly after their launch, as seen in this image. The brightness of these satellites will decrease as they ascend to their designated orbital altitude.

216
Andromeda seen through long-exposure photographs taken by Dutch photographer Kees Scherer from a garden observatory in Portugal. The image is a composite of 223 separate photos, each with a 300-second exposure.[124] Notable imperfections are present, such as bright parallel aeroplane trails, lengthy and uninterrupted satellite trails, short cosmic ray streaks, and fault pixels. Astronomers often face difficulties from light pollution present in the busy skies and edit them to achieve a clear image.

216

217
The double star Albeiro in Cygnus can be seen behind Starlink satellites travelling across the field. Numerous commercial organisations have initiated and announced plans to launch hundreds or even thousands of satellites.[125] These extensive constellations will negatively impact astronomical observations. The number is expected to exceed the existing brightness limits recommended for such satellite constellations.[126]

218
Even before the recent increase in satellite launches, many were already visible in the night sky. The streaks seen are from satellites reflecting sunlight.

219
Orion can be seen at the left amidst a dark sky. On the right, Orion is barely visible from the city of Orem, United States, a city of 500,000 people.

217

218

219

220

"Towering shafts of light defy the darkness and thousands of lighted windows symbolise man's successful struggle against nature."[127] – Matthew Luckiesh

Luckiesh was the physicist and Director of General Electric's Lighting Research Laboratory in 1920.

221

Illuminations captured in 1906, seen from the Writers' Building in Kolkata, India.

221   **220**

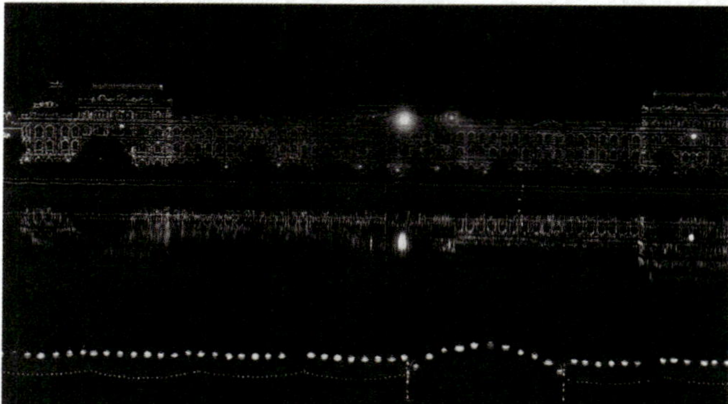

222

222
The 1904 World's Fair in St. Louis, United States, showing The Palace of Electricity by night.

223
Fireworks display at Covent Garden, London, on September 10, 1690, for the celebration of the return of King William III from Ireland.

224
"The Tower of Jewels, the dominating piece of architecture of the entire Panama-Pacific Exposition, is shown here, illuminated for the first time. That it does not belie its title is evidenced by its beauty when it is illuminated. There are 125,000,000 jewels backed by a mirror the size of a 25-cent piece."[128] – Hugo Gernsback

223

224

ARCHEOLOGY OF LIGHT

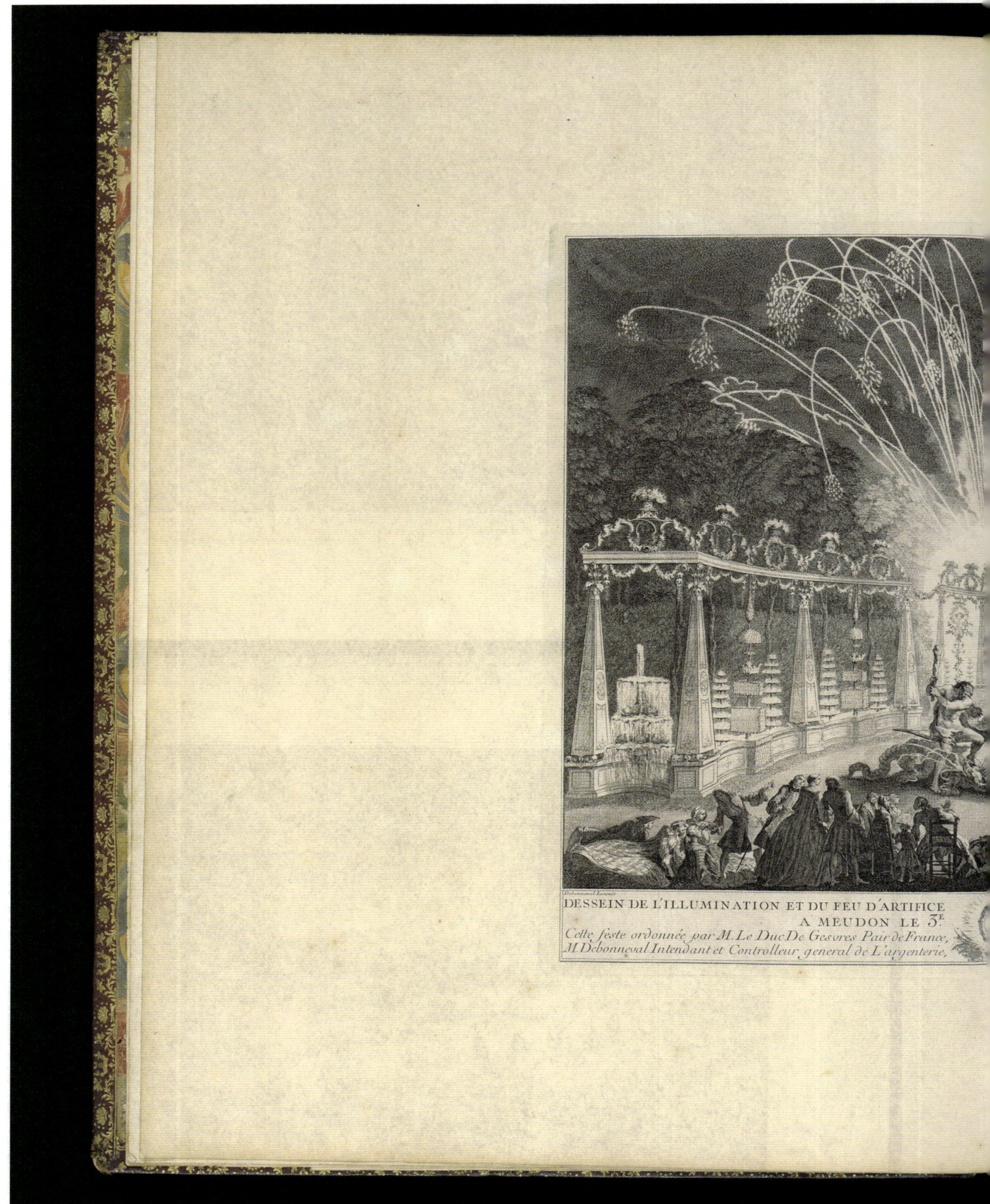

225 A view of the gardens at the Palace of Versailles during a fireworks celebration for Louis XV in 1735.

DONNÉ A MONSEIGNEUR LE DAUPHIN
SEPTEMBRE 1735.
Premier Gentilhomme de la Chambre Du Roy, à esté conduite par
Menuë plaisirs et affaires de La Chambre de Sa Majesté.

226

226

The Moulin Rouge, Paris, in 1958. In his exploration of lighting signs, French historian Philippe Artières references a 1927 text in the *Frankfurter Zeitung*, in which German sociologist Siegfried Kracauer states, "The neon signs of [Pigalle] are mechanical fires that tremble with venal sensuality. Pyrotechnic flares crossing each other under a canopy, clearly pointing towards the centre, to where everything flows, and the wheel of Moulin Rouge turns, but grinds no grain." [129]

227

McDonald's in Times Square, United States, in 2006.

228

Binion's Horseshoe, a casino in Downtown Las Vegas, United States.

229

"Las Vegas is the only town in the world whose skyline is made up neither of buildings, like New York, nor of trees, like Wilbraham, Massachusetts, but signs. One can look at Las Vegas from a mile away on Route 91 and see no buildings, no trees, only signs. But such signs. They tower. They revolve, they oscillate, they soar in shapes before which the existing vocabulary of art history is helpless… Boomerang Modern, Palette Curvilinear, Flash Gordon Ming-Alert Spiral, McDonald's Hamburger Parabola, Mint Casino Elliptical, Miami Beach Kidney. Las Vegas sign makers work so far out beyond the frontiers of conventional studio art that they have no names themselves for the forms they create." [130] – Thomas Kennerly Wolfe

American author Wolfe described Las Vegas as a Pop city, alive through its electric signs.

227

228

HORSESHOE
HORSESHOE

229

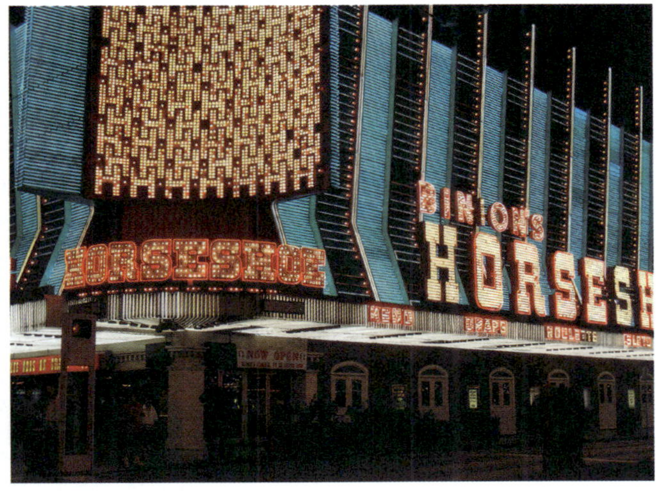

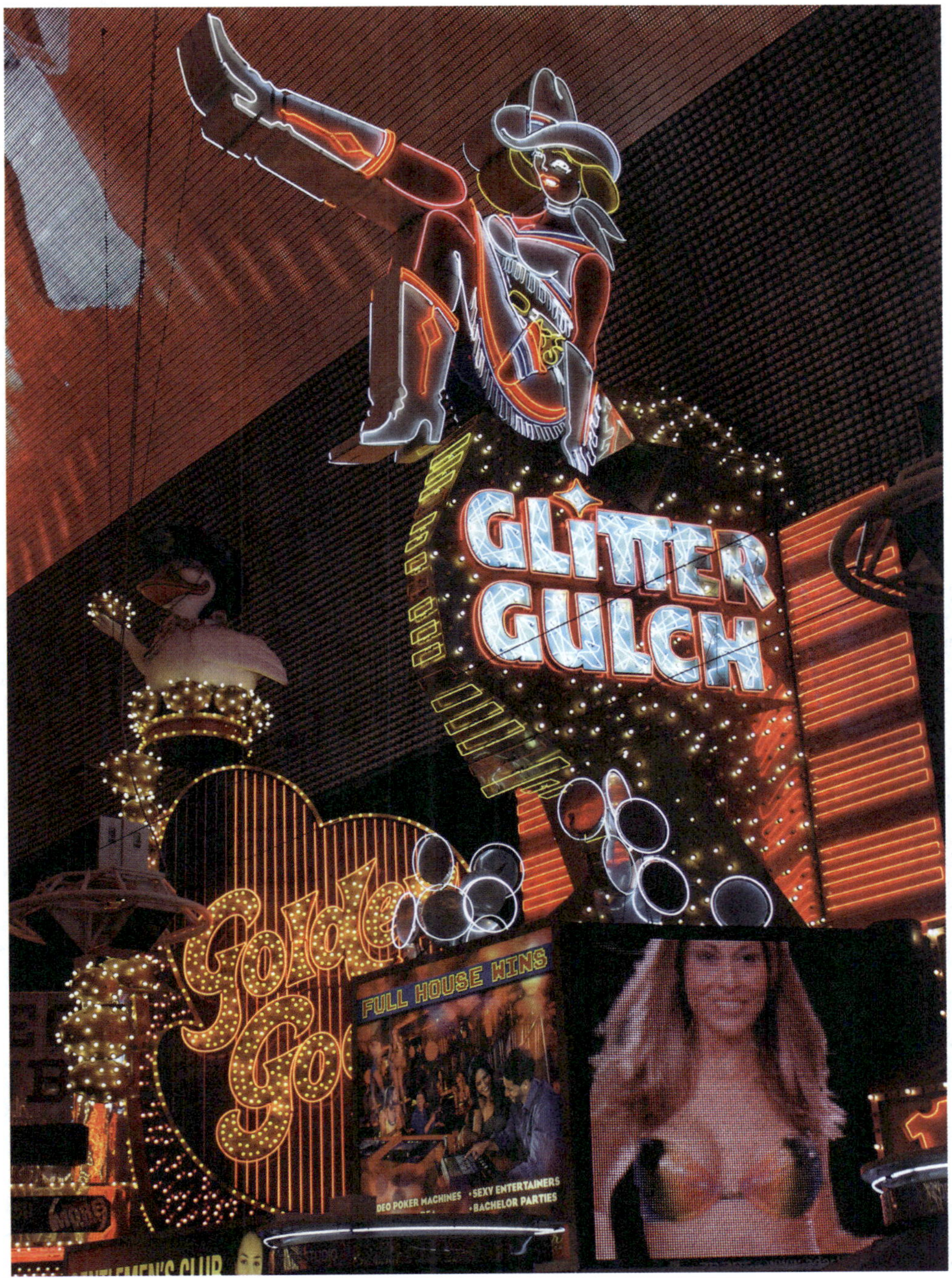
GLITTER
GULCH
FULL HOUSE WINS
SEXY ENTERTAINERS
BACHELOR PARTIES

230

231

230

Las Vegas and its lights can be seen from eight different national parks in the United States.[131] It officially became a city in 1911, with Fremont Street serving as the principal artery to the railroad station.[132] The street's first illuminated signs emerged in 1906, luring new visitors with an increasing array of advertisements. The city quickly became characterised by neon lights, towering signs, and round-the-clock casinos that transformed the city from day to night. Las Vegas epitomises spectacle—a continuous flow of visual and kinographic communication, and a hub of gambling. In the 1972 book *Learning from Las Vegas*, American architects Robert Venturi, Denise Scott Brown, and Steven Izenour dissect the city's architectural landscape through a postmodernist lens, highlighting the preference for symbolic over formal expression—in other words, bright signage and ornate facades that cater to the moving viewer on the highway over more traditional architectural forms.[133]

231

"No urban nights are like the nights there. I have looked down across the city from high windows. It is then that the great buildings lose reality and take on their magical powers. They are immaterial; that is to say one sees but the lighted windows. Squares after squares of flame, set and cut into the ether. Here is our poetry, for we have pulled down the stars to our will."[134] – Ezra Pound

In 1912, American poet Pound described New York as "the most beautiful city in the world."[135]

232

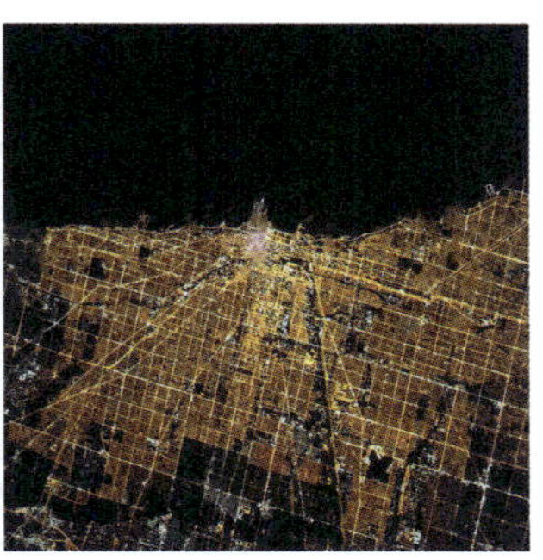

233

234

232
Boston, captured from the International Space Station on January 7, 2021.

233
Chicago, captured from the International Space Station on April 5, 2016.

234
Kuwait City and surrounding suburbs, captured from the International Space Station on March 2, 2024.

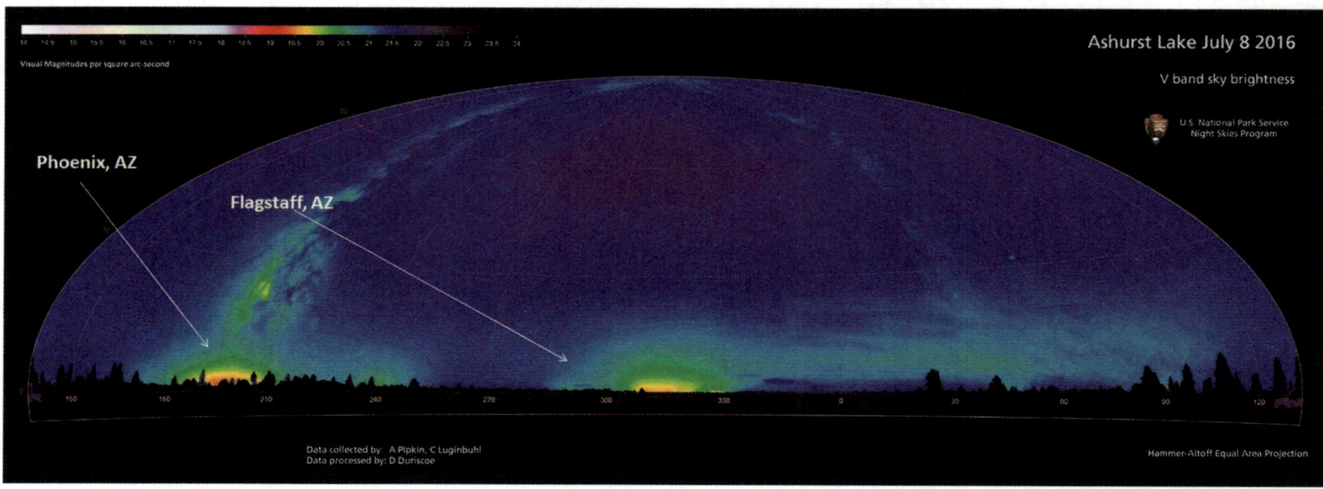

235

235
A detailed all-sky map near Ashurst Lake, United States, illustrates the extent of light pollution emanating from urban areas. This pollution produces a skyglow that obscures the stars and can adversely affect regions far beyond city limits, up to 320 kilometres away.[136] Such light pollution extends into protected natural areas including national parks, nature reserves, and other conservation areas, negatively impacting ecosystems.

236

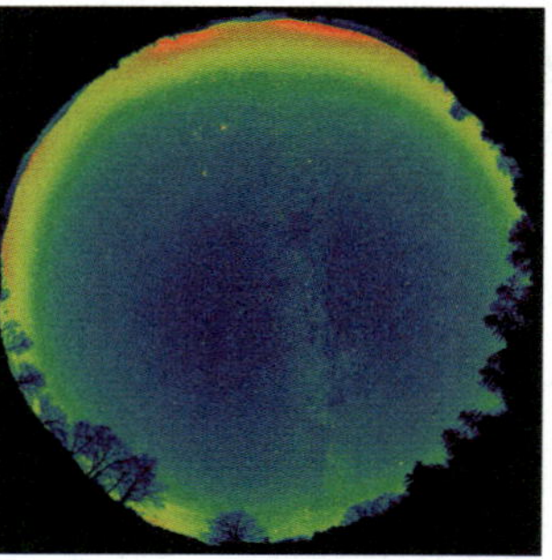

237

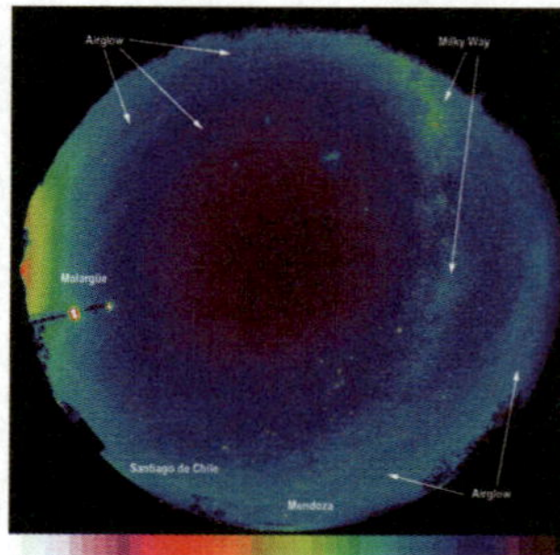

236
An all-sky brightness map, developed from an image captured near Chřibská, in Bohemian Switzerland National Park. Reports indicate that "orange and pink sky glow spreads further and further out from our towns and cities," spreading into our unlit countryside.[137] This form of mapping is instrumental in detecting sky glow that radiates from brightly lit urban regions into darker, rural landscapes.

237
All sky map of the night sky at Los Leones, Argentina. This issue reveals the persistent and troubling truth: it is not that the stars are vanishing, but rather that earth is becoming progressively brighter.[138] Unfortunately, light pollution poses more than just an inconvenience, it is a profound threat to human health, economic well being, and the flora and fauna. It disconnects humanity further from the natural environment.

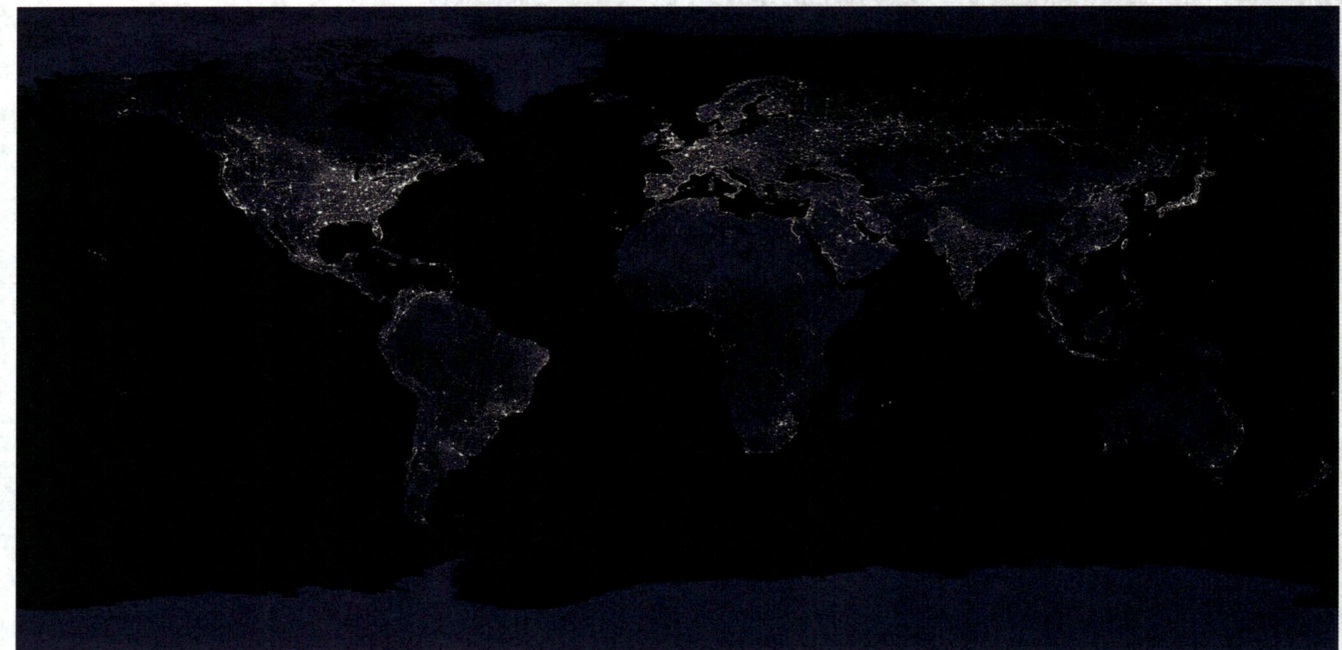

239

238

238
This image of earth's city lights uses data from the Defense Meteorological Satellite Program (DMSP) Operational Linescan System (OLS), which, although originally intended for cloud observation by moonlight, also serves to identify permanent light sources on earth's surface.[139] The most lit areas indicate heavy urbanisation but not necessarily high population density. Urban growth often aligns with coastlines and major transport routes. More than a century after the invention of electricity, some regions like Antarctica remain completely dark, and the interiors of Africa and South America and deserts, mostly unlit.

239
Light pollution has spilled into our oceans. Researchers have now measured underwater light levels in coastal areas globally, noting that low intensity artificial light and specific wavelengths, especially blue and green light, are detrimental to sensitive marine organisms. They discovered that around 1.9 million square kilometres of ocean waters are affected by biologically significant levels of light pollution down to a depth of one metre. Significant portions of oceanic waters are exposed to light down to depths of ten and twenty metres, and even deeper in some regions. In parts of the South China Sea near Malaysia where the water is exceptionally clear, nighttime light can reach depths exceeding forty metres.[140] Copepods show sensitivity to moonlight, which triggers their daily vertical migrations within the water column for feeding. All creatures that have visual orientation systems may be vulnerable. Studies have shown that light pollution affects the behaviour, reproduction, and survival of marine invertebrates, amphibians, fish, and birds.

240
"The beacon's blaze allures
The bird of passage, till he madly strikes
Against it, and beats out his weary life." [141]

– Alfred Tennyson

[119] Macfarlane, *The Wild Places*, 201.

[120] Davies and Smyth, "Why Artificial Light at Night Should Be a Focus for Global Change Research in the 21st Century," 873.

[121] "The Formation of the Andromeda Galaxy Finally Elucidated," Observatoire de Paris, December 21, 2001, https://www.observatoiredeparis.psl.eu/the-formation-of-the.html?lang=en.

[122] Hafez et al., "The Investigation of Stars, Star Clusters and Nebulae in Abd al-Rahman al-Sufi's *Book of the Fixed Stars*," 143.

[123] "Trails Made by Starlink Satellites," International Astronomical Union, June 3, 2019, https://www.iau.org/public/images/detail/ann19035a/.

[124] "Andromeda Before Photoshop," NASA Astronomy Pictures of the Day, October 14, 2019, https://apod.nasa.gov/apod/ap191014.html.

[125] Hainaut and Williams, "Impact of Satellite Constellations on Astronomical Observations," 1.

[126] Hall, "Semi-Empirical Astronomical Light Pollution Evaluation of Satellite Constellations," 1900.

[127] Luckiesh, "The Lights of New York City," https://wellcomecollection.org/works/ev6jxp2t/images?id=kdx7ekh5.

[128] Gernsback, "The Tower of Jewels at Frisco's Exposition," *The Electrical Experimenter* (June 1915): 45.

[129] Kracauer, cited in Miranda, *Being and Neonness*, 18.

[130] Wolfe, cited in Dekoven, *Utopia Limited*, 77.

[131] "Lightscape / Night Sky," United States National Parks Service, https://www.nps.gov/grba/learn/nature/lightscape.htm.

[132] Schielke, "Light Matters: A Flash Back to the Glittering Age of Las Vegas at the Neon Museum," *ArchDaily* (blog), June 23, 2015. https://www.archdaily.com/645768/light-matters-a-flash-back-to-the-glittering-age-of-las-vegas-at-the-neon-museum.

[133] Jindal, "Book in Focus: Learning from Las Vegas," https://www.re-thinkingthefuture.com/rtf-architectural-reviews/a5183.

[134] Pound, cited in Lindner, *Imagining New York City*, 17.

[135] Pound, cited in Sharpe, "New York, Night, and Cultural Mythmaking," 3.

[136] Olsen, Gallaway, and Mitchell, "Modelling US Light Pollution," 885.

[137] Dunnett, "Contested Landscapes," 631.

[138] Lystrup, "The Dark Side of the Light," 507.

[139] "Earth's City Lights," NASA Visible Earth, October 23, 2000, https:// visibleearth.nasa.gov/images/55167/earths-city-lights.

[140] Pratt, "Bathed in a Sea of Artificial Light," NASA Earth Observatory, March 2, 2022, https://earthobservatory.nasa.gov/images/149518/bathed-in-a-sea-of-artificial-light.

[141] Tennyson, "The Eddysone Lantern," 1091, cited in Clarke, *Studies in Bird Migration*, frontispiece.

WITHOUT
LIGHT

LAURIAN GHINIȚOIU

WITHOUT LIGHT

BEIRUT
LAURIAN GHINIȚOIU

دون ضوء

BEIRUT

LAURIAN GHINIȚOIU

دفون ضوء

LAURIAN GHINIȚOIU

MANGO
Market

دون ضوء

212

ARCHAVIL
كاريتاس لبنان

LAURIAN GHINIȚOIU

دون ضوء

LAURIAN GHINIŢOIU

WITHOUT LIGHT

LAURIAN GHINIȚOIU

WITHOUT LIGHT

BEIRUT

LAURIAN GHINIȚOIU

دون ضوء

WITHOUT LIGHT

BEIRUT – 2020-2022

*The persistent electricity crisis plunged the city into a state of profound
uncertainty. Without light, the city's architecture took on new forms, where
details faded and the play of shadow created an enigmatic tapestry. Once light
is transformed into shadow, our perception changes. Our senses evolve, our eyes
adapt, and darkness becomes a friend. The photographic essay captures the
paradoxical beauty and unsettling mystery of Beirut's darkened streets.
It reveals a different dimension, one where anonymity and the unknown
redefine our perception and understanding of a place.*

LAURIAN GHINIȚOIU

STONE GARDEN
LINA GHOTMEH

دون ضوء

بدون ضوء

CMA COM

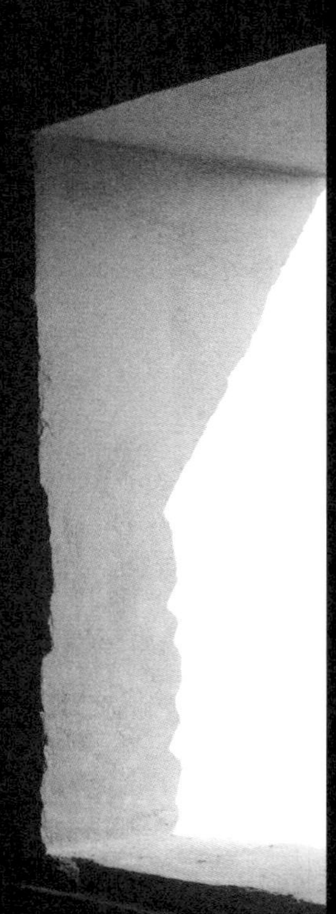

STONE GARDEN — 2011-2020

I documented Stone Garden, a project I designed and completed with my practice Lina Ghotmeh — Architecture, during its construction. The building stands on the Lebanese coastline, near the industrial port of Beirut, just one mile from the site of the 2020 explosion that devastated the city. Throughout history, windows have fascinated poets like Baudelaire and Mallarmé as symbols of freedom, perspective, and poetic experience. Similarly, Egyptians saw windows as gateways for the morning sun. As old as architecture itself, windows have evolved both technically and symbolically in tandem. They encapsulate a dialogue between past and present, light and shadow, public and private, allowing the mind to travel and the eye to see. The windows of Stone Garden, as measures of light, reveal and frame a city marked by conflict and renewal. I hope that Stone Garden, standing alongside traditional homes and modern architecture in Beirut, tells the story of resilience, transforming how we perceive space, memory and the role of contemporary architecture in Beirut's dynamic landscape.

LINA GHOTMEH

MATERIAL
LIGHT

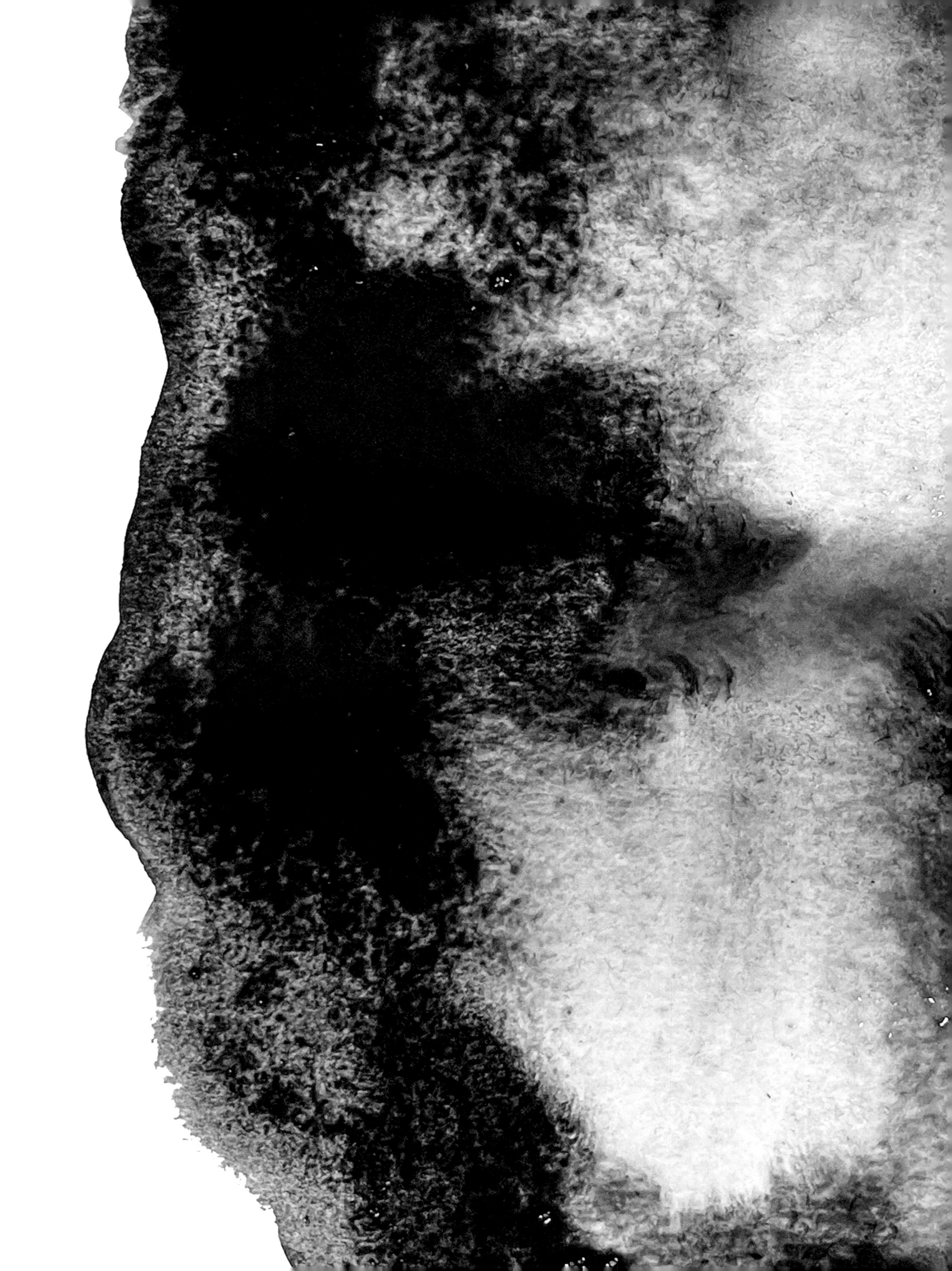

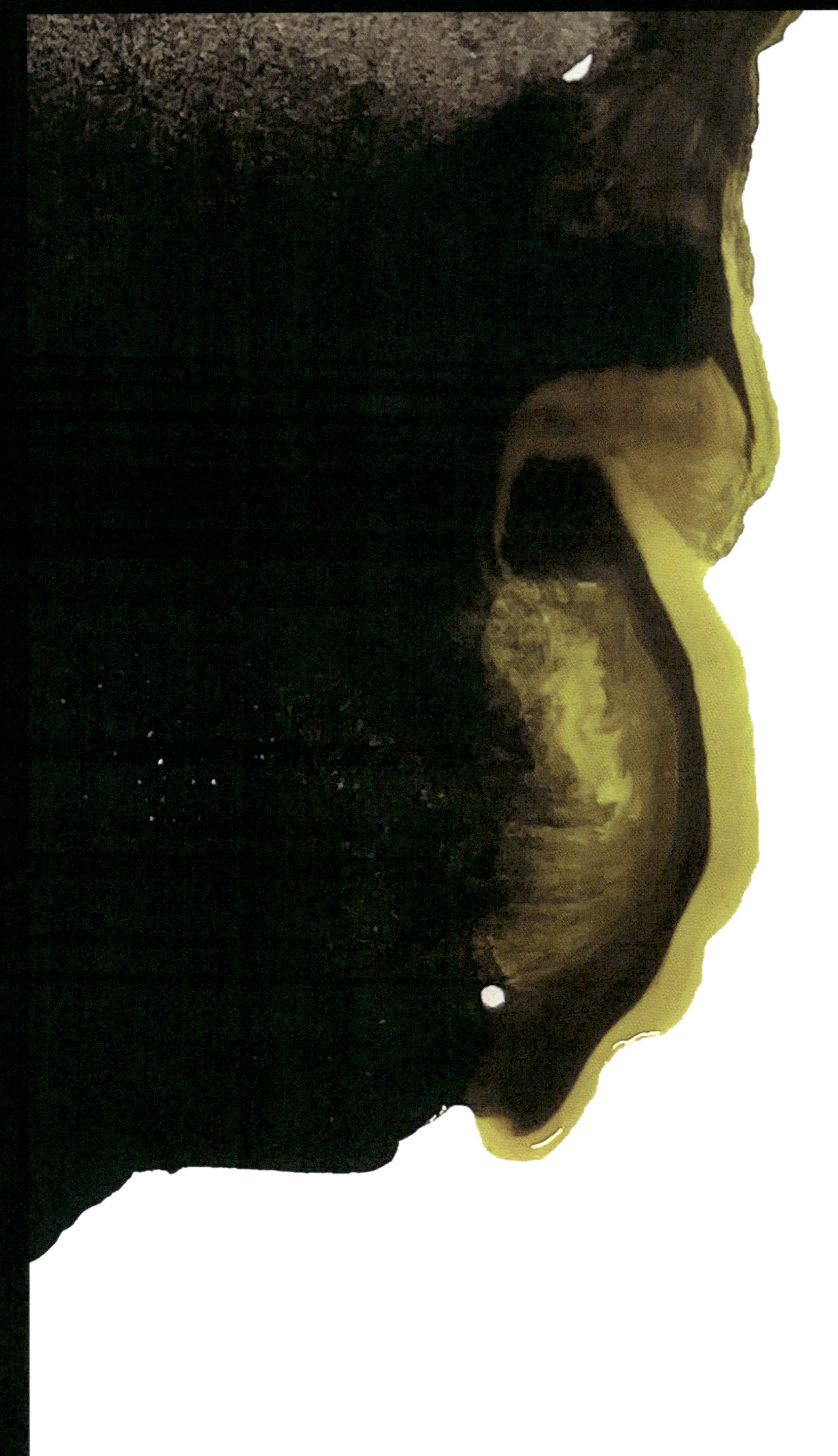

LINA GHOTMEH

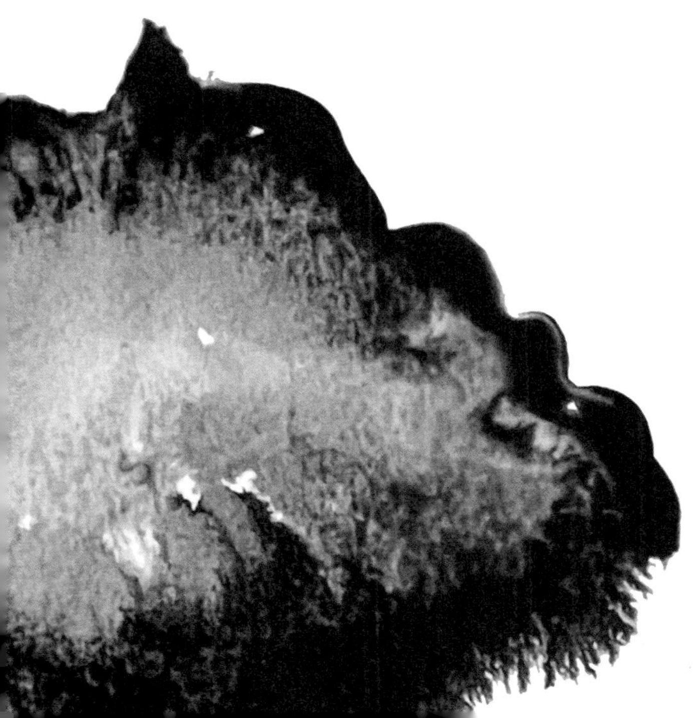

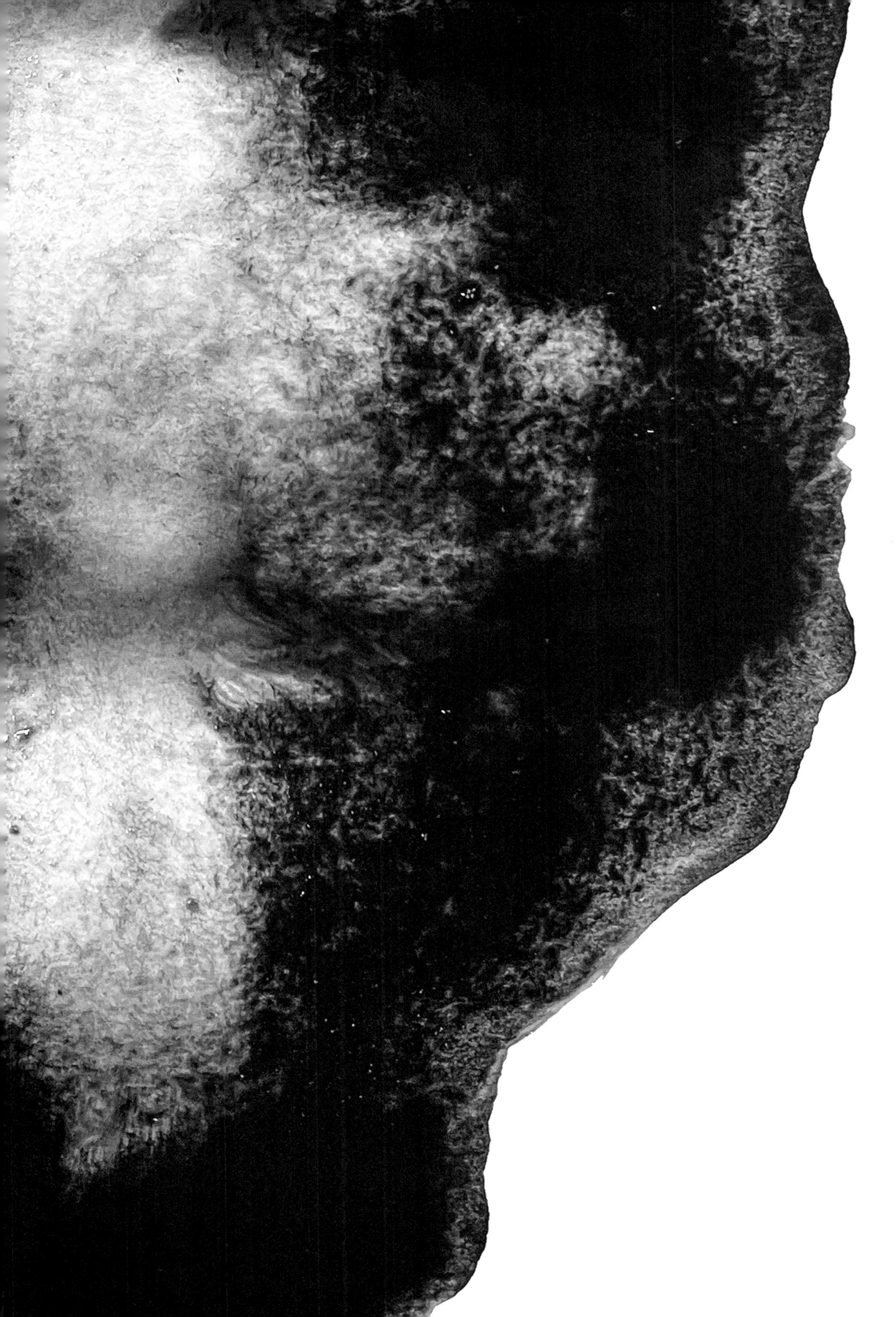

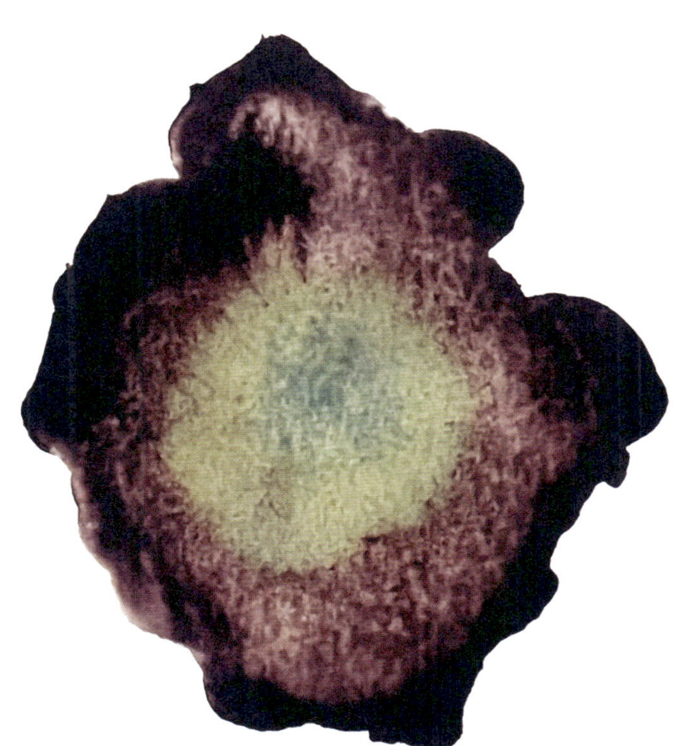

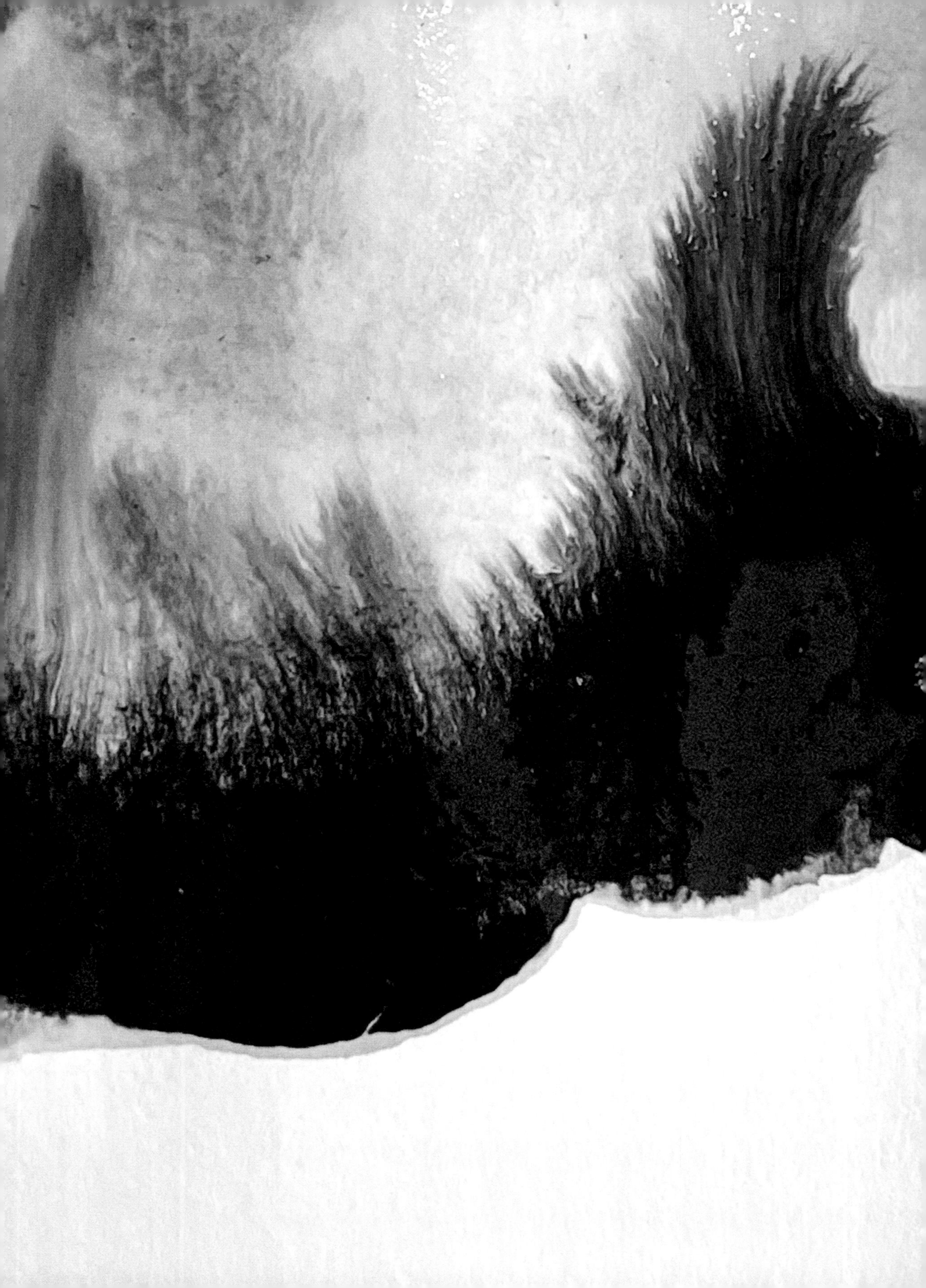

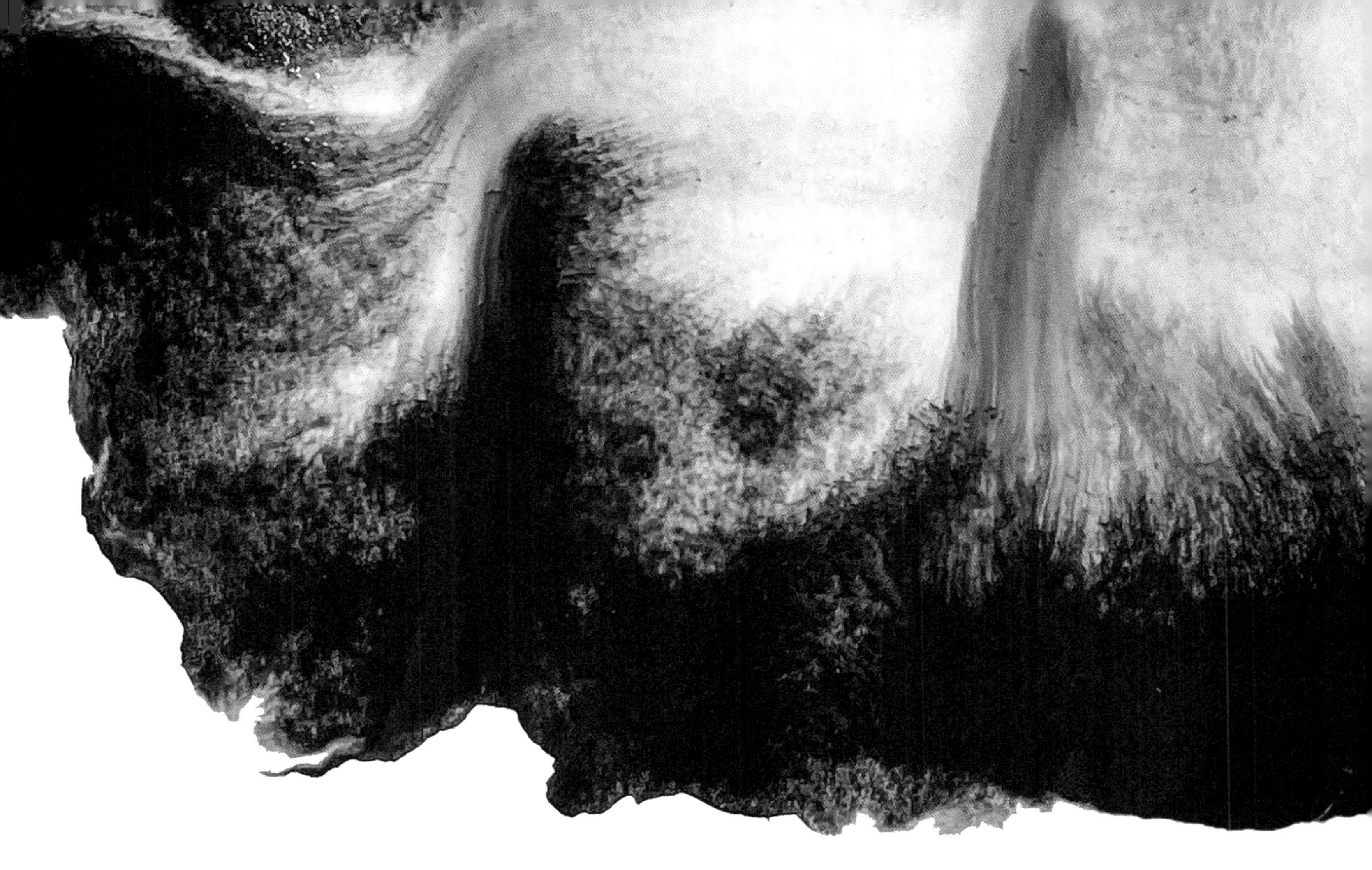

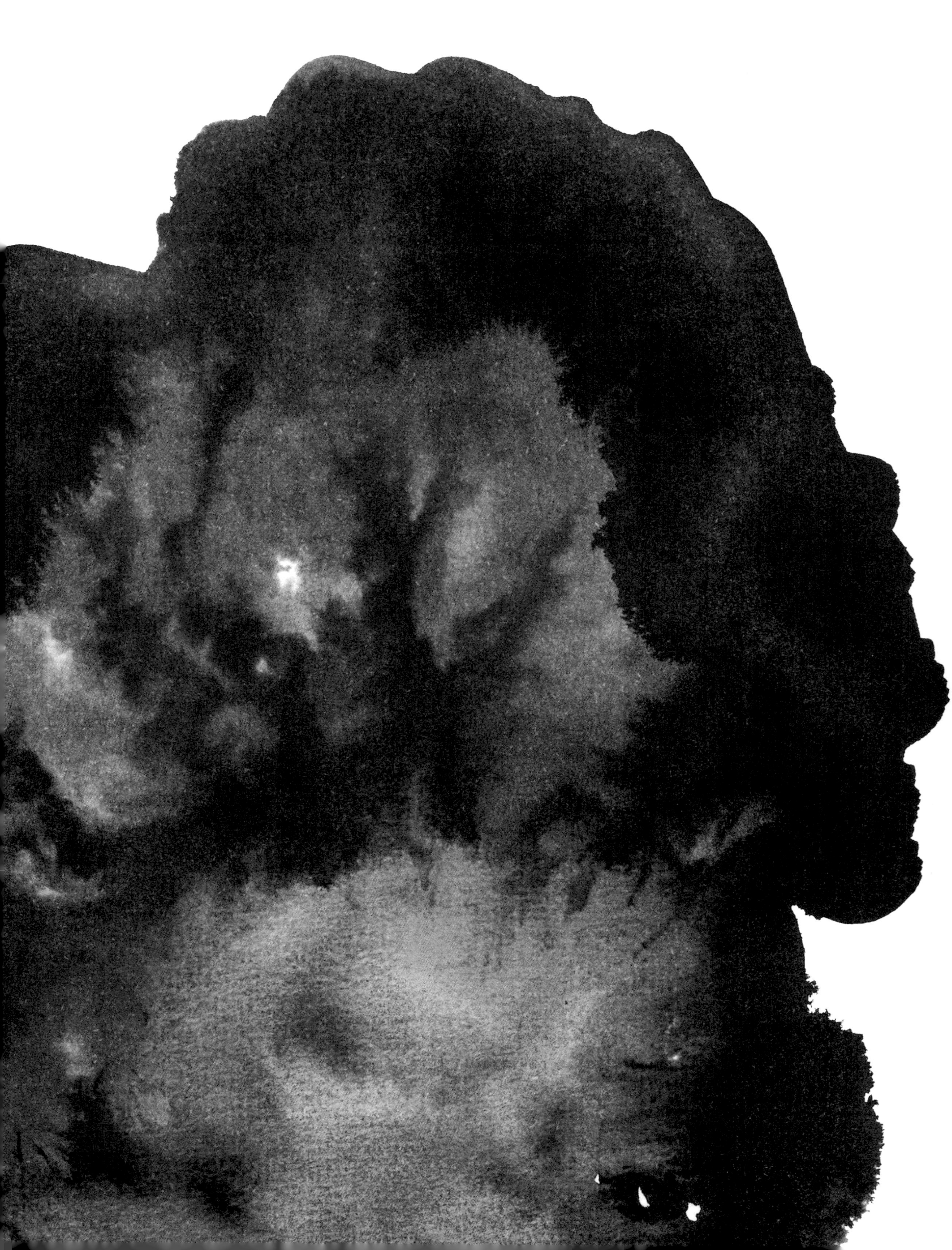

مادة الضوء

MATERIAL LIGHT

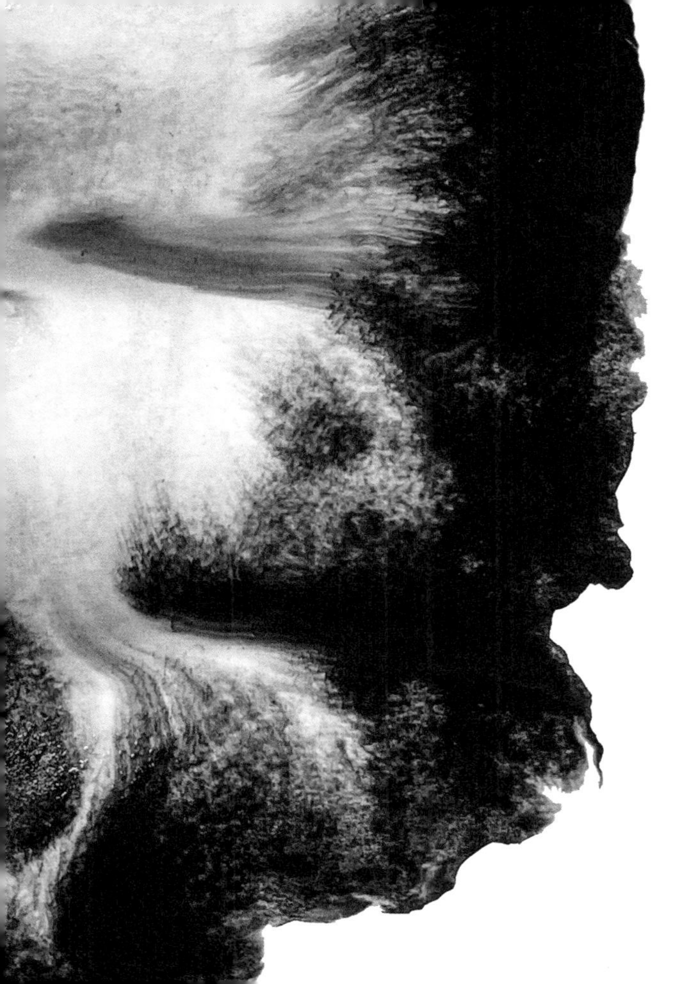

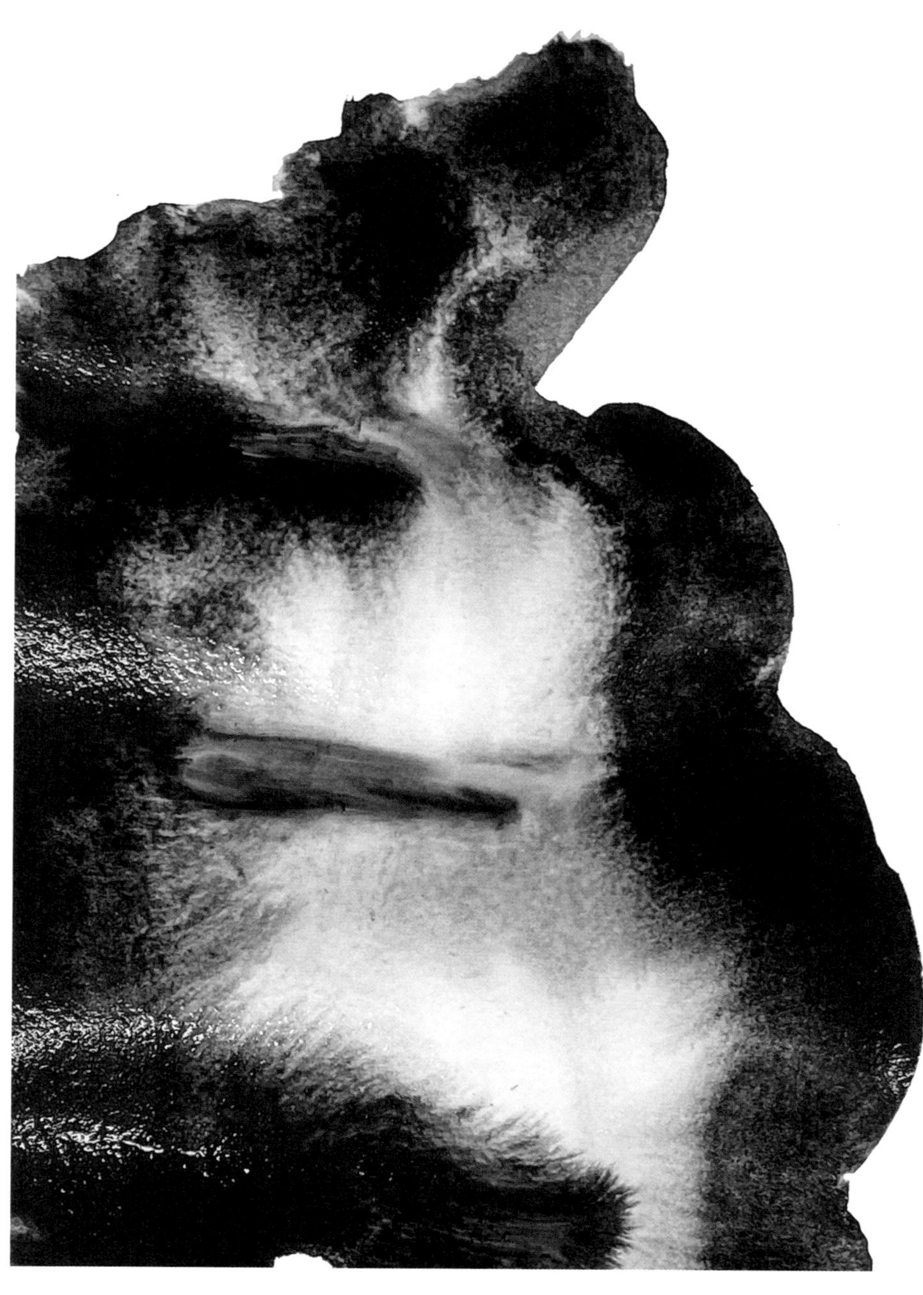

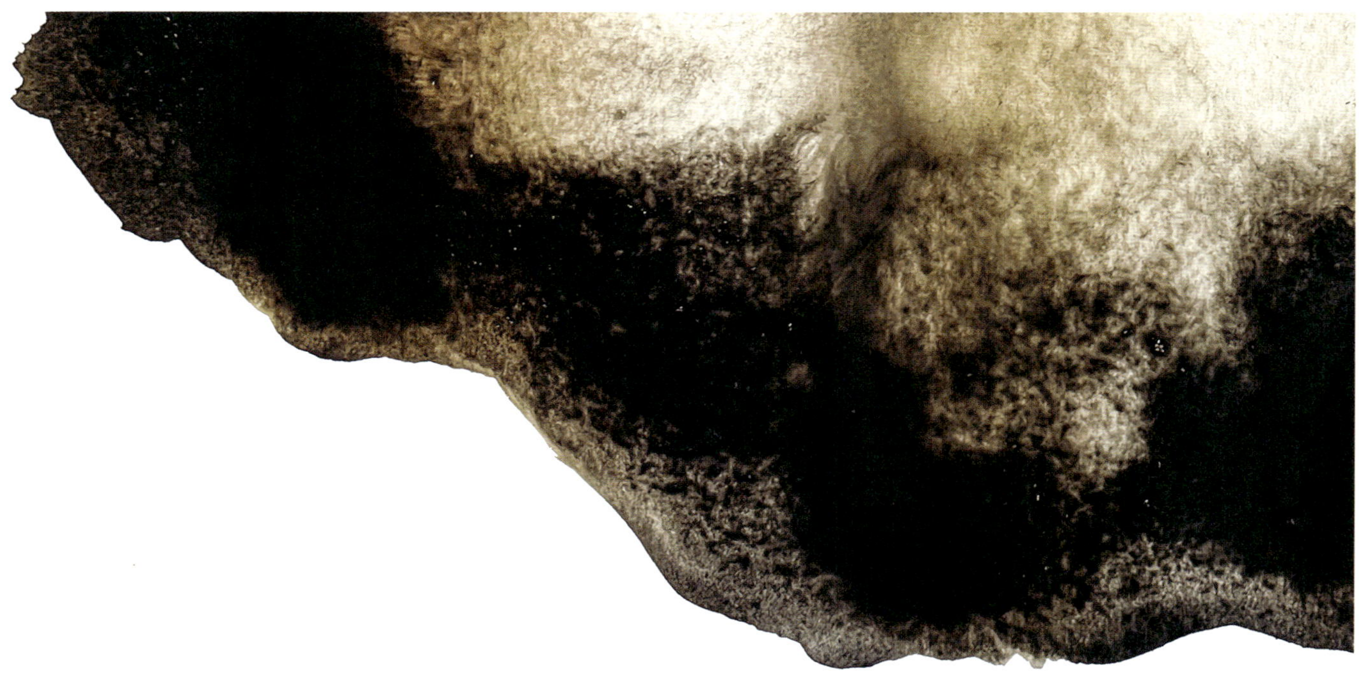

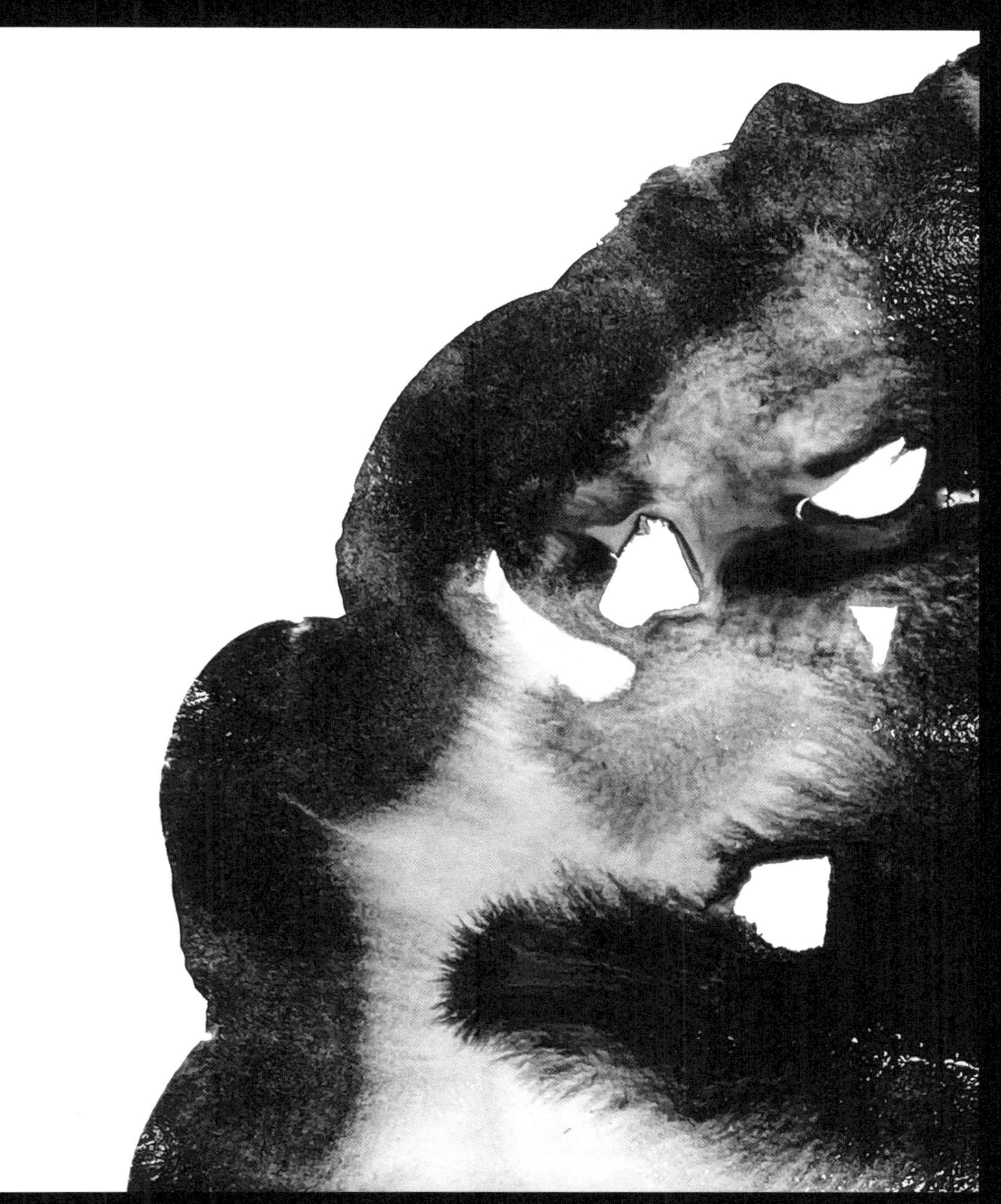

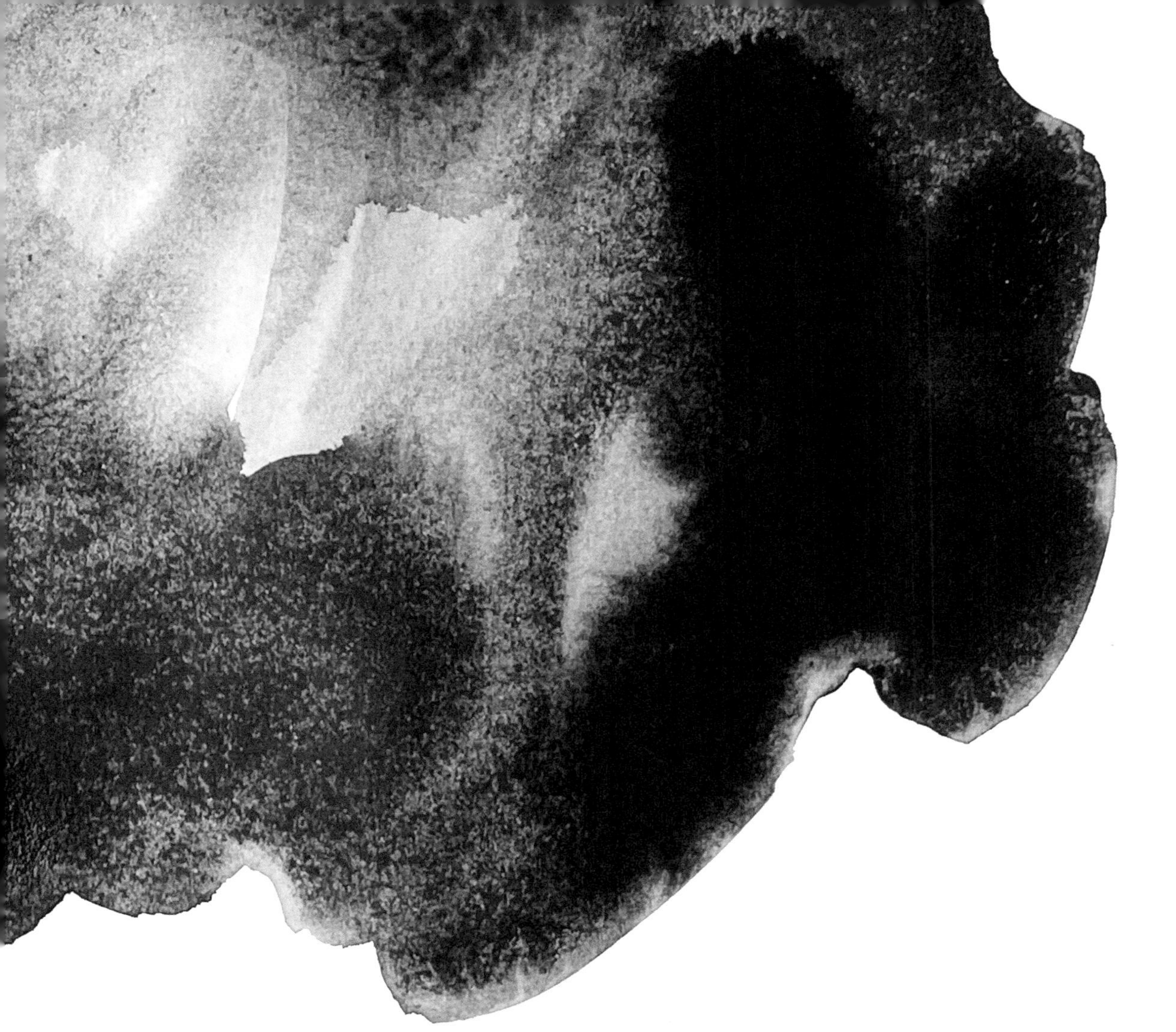

FLOWS – 2024

*This series of ink drawings, created during the making
of this publication, serves as contemplative notes on light as a material
on paper. The preliminary stroke or scatters of ink, became an initial
transcription that predicted the remainder of the expression.
Moments of alteration or removal marked not only presence
but acts of thinking by design, establishing a language
reminiscent of the book's early images of the sun and bacteria.
These drawings became a form of note-taking, exploring spatial
composition and the possibilities of light through transparency.
Composed on pages, they have been assembled, disassembled,
and reassembled to seek new forms. Documented not in their
final state, as they lose tonalities and transparencies
as they dry, they capture the elusive, spiritual qualities
of ink, water, and paper–forming a pictorial
and visual language, a writing of ink and light.*

LINA GHOTMEH

IMAGE CREDITS

000 (P.4-5) - NASA/Wilkinson Microwave Anisotropy Probe Science Team, Nine Year Microwave Sky, n.d. WMAP # 121238, NASA. Public Domain.

001 (P.22) - NASA Goddard Space Flight Center/ Lockheed Martin Solar and Astrophysics Laboratory/ Interface Region Imaging Spectrograph, IRIS First Light, 2013. NASA. Public Domain.

002 (P.23) - ATG medialab under contract for ESA, Solar Orbiter, 2019. 431632, European Space Agency. CC BY-SA 3.0 IGO.

003 (P.24) - Solar Orbiter/EUI Team/ ESA & NASA; CSL, IAS, MPS, PMOD/WRC, ROB, UCL/MSSL, Solar Orbiter's First Views of the Sun, 2020. 441337, European Space Agency. ESA Standard Licence.

004 (P.25) - Solar Orbiter/EUI Team/ ESA & NASA; CSL, IAS, MPS, PMOD/WRC, ROB, UCL/MSSL, Solar Orbiter's First Views of the Sun, 2020. 441333, European Space Agency. ESA Standard Licence.

005 (P.26) - NASA/Astronaut Garriott (Skylab-3), Skylab, 1973. 9606705, NASA. Public Domain.

006 (P.28) - Ed Ward, Mixed cyanobacteria from Mississippi River, Red Wing, Minnesota, USA, 2006. Micrograph. Image courtesy of Ed Ward. © Ed Ward.

007 (P.28) - Luke Thompson, TEM Image of Prochlorococcus MED4 with Overlay Green Colouring, 2007. Micrograph. Chisholm Lab, Massachusetts University of Technology. Flickr. Public Domain.

008 (P.28) - Josef Reischig, Cyanobacteria: Native Preparation, n.d. Micrograph, magnification: 2400x. Wikimedia Commons. CC BY-SA 3.0 DEED.

009 (P.30) - Commonwealth Scientific and Industrial Research Organisation, Cylindrospermum - Blue Green Algae, n.d. Micrograph. CSIRO Alumni. © Copyright CSIRO Australia.

010 (P.30) - Kevin Mackenzie (University of Aberdeen), Chloroplast in a Bean Leaf, TEM, n.d. Micrograph. Wellcome Collection. CC BY 4.0.

011 (P.31) - Debbie Marshall, Scanning Electron Micrograph of an Open Stoma on the Leaf of a Lettuce (Lactuca sativa), n.d. Wellcome Collection. CC BY 4.0.

012 (P.31) - Nigel Chaffey, Stoma and Chloroplasts of Maize Leaf, n.d. Micrograph. Wellcome Collection. CC BY 4.0.

013 (P.31) - Fernán Federici, Arabidopsis thaliana Plant Cells Containing Chloroplasts, n.d. Micrograph. Wellcome Collection. CC BY 4.0.

014 (P.32) - Lauren Holden, Open Stoma on an Orchid Leaf (Phalaenopsis sp.), n.d. Micrograph. Wellcome Collection. CC BY 4.0.

015 (P.33) - Mary Morphew and Richard J. McIntosh, Chlamydomonas reinhardtii, Plant Cell, 2021. Micrograph. 11363, Cell Image Library. UC San Diego Library Digital Collections. Public Domain.

016 (P.34) - Fayette A. Reynolds, Aquatic Monocot Stem: Epidermis in Elodea, 2014. Micrograph, magnification: 400x. Berkshire Community College Bioscience Image Library. Public Domain.

017 (P.35) - Luca Santangeli, Diatom Chain of Thalassiosira, 2020. Micrograph. European Molecular Biology Laboratory (EMBL). Courtesy of Luca Santangeli and EMBL. © Luca Santangeli (Arendt Lab, EMBL Heidelberg).

018 (P.36) - Orin Zebest, Comb Jelly (Ctenophora), 2014. Micrograph. Flickr. CC BY 2.0.

019 (P.36) - Nick Hobgood, Pyrosome Pelagic Colonial Tunicate or Salp Encountered Off Atauro Island, East Timor, 2005. Micrograph. Wikimedia Commons. CC BY-SA 3.0 DEED.

020 (P.37) - Kevin Raskoff (Monterey Bay Aquarium Research Institute, NOAA Office of Ocean Exploration and Research), Light Refracts off the Comb-rows of the Ctenophore Mertensia ovum Producing Stripes of Rainbow Color, 2002. Micrograph. NOAA Ocean Explorer. Courtesy of Kevin Raskoff. © Kevin Raskoff.

021 (P.38) - NOAA Okeanos Explorer Program, Gulf of Mexico 2012 Expedition, Lobate Ctenophore Displaying Bioluminescence, 2012. Micrograph. Expl8238, NOAA Photo Library. CC BY 2.0 DEED.

022 (P.38) - NOAA Oceanic and Atmospheric Research/National Undersea Research Program, Lobate Ctenophores are Translucent and Give Off a Bioluminescent Glow. Bolinopsis infundibulum, 2009. Micrograph. nur01004, NOAA Photo Library. Public Domain.

023 (P.38) - Uwe Kils, Planctonic Polychaete Worm from Genus Tomopteris, 2005. Micrograph. Wikimedia Commons. CC BY-SA 3.0 DEED.

024 (P.39) - Andrei Savitsky, Copepods of Different Species, 2019. Micrograph. Courtesy of Andrei Savitsky. © Andrei Savitsky.

025 (P.41) - Joseph Pallante, Bioluminescent Armillaria Novae-Zelandiae, 2021. Courtesy of Joseph Pallante. © Joseph Pallante.

026 (P.41) - Alan Rockefeller, A Fruit Body of the Bioluminescent Fungus Mycena Nebula, 2012. Digital photograph. 306597, Mushroom Observer. Courtesy of Alan Rockefeller. © Alan Rockefeller.

027 (P.41) - Thomas Fuhrmann, Área de Proteção Ambiental Quilombos do Médio Ribeira, 2021. Courtesy of Thomas Fuhrmann. © Thomas Fuhrmann.

028 (P.41) - Alexey Sergeev, Omphalotus Subilludens (Murrill) H.E. Bigelow, 2017. 299179, Mushroom Observer. CC BY-SA 3.0 DEED.

029 (P.42-43) - Judson McCranie, Fireflies in South Georgia, U.S., at the Butler Island Plantation, 2017. Digital photograph. Courtesy of Judson McCranie. © Judson McCranie.

030 (P.44-45) - Eddie Yip, Tai Po Fireflies in Hong Kong, 2018. Flickr. CC BY-SA 2.0.

031 (P.45) - David Fant, Fireflies, 2009. Flickr. CC BY 2.0.

032 (P.46) - NASA/Goddard/Jeff Schmaltz/MODIS Land Rapid Response Team, Phytoplankton Bloomed in the North Atlantic Ocean, 2010. NASA. CC BY 2.0.

033 (P.47) - European Space Agency, Japan in bloom, 2021. 452718, European Space Agency. Courtesy of ESA. © Contains modified Copernicus Sentinel data (2019), processed by European Space Agency.

034 (P.48) - The Sea Down to 900 Metres, No. 4, at 600m Deep, from Liebig Chromos Series 1360, 1937. Trade Card, 11 × 7.1 cm. PM 110618, Private collection of Paul M.R. Maeyaert. Wikipedia Commons. CC BY-SA 4.0 DEED.

035 (P.49) - The Sea Down to 900 Metres, No. 5, at 800m Deep, from Liebig Chromos Series 1360, 1937. Trade Card, 11 × 7.1 cm. PM 110619, Private collection of Paul M.R. Maeyaert. Wikipedia Commons. CC BY-SA 4.0 DEED.

036 (P.50) - Neolithic Representation of Solar Symbols, Spain, n.d. Wellcome Collection. CC BY 4.0.

037 (P.50) - Flint, ca. 200-700 CE. Flint, 7.29 cm. 36.30.9, The Metropolitan Museum of Art. Public Domain.

038 (P.51) - Adolf Hofer, Object Image, 1935. Bild-1935.01.0026, National Museums of World Culture – Museum of Ethnography, Sweden. CC BY 2.5.

039 (P.52) - Unknown, Drawing with Scene from the Paleolithic. People Working in Cave, ca. 1839-1939. Glass slide. KU Leuven. Public Domain.

040 (P.53) - Unknown, Drawing with Scene from the Paleolithic. People Working in Cave II, ca. 1839-1939. Glass slide. KU Leuven. Public Domain.

041 (P.54) - Cave of Beasts. Photograph by Clemens Schmillen, 2014. Wikimedia Commons. CC BY-SA 3.0 DEED.

042 (P.54) - Hands at the Cuevas de las Manos. Photograph by Mariano Cecowski, 2005. Wikimedia Commons. CC BY-SA 3.0 DEED.

043 (P.55) - E. A. Abbey (from a sketch by Theo. R. Davis), Around the Council Fire, The Young Brave's Speech, from "Harper's Weekly," 1873. Print, 25.6 × 36.5 cm. 29.88.9(16), The Metropolitan Museum of Art. Public Domain.

044 (P.56-57) - Unknown, Four Priests Perform a Yagna, a Fire Sacrifice, an Old Vedic Ritual Where Offerings Are Made to the God of Fire, Agni, 1800-1899. Gouache painting, 12.4 × 18.5 cm. 577128i, Wellcome Collection. Public Domain.

045 (P.58-59) - Unknown, History of Inventions, published in Walter Hough, Synoptic Series of Objects, 1922. National Museum of Natural History (Smithsonian Institution). Public Domain.

046 (P.60) - Ibrahim Rashid, Heatwave, 2024. Acrylic on canvas, 60 × 45 cm. Courtesy of Ibrahim Rashid. © Ibrahim Rashid.

047 (P.61) - Ibrahim Rashid, Heatwave II, 2024. Acrylic on canvas, 60 × 45 cm. Courtesy of Ibrahim Rashid. © Ibrahim Rashid.

048 (P.61) - Ibrahim Rashid, Heatwave III, 2024. Acrylic on canvas, 60 × 45 cm. Courtesy of Ibrahim Rashid. © Ibrahim Rashid.

049 (P.62) - Inscribed Brick, ca. 2112-2095 BCE. Brick: 30.9 × 30.8 × 7.4 cm, Inscription: 11 × 9.5 cm. 59.41.86, The Metropolitan Museum of Art. Public Domain.

050 (P.63) - Unknown, Tempel von Kom Ombo, 2009. Photographed by Hedwig Storch, 2009. Wikimedia Commons. CC BY-SA 3.0.

051 (P.64) - Ancient Shu People, Sun and Immortal Birds Gold Ornament, ca. 1600-1046 BCE. Jinsha Site Museum. Wikimedia Commons. Public Domain.

052 (P.64) - Pilgrim's Badge with Sun with Human Face, ca. 1400-1500. Metalwork-Lead, 3.9 × 4.2 × 0.4 cm. 1986.77.3, The Metropolitan Museum of Art. Public Domain.

053 (P.64) - The Banc Ty'nddôl Sun-Disc, n.d. Photographed by Simon Timberlake, 2003. National Museum of Wales in Cardiff, Department of Archeology. Reproduced with permission of Simon Timberlake and the Early Mines Research Group. © Simon Timberlake.

054 (P.65) - Nebra Sky Disk, 1800-1600 BCE. Photograph by Frank Vincentz, 2022. Wikimedia Commons. CC-BY-SA-4.0.

055 (P.65) - Solvognen, Night Side Visible, Bronze Age. Photograph by John Lee. B7703, Nationalmuseet, Denmark. CC BY-SA 4.0 DEED.

056 (P.66) - Victory Stele of Naram-Sin, King of Akkad, ca. 2250 BCE. Department of Near Eastern Antiquities – Mesopotamia, Musée du Louvre. Photographed by Fred Romero, 2016. Flickr. CC BY 2.0 DEED.

057 (P.67) - Unknown, Aztec Calendar Stone, 1880-1897. Photographed by William Henry Jackson, 1843-1897. Detroit Publishing Company Photograph Collection, Library of Congress Prints and Photographs Division. Public Domain.

058 (P.67) - Pilgrim's Badge in the Form of a Solar Disk, ca. 1300-1400 CE. Metalwork-Lead, 0.1 cm × 2.5 cm. 1986.77.5, The Metropolitan Museum of Art. Public Domain.

059 (P.67) - Babylonian Kudurru Boundary Stele, Reign of King Melisipak, 1186-1172 BCE. Musée du Louvre. Photographed by Gary Todd, 2016. Flickr. Public Domain.

060 (P.69) - Unknown, Saint Eufrasia, 1558. Woodcut. 4843i, Wellcome Collection. Public Domain.

061 (P.69) - Unknown, Candi Ceto Majapahit Sun, 1264. Photographed by Michael Gunther, 2008. CC-BY-SA-4.0. Wikimedia Commons.

062 (P.70) - Furniture Plaque Carved in Relief with a Male Figure Grasping a Tree; Winged Sun Disc Above, ca. 700-800 BCE. Relief, 26.7 × 11.4 × 0.8 cm. 59.107.6, The Metropolitan Museum of Art. Public Domain.

063 (P.71) - Unknown, Hasegawa Settan, The Rising Sun, 1824. Photographed by M. Forrer, 2013. RP-P-1999-257-2, Goslings Collection, Rijksmuseum. Public Domain.

064 (P.71) - Unknown, Stela of Aafenmut, ca. 924-889 BCE. 23 × 18.2 × 3.5 cm. 28.3.35, The Metropolitan Museum of Art. Public Domain.

065 (P.72) - Adriaen Collaert (after a drawing by Maerten de Vos), Fire: The Four Elements, 1580-1584. Print Album Leaf. RP-P-2005-214-17-2, Rijksmuseum. Public Domain.

066 (P.72) - Giovanni di Paolo (Giovanni di Paolo di Grazia), The Creation of the World and the Expulsion from Paradise, 1445. Oil painting, 46.4 × 52.1 cm. 28.3.35, The Metropolitan Museum of Art. Public Domain.

067 (P.73) - The Sun from Persian Manuscript 373, n.d. Wellcome Collection. CC BY 4.0.

068 (P.73) - Jacob Gole (after design by Cornelis Dusart), Lodewijk XIV, koning van Frankrijk, 1691. Print, 14.6 × 10.7 cm. RP-P-BI-7331, Rijksmuseum. Public Domain.

069 (P.74) - Watanabe Nobukazu, The Eastern Expedition of Emperor Jinmu, 1890-1895. Colour woodcut, 35.8 × 71.9 cm. RP-P-1985-485, Rijksmuseum. Public Domain.

070 (P.74) - Hans Kaufmann, Prinz Heinrich-Flug, 1914. Poster, 85.1 × 58.1 cm. 2673379, Graphic Design Collection, Staatliche Museen zu Berlin. Public Domain.

071 (P.74-75) - Unknown, Irworobongdo, ca. 1850-1950. Folding screen, 195.4 × 359.8 cm. The Royal Family of Joseon, National Palace Museum of Korea. Wikimedia Commons. Public Domain.

072 (P.75) - Unknown, Surya the Sun Deity Driving in His Chariot, n.d. Gouache drawing. 27740i, Wellcome Collection. Public Domain.

073 (P.76) - Seated Goddess with a Child, ca. 1400-1200 BCE. Gold pendant, 4.3 × 1.7 × 1.9 cm. 1989.281.12, The Metropolitan Museum of Art. Public Domain.

074 (P.77) - Fred Kabotie, Sunface Mural at the Painted Desert Inn, 2006. Digital photograph. Petrified Forest, National Park Arizona. Public Domain.

075 (P.78-79) - Anders Zorn, A Musical Family, 1905. Oil on canvas, 130 × 100 cm. Photograph by Cecilia Heisser. NM 1950, National Museum of Sweden. Public Domain.

076 (P.80) - Jan Saenredam (after Cornelis van Haarlem), Plato's Allegory of the Cave, 1604. Photographed by Arthur Strathearn, 2004. Flickr. Public Domain.

077 (P.80) - Katsushika Ōi, Courtesans Showing Themselves to the Strollers through the Grille, ca. 1818-1844. Hanging scroll, colour on paper. Collection 5, Ōta Memorial Museum of Art, Japan. Wikimedia Commons. Public Domain.

078 (P.81) - Michelangelo Buonarroti, The Creation Of The Sun, The Moon And The Plants, 1508-1512. Catholic University of Leuven. Public Domain.

079 (P.82-83) - Suhrawardi, copied by Shams bin Jamal Al-Hatani, Well-known treatise on theosophy, Arabic manuscript on paper, 1220 (manuscript), 1220. Paper, 23.4 × 14.5 cm. CH8940673, Christies. Photo © Christie's Images / Bridgeman Images.

080 (P.88) - Unknown, Ancient Egyptian Sundial, 1908. Courtesy of the University of Basel King's Valley Project. © University of Basel King's Valley Project.

081 (P.89) - Unknown, Museum Side Roman Sundial, n.d. Photographed by Ad Meskens in 2010. Courtesy of Ad Meskens. © Ad Meskens.

082 (P.90) - Henri Le Secq, Sculpture of an Angel with a Sundial on the Façade of Chartres Cathedral, ca. 1900-1905. Collotype on paper, 17.6 × 11.6 cm. RP-F-2001-7-509-122, Rijksmuseum. Public Domain.

083 (P.91) - Giovanni Maggi, Lateran Obelisk behind the St. John Lateran in Rome, 1600. Etching on paper, 21.5 × 15.5 cm. RP-P-2016-748-83, Rijksmuseum. Public Domain.

084 (P.91) - Unknown, Turning the Obelisk, 1882. Collotype on paper, 27.9 × 21.7 cm. RP-F-2001-7-1549-20, Rijksmuseum. Public Domain.

085 (P.91) - Unknown, The Obelisk Horizontal, 1879. Collotype on paper, 35.1 × 27.9 cm. RP-F-2001-7-1549-8, Rijksmuseum. Public Domain.

086 (P.92-93) - Unknown, Disembarking the obelisk, 1880. Collotype on paper, 19.3 cm × 26.2 cm. RP-F-2001-7-1549-15, Rijksmuseum. Public Domain.

087 (P.94) - Unknown, Astrolabe When Components Are Together Showing the Front, n.d. Wellcome Collection. CC BY 4.0.

Unknown, The Back of an Astrolabe, n.d. Wellcome Collection. CC BY 4.0.

088 (P.94) - Unknown, Planispheric Astrolabe, ca. 800-900 CE. Brass, cast, with fretwork rete, and surface engraving, 18.5 × 13.2 cm. SCI 430, Khalili Collections. CC-BY-SA 3.0 IGO.

089 (P.95) - Unknown, Astrolabe-Quadrant, 1840-1841 CE. Solid walnut, red and black ink, yellowish varnish, brass socket for the plumb line, 16.8 × 12.8 × 3 cm, radius of quadrant 12.5 cm. SCI 40, Khalili Collections. CC-BY-SA 3.0 IGO.

090 (P.95) - Unknown, Mediaeval Quadrant: Horary Quadrant, 1200-1400. Copper alloy, 4.8 × 5.1 × 0.1 cm. Photograph by Anni Byard. BERK-C673DD, Portable Antiquities Scheme, Wikimedia Commons. CC BY 2.0.

091 (P.96) - Gunter Edmund, Navigation: An Astrolabe, a Cross-Staff, and a Back-Staff or Davis's Sextant, 1624. Pencil drawing. 46655i, Wellcome Collection. Public Domain.

092 (P.96) - Unknown, Text and astrolabe from the book of the birth of Iskandar, n.d. Wellcome Collection. CC BY 4.0.

093 (P.97) - Thomas E. Sargent, Sextant. Metal box, 32.8 × 27.3 × 12.5 cm, sextant radius: 21.6 cm. Photograph by Claes Claesson. S 2882, Sjöhistoriska museet. CC BY 4.0.

094 (P.97) - Woodrow Wilson Gholston, Lieutenant Commander Ray Schoppe (Commanding Officer of USC&GS Surveyor) Measuring Horizontal Sextant Angle During Inshore Ship Hydrographic Operations, 1940. Coast & Geodetic Survey, Photo Library National Ocean and Atmospheric Administration. Public Domain.

095 (P.97) - Unknown, Taking Sextant Angles for Positioning Vessels. Coast & Geodetic Survey, Photo Library National Ocean and Atmospheric Administration. Public Domain.

096 (P.97) - Unknown, A Woman Seated in a Chamber Having Her Exceptionally High Wig Dressed by a French Hairdresser Who Stands on the Top of a Step-Ladder; The Woman's Husband, A Naval Officer, is Holding a Sextant to his Eye to Ascertain the Altitude of the Adornment, 1771. 31715i, Wellcome Collection. Public Domain.

097 (P.98) - Unknown, Astronomers Manipulating a Huge Armillary Sphere and Tools to Measure Longitude and Latitude. Miniature printed in manuscript Sehinsahname (The Story of the King of Kings), 1581. Istanbul University Library. Photograph by Luisa Ricciarini / Bridgeman Images. LRI4661267, Bridgeman Images.

098 (P.98) - Unknown, The Nimrud Lens, The Layard Lens, inlay, Neo-Assyrian, North West Palace, 750-710 BCE. Rock Crystal. 90959, The British Museum. © The Trustees of the British Museum.

099 (P.98) - Unknown, Ancient Greece Antikythera Mechanism. Photograph by Gary Todd, 2016. Flickr. Public Domain.

100 (P.99) - Sandro Botticelli, Sant'Agostino in the Study, ca. 1480. Detached wall painting on fibreglass support with aluminium. GR 13121, Opificio delle Pietre Dure, Florence. Public Domain.

101 (P.99) - F. Friedrich and K. Preuss, Astronomical Clock on the Southern Wall of Prague's Old Town Hall, ca. 1855-1900. Albumen print, 25.9 × 20.6 cm. RP-F-F16054, Rijksmuseum. Public Domain.

102 (P.100) - Sarkisianarto, Zorats Karer, 2022. Wikimedia Commons. CC BY 4.0.

103 (P.100) - Josef Kořenský, Stonehenge, 1801. Paper, 22.5 × 29 cm. Náprstek Museum of Asian, African and American Cultures. CC BY 4.0.

104 (P.101) - Unknown, Professor Adolphus Hall of the U.S. Naval Observatory looking through the 26" telescope, 1924. National Museum of the U.S. Navy. Public Domain.

105 (P.102) - Thomas Daniell, Astronomy: The Open Air Observatory at Delhi, 1815. Coloured aquatint. 46655i, Wellcome Collection. Public Domain.

106 (P.102) - Allan Grey, Jantar Mantar, Jaipur, 2009. Digital image. Flickr. CC BY-SA 2.0.

107 (P.103) - Unknown, Sciences and Islam: Description of the Astronomical Observatory of the Arab Scientist Taqi al-Din, 1581. Istanbul University Library. Photograph by Luisa Ricciarini / Bridgeman Images. LRI4661302, Bridgeman Images.

108 (P.103) - Unknown, Nasireddin's Observatory at Meraga, Nasireddin Tusi (d. 1274) and the four men who set up the observatory, ca. 1562-1563. BL3311603, British Library archive / Bridgeman Images.

109 (P.104) - Unknown, Astronomy: The Open Air Observatory at Peking, 1797. Engraving. 46266i, Wellcome Collection. Public Domain.

110 (P.104) - Tycho Brahe's observatory at Stjerneborg, Hven, 1584. 10322304, Science & Society Picture Library. © Science Museum Group.

111 (P.105) - Unknown, Astronomy: A Large Telescope, at Greenwich Observatory. Coloured wood engraving, 10.5 × 12.1 cm. 46255i, Wellcome Collection. Public Domain.

112 (P.105) - Peter H. Feist, 003.28, 1975. 1299, Media Library of the Institute for Art and Visual History, Berlin University. CC BY SA 4.0.

113 (P.105) - N'Dalla Tando, Observatório Meteorológico, ca. 1902. Postcard, 14 × 9 cm. PI 21118, Iconography, National Library of Portugal. Public Domain.

114 (P.106) - Andrea Pisano and help, Firenze - Duomo, Campanile, formella con Tolomeo e l'Astronomia, ca. 1343-1360. Photographic print, 24.8 × 19.0 cm. Photograph by Alinari. Gam29142, Turin Gallery for Modern and Contemporary Art. CC BY 4.0.

115 (P.106) - Claude Vignon, Empedocles, ca. 1600-1699. Line engraving. 2733i, Wellcome Collection. Public Domain.

116 (P.107) - Unknown, Hemelkaart van het stelsel van Ptolemaeus, 1660 and/or 1708. RP-P-AO-29-1-5, Rijksmuseum. Public Domain.

117 (P.108-109) - Raffaello Sanzio da Urbino, The School of Athens, ca. 1509-1511. Fresco, Apostolic Palace, Vatican City, 550 × 770 cm. Photograph by Jean-Pol Grandmont. Wikimedia Commons. Public Domain.

118 (P.110) - Unknown, Stamp IQ 1962 (Iraqi postage stamp on the millennium anniversary of the founding of the city of Baghdad and in memory of philosopher Al-Kindi), 1962. Photograph by Mohammdaon. Wikimedia Commons. Public Domain.

119 (P.110) - Ptolemy, Copy of the Structure of the Human Eye According to Ibn al-Haytham, printed in Kitāb al-manāzir (The Book of Optics), ca. 1011-1021. Süleimaniye Mosque Library. Wikimedia Commons. Public Domain.

120 (P.110) - Aristotle and ibn Bakhtishu', The wise Aristotle and a student (vellum), ca. 1200-1300 CE. BL3287115, British Library archive / Bridgeman Images.

121 (P.111) - Bertel Thorvaldsen, Nicolaus Copernicus Monument, ca. 1822-1830. Photography, 10 × 8.5 cm. Catholic University of Leuven. Public Domain.

122 (P.111) - Joos van Wassenhove, Illustrated Men, ca. 1473-1477. 10 × 8.5 cm. Catholic University of Leuven. Public Domain.

123 (P.112) - Unknown, Astronomy: Galileo with His Telescope in the Piazza San Marco, Venice. Wood engraving. 46321i, Wellcome Collection. Public Domain.

124 (P.113, 117) - Johann Melchior Füssli, A Cosmological Plan Detailing Copernicus' Astronomical Vision, Surrounded by Diagrams of the Systems of Ptolemy and Tycho Brahe, 1732. Line engraving, 28.1 × 38 cm. 15962i, Wellcome Collection. Public Domain.

125 (P.113) - Unknown, Celestial Map of the Copernican System, 1708. Engraving on paper, 44 × 52.5 cm. RP-P-AO-29-1-7, Rijksmuseum. Public Domain.

126 (P.114) - Young Thomas, A Course of Lectures on Natural Philosophy and the Mechanical Arts, 1807. Uploaded JPEG by Arthunter. Wikimedia Commons. Public Domain.

127 (P.114) - Isaac Newton, Philosophiae Naturalis Principia Mathematica, 1688. L0012486, Wellcome Collection. CC BY 4.0.

128 (P.114) - Unknown, Young Diffraction, 1803. Uploaded by Graycrawford. Wikimedia Commons. Public Domain.

129 (P.115) - Ole Rømer, Observations of the First Jupiter Moon in Paris, ca. 1670 (first published in 1915). Uploaded by Hemmingsen. Wikimedia Commons. Public Domain.

130 (P.116) - Ibn Sahl, Reproduction of On Burning Mirrors and Lenses, ca. 940-1000. Milli MS 867, fol. 7r, Milli Library, Tehran. Uploaded by Thuresson. Wikimedia Commons. Public Domain.

131 (P.120) - Girolamo Cardano, De subtilitate, 1559. DIGITOOL3024364, Biblioteca Europea Di Informazione E Cultura. CC BY-SA 4.0.

132 (P.120) - Gemma Frisius Rainer, De radio astronomico et geometrico liber, n.d. BSB-ID 991037850029707356, Bavarian State Library. © Bavarian State Library.

133 (P.121) - Adolphe Ganot and Atkinson Edmund, Natural Philosophy for General Readers and Young Persons, 1876. GLAD-100902938, Internet Archive. Public Domain.

134 (P.122) - Unknown, Painted Image On Glass for Magic Lantern. Boy Tastes the Honey and Tumbles into the Barrel, 1975. Glass negative, colour. TEKA0111619, Tekniska museet. Public Domain.

135 (P.122) - John J. Thomson, Peking, Pechili Province, China: A Magic Lantern Show, 1869. Glass photonegative, wet collodion. 19716i, Wellcome Collection. Public Domain.

136 (P.122) - Willem Jacobs Gravesande, Physices elementa mathematica, experimentis confirmata. Sive Introductio ad philosophiam Newtonianam, 1742. Wellcome Collection. Public Domain.

137 (P.123) - René Descartes, Discourse On the Method for Conducting One's Reason Well, and Seeking Truth in the Sciences, 1637. Wellcome Collection. Public Domain.

138 (P.124) - Charles Paxson, Wilson, Branded Slave from New Orleans, 1863. Albumen silver print from glass negative, 8.4 × 5.3 cm. 2019.521, The Metropolitan Museum of Art. Public Domain.

139 (P.124) - Honoré Daumier, Nadar Raising Photography to the Height of Art, 1862. Lithograph, 44.5 × 31.3 cm. 26.52.4, The Metropolitan Museum of Art. Public Domain.

140 (P.125) - Paul Henry, A Section of the Constellation Cygnus, 1885. Albumen silver print from glass negative, 25.8 × 21.2 cm. 2005.100.124, Gilman Paper Company Collection, The Metropolitan Museum of Art. Public Domain.

141 (P.126-127) - M. Henry and Michel Berthaud, Photographie d'une portion de la carte du ciel, ca. 1881-1891. Paper, 32 × 25.9 cm. RP-F-2001-7-1101A-28, Rijksmuseum. Public Domain.

142 (P.128) - Unknown, Total Eclipse of the Sun, Dec. 12, 1871, ca. 1882. Paper, 9 × 9 cm. RP-F-2001-7-1093-1, Rijksmuseum. Public Domain.

143 (P.128) - Warren de la Rue, Fotoreproductie van foto door Warren de la Rue van vlekken op de maan, 1887-1888. Paper, 6.8 × 6.8 cm. Photograph by Marinus Pieter Filbri. RP-F-F01133-X, Rijksmuseum. Public Domain.

144 (P.128) - Pierre Jules César Janssen, Photographie du disque solaire, ca. 1867-1877. Paper, 17.6 × 11.8 cm. Printed by Goupil & Cie. RP-F-2001-7-498-2, Rijksmuseum. Public Domain.

145 (P.128) - John William Draper, Draper's Moon Daguerreotype, 1840. MC 298. Provided by NYU Special Collections. © NYU Special Collections.

146 (P.128) - H. A. Lawrence and C. Ray Woods, Solar Eclipse from Caroline Island, 1883. Gelatin silver print, 13.3 × 13.1 cm. 2018.382, The Metropolitan Museum of Art. Public Domain.

147 (P.129) - Otto Bütschli, Twaalf microscoopopnamen van gestolde zwavel, ca. 1890-1900. Paper, 31.2 × 46.7 cm. RP-F-2001-7-782-1, Rijksmuseum. Public Domain.

148 (P.129) - Otto Bütschli, Zestien microscoopopnamen van zwavel, ca. 1890-1900. Collotype on paper, 31.2 × 46.7 cm. RP-F-2001-7-782-2, Rijksmuseum. Public Domain.

149 (P.130) - Eadweard Muybridge, Attitudes of Animals in Motion, 1879, printed 1881. Albumen silver print, 16 × 25.3 cm. 2015.778.33, Collection 72, The Metropolitan Museum of Art. Public Domain.

150 (P.130) - Eadweard Muybridge, Animal Locomotion. An Electro-Photographic Investigation of Consecutive Phases of Animal Movements, 1887. 1991.1135.9, The Metropolitan Museum of Art. Public Domain.

151 (P.131) - Daguerre Louis, Intérieur d'un cabinet de curiosités, 1837. Daguerreotype, 16.7 × 21.2 cm. frSFP_0092im_DG_0001, Collection Société française de photographie. © Collection Société française de photographie (coll. SFP), Paris.

152 (P.131) - Joseph Nicéphore Niépce, Untitled 'point de vue', 1827. Heliograph on pewter, 16.7 × 20.3 × 0.15 cm. Gernsheim Collection, Harry Ransom Center, The University of Texas at Austin. Public Domain.

153 (P.132) - William Henry Fox Talbot, The Open Door, 1844. Salted paper print from paper negative, 14.3 × 19.4 cm. 2005.100.498, Gilman Collection, The Metropolitan Museum of Art. Public Domain.

154 (P.132) - Johannes Kepler, Astronomiae pars optica, 1604. DIGITOOL158093, Biblioteca Europea Di Informazione E Cultura. CC BY-SA 4.0.

155 (P.133) - Modern "Vivex" colour print (c. 1930s) made from what is believed to be the first set of tri-colour separation negatives made, i.e. those of James Clerk Maxwell of 1861. 10714930, Science Museum. © Science Museum Group.

156 (P.134-135) - Étienne-Gaspard Robertson, Fantasmagorie de Robertson dans la Cour des Capucines en 1797, printed in Mémoires récréatifs, scientifiques et anecdotiques du physicien-aéronaute E.G. Robertson, 1831. Engraving. Uploaded by Marisa Snyder. Internet Archive. Public Domain.

157 (P.138) - Benjamin West, Benjamin Franklin Drawing Electricity from the Sky, ca. 1816. Oil on slate, 34 × 25.6 cm. 1958-132-1, Philadelphia Museum of Art. Public Domain.

158 (P.138) - Benjamin Franklin 1956 Issue 3c, 1956. Uploaded by Gwillhickers. Wikimedia Commons. Public Domain.

159 (P.139) - Thomas Browne, Pseudodoxia Epidemica, 1658. Image courtesy of Dreweatts 1759. © Dreweatts.

160 (P.140) - Ion Gauge Used by Scientists At Ames, 2013. United States Department of Energy. Public Domain.

161 (P.141) - Maha Mustafa, Deadline, Malmö, 2003. Installation, heat coil at 220V. Courtesy of Maha Mustafa. © Maha Mustafa.

162 (P.141) - Thomas A. Edison, Kohlefadenglühlampe - New Type Edison Lamp 16c, 1880. EVZ:1980/0014-051, Technomuseum. Public Domain.

163 (P.141) - William J. Hammer, Early Paper Filament Incandescent Electric Light Bulbs, 1904. Uploaded by Chetvorno. Wikimedia Commons. Public Domain.

164 (P.141) - Friemann & Wolf. Zwickau IS, Säkerhetslykta, 1936. Metal, iron metal, copper alloy, glass, 27 cm × (diameter) 9.5 cm. TEKS0013666, Tekniska museet. CC BY 4.0.

165 (P.141) - Swan Joseph Wilson, Kohlefadenglühlampe - Swan'sche Lampe, ca. 1884-1900. EVZ:1980/0014-309, Technomuseum. Public Domain.

166 (P.142) - Thomas Rowlandson, A Peep at the Gas-lights in Pall Mall, 1809. Engraving. Uploaded by Churchh. Wikimedia Commons. Public Domain.

167 (P.142) - Wasastjerna Torsten, Pohjoissataman luistinrata, 1891-1892. Gouache on paper, 37.5 × 32 cm. 2478286, Helsinki City Museum. CC BY 4.0.

168 (P.143) - Unknown, Le Général d'Alton poursuivi par les Réverbères Patriotiques, 1789. Etching, 21.5 × 13.8 cm. G.26346, Carnavalet Museum, History of Paris. CC0 1.0 DEED.

169 (P.143) - Unknown, Jablochkoff Candles on the Victoria Embankment, 1878. Uploaded by Dan Michael O. Wikimedia Commons. Public Domain.

170 (P.144) - Unknown, Tikkunekkukauppaa Elannon myymälän tiskillä. 2282840, Helsinki City Museum. CC BY 4.0.

171 (P.144) - Honoré Daumier, Curious People In Front of a Shop Window, ca. 1800-1900. Oil on panel, 10 × 8.5 cm. 9990676460101488, University of Louvain. Public Domain.

172 (P.144) - Unknown, Lysrör på fabrik? Man vid arbetsbord. Photograph. TEKA0006020, Tekniska museet. Public Domain.

173 (P.145) - Otto Holmström, Fotografi, 1962. Photograph, 13 × 18 cm. 62_273, Helsingborg Museum. Public Domain.

174 (P.145) - Viktor Mussik, Neonové reklamy, 1935. Photograph, 9 × 6 cm. As I 5021, Náprstek Museum of Asian, African and American Cultures. CC BY 4.0.

175 (P.146-147) - Matt Wiebe, Battle of the Light Bulbs. Halogen (gold) vs LED (silver), 2016. Photograph. Flickr. CC BY 2.0 DEED.

176 (P.148) - Unknown, Electrical Appliances Exhibited at the 1882 Electrical Exhibition, Including Chandeliers and the First Telegraph Instrument, 1882. Wood engraving, 29.5 × 22.1 cm. 578799i, Wellcome Collection. Public Domain.

177 (P.149) - Hugo Gernsback, The Electrical Experimenter, 1913-1920. (OCoLC)ocm08740783, Smithsonian Libraries and Archives. Public Domain.

178 (P.149) - Hugo Gernsback, The Electrical Experimenter, 1913-1920. (OCoLC)ocm08740783, Smithsonian Libraries and Archives. Public Domain.

179 (P.149) - Hugo Gernsback, The Electrical Experimenter, 1913-1920. (OCoLC)ocm08740783, Smithsonian Libraries and Archives. Public Domain.

180 (P.150) - 1-watt Red Power LED, 2022. Uploaded by Ashkananisi7. Wikimedia Commons. CC BY-SA 4.0 DEED.

181 (P.150) - Steve Jurvetson, Rows and Rows, 2005. Photograph. Flickr. CC BY 2.0 DEED.

182 (P.150) - Oak Ridge National Laboratory, VULCAN diffractometer, 2010. Photograph. Flickr. CC BY 2.0 DEED.

183 (P.151) - Paul Griggs, Red laser, 2010. Photograph. thst3rc, Wellcome Collection. CC BY 4.0.

184 (P.152) - Maurice Dessertenne, Lighting Through the Ages, ca. 1900. Uploaded by Michel Vuijlsteke. Wikimedia Commons. Public Domain.

185 (P.154) - James R. Biard, The 1N650 series of GaAs tunnel diodes, Texas Instruments Press Releases, January - March 1960. Semiconductor Components Division at Texas Instruments. A2005.0025, Texas Instruments Records, DeGolyer Library, Southern Methodist University. Courtesy of DeGolyer Library. © DeGolyer Library, SMU.

186 (P.154) - James R. Biard, SNX-100, Texas Instruments Press Releases, January - March 1960. Semiconductor Components Division at Texas Instruments. A2005.0025, Texas Instruments Records, DeGolyer Library, Southern Methodist University. Courtesy of DeGolyer Library. © DeGolyer Library, SMU.

187 (P.156) - Unknown, Solar Machine Designed by Frenchman Auguste Mouchot, 1878, printed in Le Monde Illustré, 1878. Pam 95.428, Tekniska museet. Public Domain.

188 (P.157) - Hugo Gernsback, The Electrical Experimenter, 1913-1920. (OCoLC)ocm08740783, Smithsonian Libraries and Archives. Public Domain.

189 (P.158) - Mateo Flecha, Noto Bifacial Plant, 1998. Photograph. Wikimedia Commons. CC BY-SA 4.0.

190 (P.158) - Jesse Allen (NASA Earth Observatory), Topaz Solar Farm, California, 2015. Photograph. NASA Earth Observatory. Public Domain.

191 (P.159) - Hugo Gernsback, The Electrical Experimenter, 1913-1920. (OCoLC)ocm08740783, Smithsonian Libraries and Archives. Public Domain.

192 (P.160) - NASA Glenn Research Center, Photovoltaic Hardware - Prototype Organic Solar Cell Module, 2007. Photograph. GRC-2011-C-00363, NASA GRC. Public Domain.

193 (P.161) - NASA, ISS-52 Roll Out Solar Array (ROSA) (4), 2017. Photograph. NASA. Public Domain.

194 (P.162) - NASA, Impact!, 1963. Photograph. NASA. Public Domain.

195 (P.163) - Crescent Dunes, 2012. Photograph. Uploaded by Random Tree. Wikimedia Commons. Public Domain.

196 (P.163) - NASA/GSFC/METI/ERSDAC/JAROS, and U.S./Japan ASTER Science Team, Ivanpah Solar Energy Plant, California, 2013. Photograph. NASA Jet Propulsion Laboratory. Public Domain.

197 (P.163) - Carlo Altamirano (United States Department of Energy), Solar PV Panels on Top of the Mountains in Colorado During Winter, 2017. Photograph. United States Department of Energy. Public Domain.

198 (P.163) - Nevada Bureau of Land Management, Crescent Dunes Solar Energy Project, Nevada, USA, 2015. Photograph. Bureau of Land Management. CC BY 2.0 DEED.

199 (P.164) - NASA, Nancy Grace Roman with Space Telescope Model, ca. 1980. Photograph. NASA. Courtesy of the Roman Family. Public Domain.

200 (P.164) - NASA Marshall Space Flight Center, History of Hubble Space Telescope (HST), 1986. Photograph. 8663388, NASA Marshall Space Flight Center. Public Domain.

201 (P.164) - NASA, Early Construction of the Frame of the Hubble Space Telescope. Photograph. NASA. Public Domain.

202 (P.165) - NASA Johnson Space Center, View of the HST After Being Released from the Shuttle Atlantis, 2009. Photograph. s125e011825, NASA Johnson Space Center. Public Domain.

203 (P.165) - NASA/Jet Propulsion Laboratory-Caltech, Completed CADRE Rover in the Clean Room, 2024. Photograph. PIA26169, NASA Jet Propulsion Laboratory. Public Domain.

204 (P.165) - Nick Galante (NASA), Pathfinder in Flight over Hawaii, 1997. Photograph. EC96-43817-11, NASA Armstrong Flight Research Center. Public Domain.

205 (P.165) - Carla Thomas (NASA), Pathfinder Aircraft Flight #1, 1996. Photograph. EC97-44287-2, NASA Armstrong Flight Research Center. Public Domain.

206 (P.166) - Allison Bills (NASA Jet Propulsion Laboratory/Space Dynamics Laboratory), Completed SunRISE SmallSats Pictured Together, 2023. Photograph. PIA25789, NASA Jet Propulsion Laboratory. Public Domain.

207 (P.167) - NASA Johnson Space Center, Apollo 12 Mission Image–Close-Up View of the Solar Wind Panel, 1969. Photograph. as12-47-6898, NASA Johnson Space Center. Public Domain.

208 (P.168) - NASA, ESA, J. Hester and A. Loll (Arizona State University), Crab Nebula, 2017. Digital image. GSFC_20171208_Archive_e002159, NASA Goddard. Public Domain.

209 (P.168) - NASA/DOE/Fermi LAT Collaboration, CXC/SAO/JPL-Caltech/Steward/O. Krause et al., and NRAO/AUI, Cassiopeia A supernova, 2017. GSFC_20171208_Archive_e002183, NASA Goddard. Public Domain.

210 (P.169) - NASA/ESA/IAC/HFF Team, STScI, Hubble Sees 'Ghost Light' From Dead Galaxies, 2017. Digital image. GSFC_20171208_Archive_e000914, NASA Goddard Public Domain.

211 (P.169) - NASA/JSC, Aurora Australis Taken From the shuttle Discovery during STS-85 Mission, 1997. Photograph. sts085-365-006, NASA Johnson Space Center. Public Domain.

212 (P.169) - NASA/JPL/University of Arizona, L, Saturn Polar Aurora, 2008. Digital image. PIA11396, NASA Jet Propulsion Laboratory. Public Domain.

213 (P.172) - Kevin M. Gill, Andromeda Galaxy, 2021. Digital photograph. Flickr. CC BY 2.0 DEED.

214 (P.173) - TIO/NOIRLab/NSF/AURA/DECam DELVE Survey, Clara Martínez-Vázquez, and Cliff Johnson, Starlink Satellites Imaged from CTIO, 2019. Collage. iotw1946a, TIO/NOIRLab/NSF/AURA/DECam DELVE Survey. CC BY 4.0.

215 (P.174) - Victoria Girgis (Lowell Observatory), Trails Made by Starlink Satellites. Digital image. International Astronomical Union. Lowell Observatory Archives. CC BY 4.0 International. © Lowell Observatory Archives.

216 (P.175) - Kees Scherer, Andromeda before Photoshop, 2019. Digital image. Flickr. Public Domain.

217 (P.176) - Rafael Schmall, Albireo in Cygnus with Starlink Satellites, 2021. Digital photograph. ann21021, TIO/NOIRLab/NSF/AURA/DECam DELVE Survey. CC BY 4.0.

218 (P.176) - Steve Elliot, There is a lot of stuff up there, 2020. Digital image. Flickr. CC BY-SA 2.0.

219 (P.177) - Jeremy Stanley, Light Pollution It's Not Pretty, 2009. Digital photograph. Flickr. CC BY 2.0 DEED.

220 (P.178) - Matthew Luckiesh, The Lights of New York City, 1920. Photograph. ev6jxp2t, Wellcome Collection. CC BY 4.0 International.

221 (P.178) - Unknown, Writers' Buildings, Dalhousie Square, Calcutta, India: Illuminated at Night, 1906. Photoprint sheet, 18.3 × 31.1 cm. 571146i, Wellcome Collection. Public Domain.

222 (P.178) - Unknown, The 1904 World's Fair, St. Louis, Missouri: The Palace of Electricity by Night, 1904. Photoprint sheet, 17.5 × 22.5 cm. 572406i, Wellcome Collection. Public Domain.

223 (P.179) - Bernard Lens (II), Vuurwerk in Covent Garden, 1690. Mezzotint, 25.4 × 34.8 cm. RP-P-1907-2735, Rijksmuseum. Public domain.

224 (P.179) - Matthew Luckiesh, Panama-Pacific Exposition, 1920. Photograph. kdwvyfx3, Wellcome Collection. CC BY 4.0.

225 (P.180-181) - Charles-Nicolas Cohin the younger, Design of the Illumination and Fireworks. Dedicated to his Grace the Dauphin at Meudon, 1735. Etching and engraving on paper, 61.1 × 91.4 cm. 1921-6-205-2, Cooper Hewitt, Smithsonian Design Museum. Public Domain.

226 (P.182) - Peter H. Feist, Paris, Moulin Rouge, Place Blanche, 1958. 35 mm reversal film, slide frame, 5 × 5 cm. 3726, Image Repository of the Media Library of the Institute for Art and Visual History, Berlin University. CC BY 4.0 SA International.

227 (P.182) - Ramy Majouji, McDonald's in Times Square, 2006. Wikimedia Commons. Public Domain.

228 (P.183) - Eric Ishii Eckhardt, Binion's Horseshoe, On the Old Las Vegas Strip, 2005. Digital photograph. Flickr. CC BY 2.0 DEED.

229 (P.183) - Holiday Point, Glitter Clutch, Fremont Street Experience, Las Vegas, 2012. Digital photograph. Flickr. CC BY 2.0 DEED.

230 (P.184) - Wilford Peloquin, Times Square, New York City, 1963. Flickr. CC BY 2.0 DEED.

231 (P.184) - Carol M. Highsmith, Times Square, Which Is Actually Triangular, in New York City, New York, 1996. Colour film transparency, 10.2 × 12.7 cm. 2011632416, Carol M. Highsmith Archive, Library of Congress. Public Domain.

232 (P.185) - NASA, Behold: The City of Boston at Night!, 2021. Digital image. NASA. Public Domain.

233 (P.185) - Tim Kopra, Night Image of Chicago, 2016. Digital image. NASA. Public Domain.

234 (P.185) - NASA Johnson Space Center, The City Lights of Kuwait City, 2024. Digital image. NASA. Public Domain.

235 (P.186) - A. Pipkin, D. Duriscoe, C. Luginbuhl, and United States National Park Service, A Calibrated All-sky Map of the Skyglow from Near Ashurst Lake, AZ, USA, 2016. Digital image. United States National Park Service. Wikimedia Commons. Public Domain.

236 (P.186) - Míla Moudrá, All-Sky Brightness Map, 2011. Digital image, processed from image taken near Chřibská village in the Bohemian Switzerland National Park. Wikimedia Commons. Courtesy of Míla Moudrá. © Míla Moudrá.

237 (P.186) - Martin Mašek, All-Sky Map of Night Sky Brightness, Pierre Auger Observatory, Los Leones, Argentina, 2015. Digital image. Wikimedia Commons. CC BY 4.0.

238 (P.188) - Craig Mayhew and Robert Simmon, Earth's City Lights, 2000. Digital image. NASA Goddard Space Flight Center. Public Domain.

239 (P.188) - Joshua Stevens, Bathed in a Sea of Artificial Light, 2022. Digital image. NASA Earth Observatory. Public Domain.

240 (P.190-191) - Marian Eagle Clarke, The Eddystone Lantern, 1901. Painting. Wikimedia Commons. Public Domain.

Abbasi, Mubashir Ul-Haq, and Sreeramuka Rajeswara Sarma. "An Astrolabe by Muhammad Muqīm of Lahore Dated 1047 AH (1637-38 CE)." *Islamic Studies* 53, no. 1/2 (2014): 37-65. https://www.jstor.org/stable/44627366.

Agrawal, Govind. "Optical Communication: Its History and Recent Progress." In *Optics in Our Time*, edited by M. Al-Amri, M. El-Gomati, and M. Zubairy. Springer, Cham, 2016. https://doi.org/10.1007/978-3-319-31903-2.

Allen, Diogenes, and Eric O. Springsted. *Philosophy for Understanding Theology.* Louisville, KY: Westminster John Knox Press, 1985.

Allen, Jesse. "Topaz Solar Farm, California." NASA Earth Observatory. March 5, 2015. https://earthobservatory.nasa.gov/images/85403/topaz-solar-farm-california.

Archeological Survey of India. "Nomination of The Jantar Mantar, Jaipur (for inclusion on World Heritage List)." UNESCO. Accessed May 21, 2024. https://whc.unesco.org/uploads/nominations/1338.pdf.

Aversa, Raffaella, Relly Victoria Petrescu, Antonio Apicella, and Florian Ion Tiberiu Petrescu. "Under Water." *Online Journal of Biological Sciences* 17, no. 2 (2017): 70-87. https://doi.org/10.3844/ojbsci.2017.70.87.

Ayduz, Salim. "Taqi al-Din Ibn Ma'ruf: A Bio-Bibliographical Essay." Muslim Heritage. June 26, 2008. https://muslimheritage.com/taqi-al-din-bio-essay/.

Bachelard, Gaston. *The Psychoanalysis of Fire.* Boston: Beacon Press, 1964.

Ballato, John, and Peter Dragic. "Glass: The Carrier of Light - A Brief History of Optical Fiber." *International Journal of Applied Glass Science* 7, no. 4 (2016): 413-422. https://doi.org/10.1111/ijag.12239.

Barton, Andrew D., Andrew J. Irwin, Zoe V. Finkel, and Charles A. Stock. "Anthropogenic Climate Change Drives Shift and Shuffle in North Atlantic Phytoplankton Communities." *Proceedings of the National Academy of Sciences* 113, no. 11 (2016): 2964-2969. https://doi.org/10.1073/pnas.1519080113.

Barton, Andrew D., Zoe V. Finkel, Ben A. Ward, David G. Johns, and Michael J. Follows. "On the Roles of Cell Size and Trophic Strategy in North Atlantic Diatom and Dinoflagellate Communities." *Limnology and Oceanography* 58, no. 1 (January 2013): 254-266. https://doi.org/10.4319/lo.2013.58.1.0254.

Baudrillard, Jean. *The Consumer Society: Myths and Structures.* London: SAGE, 2016.

Beman, J. Michael, Kevin R. Arrigo, and Pamela A. Matson. "Agricultural Runoff Fuels Large Phytoplankton Blooms in Vulnerable Areas of the Ocean." *Nature* 434, no. 7030 (2005): 211-214. https://doi.org/10.1038/nature03370.

Benjamin, Walter. *The Arcades Project.* Translated by Howard Eiland and Kevin McLaughlin. Cambridge, MA: Harvard University Press, 1999.

Bernatskyi, Artemii, and Vladyslav Khaskin. "The History of the Creation of Lasers and Analysis of the Impact of their Application in the Material Processing on the Development of Certain Industries." *History of Science and Technology* 11, no. 1 (2021):125-149. https://doi.org/10.32703/2415-7422-2021-11-1-125-149.

Blakemore, Erin. "Thomas Edison Didn't Invent the Light Bulb—But Here's What He Did Do." *National Geographic*, April 13, 2022. https://www.nationalgeographic.com/history/article/thomas-edison-light-bulb-history.

Blankenship, Robert E. "Early Evolution of Photosynthesis." *Plant Physiology* 154, no. 2 (2010): 434-438. https://doi.org/10.1104/pp.110.161687.

Brand, Peter. "The 'Lost' Obelisks and Colossi of Seti I." *Journal of the American Research Center in Egypt* 34 (1997): 101-114. https://doi.org/10.2307/40000801.

Burton, Harry Edwin. "The Optics of Euclid." *Journal of the Optical Society of America* 35, no. 5 (1945), 357-372. https://philomatica.org/wp-content/uploads/2013/01/Optics-of-Euclid.pdf.

Cadava, Eduardo. Words of Light: *Theses on the Photography of History*. Princeton: Princeton University Press, 1996. https://doi.org/10.1515/9780691188713.

Clarke, William Eagle. *Studies in Bird Migration.* London: Gurney and Jackson, 1912. https://ia804700.us.archive.org/16/items/studiesinbirdmig01clar/studiesinbirdmig01clar.pdf.

Cohen, Samuel. "An Interview with Nikola Tesla, Electrical Wizard," *The Electrical Experimenter.* June 1915. https://library.si.edu/digital-library/book/electricalexperi03gern.

Courlander, Harold. *The Fourth World of the Hopis.* Albuquerque: University of New Mexico Press, 1971.

Cotter, Charles H. "The Mariner's Sextant and the Royal Society." *The Royal Society Journal of the History of Science* (August 1978). https://doi.org/10.1098/rsnr.1978.0002.

Curry, Andrew. "Egypt's Eternal City." *Archaeology* 72, no. 2 (2019): 26-33. https://www.jstor.org/stable/26822810.

Daneshfard, Babak, Behnam Dalfardi, and Golnoush Sadat Mahmoudi Nezhad. "Ibn al-Haytham (965-1039 AD), the Original Portrayal of the Modern Theory of Vision." *Journal of Medical Biography* 24, no. 2 (2014): 227-231. https://doi.org/10.1177/0967772014529050.

Darwin, Charles. *The Descent of Man and Selection in Relation to Sex.* New York: Barnes & Noble Publishing, 2004.

Davies, Thomas, and Tim Smyth, "Why Artificial Light at Night Should Be a Focus for Global Change Research in the 21st Century." *Global Change Biology* 24, no. 3 (March 2018): 872-882. https://doi.org/10.1111/gcb.13927.

DeKoven, Marianne. Utopia Limited: *The Sixties and the Emergence of the Postmodern*. Durham, NC: Duke University Press, 2004.

De Macedo, Cecilia Cintra Cavaleiro. "Between Philosophy and Mysticism: Suhrawardi and the Metaphysics of Light." *Religious Studies Magazine* (2009). https://www.pucsp.br/rever/rv2_2009/i_macedo.htm.

De Miranda, Luis. *Being and Neonness.* Cambridge, MA: The MIT Press, 2019.

Dunnett, Oliver. "Contested Landscapes: The Moral Geographies of Light Pollution in Britain." *Cultural Geographies* 22, no. 4 (2015): 619-636. https://www.jstor.org/stable/26168681.

European Space Agency. "The Mother of Hubble." https://esahubble.org/about/history/the-mother-of-hubble/.

Fagan, Brian. *From Black Land to Fifth Sun: The Science of Sacred Sites.* Reading, MA: Perseus Books, 1998.

Fleming, Lora E., Barbara Kirkpatrick, Lorraine C. Backer, Cathy J. Walsh, Kate Nierenberg, John Clark, Andrew Reich, et al. "Review of Florida Red Tide and Human Health Effects." *Harmful Algae* 10, no. 2 (2011): 224-233. https://doi.org/10.1016/j.hal.2010.08.006.

Foucault, Michel. *Power/Knowledge: Selected Interviews and Other Writings, 1972-1977.* Edited by Colin Gordon. New York: Pantheon Books, 1980.

Franklin, Benjamin. *Experiments and Observations on Electricity.* Cambridge, UK: Cambridge University Press, 2018.

Frazer, James George. *Myths of the Origin of Fire.* London: Macmillan, 1930.

Freeth, Tony, Alexander Jones, John M. Steele, and Yanis Bitsakis. "Calendars With Olympiad Display and Eclipse Prediction on the Antikythera Mechanism." *Nature* 454, no. 7204 (2008): 614-617. https://doi.org/10.1038/nature07130.

Friedlander, Eli. "La Jetée: Regarding the Gaze." *boundary* 2 28, no. 1 (2001): 75-90. https://muse.jhu.edu/article/3327.

Frothingham, Arthur. "Ancient Orientation Unveiled." *Gorgias Press eBooks* (2009): 55-76. https://doi.org/10.31826/9781463220556-001.

Fulton, J. F., S. Gibson, John Farquhar Fulton, and Godfrey Rolles Driver. *A Bibliography of the Honourable Robert Boyle: By J.F. Fulton.* Oxford: Clarendon Press, 1932.

Gage, Joan Paulson. "Icons of Cruelty." *The New York Times.* August 5, 2013. https://archive.nytimes.com/opinionator.blogs.nytimes.com/2013/08/05/icons-of-cruelty/.

Ganot, Adolphe. *Natural Philosophy for General Readers and Young Persons.* London: Forgotten Books, 2018. First published in 1876. https://archive.org/details/naturalphilosoph00ganorich/mode/2up.

Garbuny, Siegfried. "Japan: Regeneration." *Current History* 11, no. 64 (1946): 493-499. http://www.jstor.org/stable/45307243.

Gernsback, Hugo. *The Electrical Experimenter.* May 1915 through April 1916. https://library.si.edu/digital-library/book/electricalexperi03gern.

Glasspool, Ian J., and Andrew C. Scott. "Phanerozoic Concentrations of Atmospheric Oxygen Reconstructed From Sedimentary Charcoal." *Nature Geoscience* 3, no. 9 (2010): 627-630. https://doi.org/10.1038/ngeo923.

Glasspool, Ian J., Andrew C Scott, David Waltham, Natalia Vladimirovna Pronina, and Longyi Shao. "The Impact of Fire on the Late Paleozoic Earth System." *Frontiers in Plant Science* 6 (2015): 1-13. https://doi.org/10.3389/fpls.2015.00756.

Gingerich, Owen. "Galileo, the Impact of the Telescope, and the Birth of Modern Astronomy." *Proceedings of the American Philosophical Society: Held at Philadelphia for Promoting Useful Knowledge* 155, no. 2 (2011): 131-141. https://dialnet.unirioja.es/servlet/articulo?codigo=4627523.

Hainaut, Olivier, and Andrew P. Williams. "Impact of Satellite Constellations on Astronomical Observations." *Astronomy & Astrophysics* 636 (April 2020). https://doi.org/10.1051/0004-6361/202037501.

Hall, Doyle T. "Semi-Empirical Astronomical Light Pollution Evaluation of Satellite Constellations." *The Journal of the Astronautical Sciences* 69, no. 6 (2022): 1893-1928. https://doi.org/10.1007/s40295-022-00358-4.

Hallegraeff, Gustaaf, and Christopher Bolch. "Unprecedented Toxic Algal Blooms Impact on Tasmanian Seafood Industry." *Microbiology Australia* 37, no. 3 (2016): 143-144. https://doi.org/10.1071/ma16049.

Hafez, Ihsan, F. Stephenson, and Wayne Orchiston. "The Investigation of Stars, Star Clusters and Nebulae in Abd al-Rahman al-Sufi's Book of the Fixed Stars." In *New Insights From Recent Studies in Historical Astronomy: Following in the Footsteps of F. Richard Stephenson*, edited by Wayne Orchiston, David Green, and Richard Strom, 143-186. Springer, 2015. https://doi.org/10.1007/978-3-319-07614-0_10.

Harry Ransom Center. "The Niépce Heliograph." https://www.hrc.utexas.edu/niepce-heliograph/#top/.

Heisler, J., P. M. Glibert, J. M. Burkholder, D. M. Anderson, W. Cochlan, W. C. Dennison, Q. Dortch, et al. "Eutrophication and Harmful Algal Blooms: A Scientific Consensus." *Harmful Algae* 8, no. 1 (2008): 3-13. https://doi.org/10.1016/j.hal.2008.08.006.

Huxley, Thomas Henry. *T. H. Huxley's Diary of the Voyage of H. M. S. Rattlesnake.* Garden City, NY: Doubleday, Doran, 1936.

International Astronomical Union. "Trails Made by Starlink Satellites." June 3, 2019. https://www.iau.org/public/images/detail/ann19035a/.

Javadi, Shohreh. "How the World Views Solar Deities." *Journal of Art and Civilisation of the Orient* 30 (2020): 1-10. https://www.jaco-sj.com/jufile?ar_sfile=1311459.

Jindal, Urja. "Book in Focus: Learning from Las Vegas by Robert Venturi, Steven Izenour, Denise Scott Brown." Rethinking the Future. https://www.re-thinkingthefuture.com/rtf-architectural-reviews/a5183.

Johnson, Frank H. "Bioluminescence (Harvey, E. Newton)." *Journal of Chemical Education* 29, no. 9 (1952): 474. https://doi.org/10.1021/ed029p474.2.

Kepler, Johannes, and Witelo. *Ad Vitellionem Paralipomena: Quibus Astronomiae Pars Optica Traditvr; Potissimum De Artificiosa Observatione et Aestimatione Diametrorvm Deliquiorumq; Solis et Lunae, Cvm Exemplis Insignivm Eclipsivm.* Frankfurt: Claudius Marnius, 1604.

King, David A. "A Survey of Medieval Islamic Shadow Schemes for Simple Time-Reckoning." *Oriens* 32 (1990): 191-249. https://doi.org/10.2307/1580631.

King, Leonard William. *A History of Sumer and Akkad: An Account of the Early Races of Babylonia from Prehistoric Times to the Foundation of the Babylonian Monarchy.* London: Chatto & Windus, 1910.

Kingsley, Peter. "Empedocles' Sun." *The Classical Quarterly* 44, no. 2 (1994): 316-324. https://www.jstor.org/stable/639636.

Komatsu, Kazuhiko. *An Introduction to Yōkai Culture: Monsters, Ghosts, and Outsiders in Japanese History.* Tokyo: Japan Publishing Industry Foundation for Culture, 2017.

Laughlin, James. "The Surya (the Sun)." *Grand Street* 60 (1997): 11. https://doi.org/10.2307/25008147.

Lilly, Laura E., Iain M. Suthers, Jason D. Everett, and Anthony J. Richardson. "A Global Review of Pyrosomes: Shedding Light on the Ocean's Elusive Gelatinous 'Fire-bodies.'" *Limnology and Oceanography Letters* 8, no. 6 (2023): 812-829. https://doi.org/10.1002/lol2.10350.

Lindberg, David C. *Theories of Vision From Al-Kindi to Kepler.* Chicago: University of Chicago Press, 1976.

Lindner, Christoph. *Imagining New York City: Literature, Urbanism, and the Visual Arts, 1890-1940.* Oxford: Oxford University Press, 2015.

Luckiesh, Matthew. "The Lights of New York City." https://wellcomecollection.org/works/ev6jxp2t/images?id=kdx7ekh5.

Luminet, Jean-Pierre. "Science, Art and Geometrical Imagination." *Proceedings of the International Astronomical Union* 5, no. S260 (2009): 248-273. https://doi.org/10.1017/s1743921311002377.

Lystrup, Eric. "The Dark Side of the Light: Rachel Carson, Light Pollution, and a Case for Federal Regulation." *Jurimetrics* 57, no. 4 (2017): 505-528. http://www.jstor.org/stable/26322762.

Macfarlane, Robert. *The Wild Places.* London: Granta Books, 2009.

Mardon, Austin A., Janani Rajendra, and Sudipta Samadder. *Decoding the Antikythera Mechanism: Mystery of the Ancient World.* Edmonton: Golden Meteorite Press, 2021.

Marcotte, Roxanne. "Suhrawardi." *Stanford Encyclopedia of Philosophy.* Revised April 4, 2012. https://plato.stanford.edu/archives/spr2013/entries/suhrawardi/.

Matulka, Rebecca, and Daniel Wood. "The History of the Light Bulb." United States Department of Energy. November 22, 2013. https://www.energy.gov/articles/history-light-bulb.

Mjoseth, Jeannine. "Sea Creatures Providing Clues on the Evolution of Vision." *The National Institute of Health Catalyst* 21 (2013): 1-20. https://irp.nih.gov/system/files/media/file/2022-01/catalyst_v21i1_0.pdf.

Morkoç, Selen. "In Between the Mind and the Heart: Kātip Çelebi's Concept of 'ilm." *University of Adelaide Press eBooks*, 2018. https://doi.org/10.20851/ilm-1-07.

NASA. "Impact!" March 23, 2008. https://www.nasa.gov/image-article/impact/.

NASA. "Ivanpah Solar Energy Plant, California." Jet Propulsion Laboratory. December 5, 2013. https://www.jpl.nasa.gov/images/pia17746-ivanpah-solar-energy-plant-california.

NASA. "Andromeda Before Photoshop." Astronomy Pictures of the Day. October 14, 2019. https://apod.nasa.gov/apod/ap191014.html.

NASA. "Earth's City Lights." Visible Earth. October 23, 2000. https://visibleearth.nasa.gov/images/55167/earths-city-lights.

NASA. "Hubble Sees 'Ghost Light' From Dead Galaxies." Image and Video Library. https://images.nasa.gov/details/GSFC_20171208_Archive_e000914.

NASA. "Nancy Grace Roman." https://science.nasa.gov/people/nancy-grace-roman-for-hubble/.

Observatoire de Paris. "The Formation of the Andromeda Galaxy Finally Elucidated." December 21, 2001. https://www.observatoiredeparis.psl.eu/the-formation-of-the.html?lang=en.

"On This Day: Louis-Jacques-Mandé Daguerre Is Born." *JSTOR* (blog). November 18, 2011. https://about.jstor.org/blog/louis-jacques-mande-daguerre/.

Olsen, Reed, Terrel Gallaway, and David Mitchell. "Modelling US Light Pollution." *Journal of Environmental Planning and Management* 57, no. 6 (June 2014): 883-903. https://doi.org/10.1080/09640568.2013.774268.

Olson, John M., and Robert E. Blankenship. "Thinking about the Evolution of Photosynthesis." *Photosynthesis Research* 80, no. 1-3 (2004): 373-386. https://doi.org/10.1023/b:pres.0000030457.06495.83.

Phillips, Pamela F., ed. *Enlightened Nightscapes: Critical Essays on the Long Eighteenth-Century Night.* London: Routledge, 2023.

Pratt, Sara E. "Bathed in a Sea of Artificial Light." NASA Earth Observatory. March 2, 2022. https://earthobservatory.nasa.gov/images/149518/bathed-in-a-sea-of-artificial-light.

Pyne, Stephen J. "Fire in the Mind: Changing Understandings of Fire in Western Civilization." *Philosophical Transactions - Royal Society. Biological Sciences* 371, no. 1696 (2016): 1-8. https://doi.org/10.1098/rstb.2015.0166.

Rahman, Saifur. "Basics of Electricity." Proceedings of the Short Course on *"Electricity-The Most Preferred Form of Energy: Need, Accessibility, Affordability and Sustainability"* (2008): 27-62. https://www.researchgate.net/publication/303309704_Basics_of_Electricity.

Rashed, Roshdi. "A Pioneer in Anaclastics: Ibn Sahl on Burning Mirrors and Lenses." *Isis* 81, no. 3 (1990): 464-491. https://doi.org/10.1086/355456.

Riebeek, Holli. "Planetary Motion: The History of an Idea That Launched the Scientific Revolution." NASA Earth Observatory. July 7, 2009. https://earthobservatory.nasa.gov/features/OrbitsHistory.

Richlen, Mindy L., Steve L. Morton, Ebrahim A. Jamali, Anbiah Rajan, and Donald M. Anderson. "The Catastrophic 2008–2009 Red Tide in the Arabian Gulf Region, With Observations on the Identification and Phylogeny of the Fish-killing Dinoflagellate Cochlodinium Polykrikoides." *Harmful Algae* 9, no. 2 (2010): 163-172. https://doi.org/10.1016/j.hal.2009.08.013.

Rimmer, S. M., S. J. Hawkins, A. C. Scott, and W. L. Cressler. "The Rise of Fire: Fossil Charcoal in Late Devonian Marine Shales as an Indicator of Expanding Terrestrial Ecosystems, Fire, and Atmospheric Change." *American Journal of Science* 315, no. 8 (2015): 713-733. https://doi.org/10.2475/08.2015.01.

Romey, Kristin. "Ancient Sundial Find Celebrated Roman Election Win." *National Geographic*. November 8, 2017. https://www.nationalgeographic.com/history/article/ancient-rome-election-victory-sundial-archaeology.

Santora, Marc. "One of the World's Oldest Clocks Stops Ticking, Briefly." *The New York Times*. January 18, 2018. www.nytimes.com/2018/01/18/world/europe/prague-astronomical-clock-orloj.html.

Schielke, Thomas. "Light Matters: A Flash Back to the Glittering Age of Las Vegas at the Neon Museum." *ArchDaily* (blog). June 23, 2015. https://www.archdaily.com/645768/light-matters-a-flash-back-to-the-glittering-age-of-las-vegas-at-the-neon-museum.

Schulte-Römer, Nona. "Research in the Dark." *Nature and Culture* 14, no. 2 (June 2019): 215-227. https://doi.org/10.3167/nc.2019.140206.

Scott, A. C. "The Pre-Quaternary History of Fire." *Palaeogeography, Palaeoclimatology, Palaeoecology* 164, no. 1–4 (2000): 281-329. https://doi.org/10.1016/s0031-0182(00)00192-9.

Scott, Andrew C., and Ian J. Glasspool. "The Diversification of Paleozoic Fire Systems and Fluctuations in Atmospheric Oxygen Concentration." *Proceedings of the National Academy of Sciences of the United States of America* 103, no. 29 (2006): 10861-10965. https://doi.org/10.1073/pnas.0604090103.

Sharpe, William. "New York, Night, and Cultural Mythmaking: The Nocturne in Photography, 1900-1925." *Smithsonian Studies in American Art* 2, no. 3 (1988): 3-21. https://doi.org/10.1086/smitstudamerart.2.3.3108955.

Shapiro, Alan. "Images: Real and Virtual, Projected and Perceived, From Kepler to Dechales." *Early Science and Medicine* 13, no. 3 (2008): 270-312. https://doi.org/10.1163/157338208x285044.

Siebert, Harald. "Transformation of Euclid's Optics in Late Antiquity." *Nuncius* 29, no. 1 (2014): 88-126. https://doi.org/10.1163/18253911-02901004.

Silvi, Cesare. "Italian Contribution to CSP With Flat or Almost Flat Reflectors." *30th ISES Biennial Solar World Congress* (January 2011). https://www.researchgate.net/publication/266890248_Italian_contribution_to_CSP_with_flat_or_almost_flat_reflectors.

Simmel, Georg. *The Philosophy of Money*. London: Routledge, 2004.

Snyder, Joel. "Picturing Vision." *Critical Inquiry* 6, no. 3 (1980): 499-526. https://doi.org/10.1086/448062.

Sobel, Dava. *The Planets*. London: HarperCollins UK, 2011.

Spence, Charles. "The Phantasmagoria: From Ghostly Apparitions to Multisensory Fairground Entertainment." *Frontiers in Communication* 7 (July 2022). https://doi.org/10.3389/fcomm.2022.894078.

Starowicz, Adam, Rusanowska, Paulina, Zielinski, Marcin. "Photovoltaic Cell - The History of Invention - Review." *Polityka Energetyczna - Energy Journal* 26 (March 2023). https://doi.org/10.33223/epj/161290.

Sutherland, Kelly R., and Anne W. Thompson. "Pelagic Tunicate Grazing on Marine Microbes Revealed by Integrative Approaches." *Limnology and Oceanography*, no. 1 (2021): 102-121. https://doi.org/10.1002/lno.11979.

Sutton, Thomas. *Photographic Notes*. London: Sampson Low, Son & Company, 1861.

Takenaka, Yasuhiro, Atsushi Yamaguchi, Naoki Tsuruoka, Masaki Torimura, Takashi Gojobori, and Yasushi Shigeri. "Evolution of Bioluminescence in Marine Planktonic Copepods." *Molecular Biology and Evolution* 29, no. 6 (2012): 1669-1681. https://doi.org/10.1093/molbev/mss009.

The Khalili Collections. "Planispheric Astrolabe." www.khalilicollections.org/collections/islamic-art/khalili-collection-hajj-and-the-arts-of-pilgrimage-planispheric-astrolabe-sci430/.

The Metropolitan Museum of Art. "Eadweard Muybridge: Attitudes of Animals in Motion." www.metmuseum.org/art/collection/search/700109.

The Metropolitan Museum of Art. "Paul Henry: A Section of the Constellation Cygnus (August 13, 1885)." https://www.metmuseum.org/art/collection/search/283255.

Thibodeau, Philip. "Ancient Optics: Theories and Problems of Vision." In *A Companion to Science, Technology, and Medicine in Ancient Greece and Rome*, edited by Georgia L. Irby, 130-144. Wiley, 2016. https://doi.org/10.1002/9781118373057.ch8.

Tyson, Neil Degrasse, and Steven Soter. *Cosmic Horizons: Astronomy at the Cutting Edge*. New York: New Press, 2001.

UNESCO. "Maragheh Observatory, Iran." Portal to the Heritage of Astronomy. https://web.astronomicalheritage.net/index.php/show-entity?identity=29&idsubentity=1.

United States National Parks Service. "Lightscape / Night Sky." https://www.nps.gov/grba/learn/nature/lightscape.htm.

Vann, Karine. "Unraveling the Mystery of the Armenian Stonehenge." *Smithsonian Magazine*, July 26, 2017. https://www.smithsonianmag.com/travel/unraveling-mystery-armenian-stonehenge-180964207.

Vermeir, Koen. "The Magic of the Magic Lantern (1660–1700): On Analogical Demonstration and the Visualization of the Invisible." *British Journal for the History of Science* 38, no. 2 (2005): 127-159. https://doi.org/10.1017/s0007087405006709.

Webster, Colin. "Ptolemy's Optics, Double-vision, and the Technological Afterimage." *Studies in History and Philosophy of Science Part A* 94 (2022): 191-200. https://doi.org/10.1016/j.shpsa.2022.06.011.

Wellcome Collection. "Electrical Appliances Exhibited at the 1882 Electrical Exhibition, Including Chandeliers and the First Telegraph Instrument. Wood Engraving, 1882." https://wellcomecollection.org/works/pvwzyswy.

White, Leslie A. "Energy and the Evolution of Culture." *American Anthropologist* 45, no. 3 (1943): 335-356. https://doi.org/10.1525/aa.1943.45.3.02a00010.

Willis, J. H. "A Bibliography of the 'Ghost Fungus', Pleurotus Nidiformis (Berk.) Sacc." *Muelleria* 1, no. 3 (1967): 213-218. https://doi.org/10.5962/p.237620.

Wrangham, Richard. "Control of Fire in the Paleolithic." *Current Anthropology* 58, no. S16 (2017): S303-S313. https://doi.org/10.1086/692113.

Wrangham, Richard W., James Holland Jones, Greg Laden, David Pilbeam, and Nancy Lou Conklin-Brittain. "The Raw and the Stolen." *Current Anthropology* 40, no. 5 (1999): 567-594. https://doi.org/10.1086/300083.

Young, Thomas. "I. the Bakerian Lecture. Experiments and Calculations Relative to Physical Optics." *Philosophical Transactions of the Royal Society of London* 94 (1804): 1-16. https://doi.org/10.1098/rstl.1804.0001.

Zahl, Paul A. "Bizarre World of the Fungi." National Geographic 128 (1965), cited in Sivinski, John M., "Phototropism, Bioluminescence, and the Diptera." *The Florida Entomologist* 81, no. 3 (1998): 282-292. https://doi.org/10.2307/3495919.

Zahl, Paul A. "The Secrets of Nature's Night Lights." *National Geographic* 140 (1975): 45-69. https://eurekamag.com/research/023/093/023093756.php.

Zanatta, Alberto, Fabio Zampieri, Cristina Basso, and Gaetano Thiene. "Galileo Galilei: Science Vs. Faith." *Global Cardiology Science & Practice* 2017, no. 2 (2017): 1-11. https://doi.org/10.21542/gcsp.2017.10.

Zewail, Ahmed H. "Micrographia of the Twenty-first Century: From Camera Obscura to 4D Microscopy." *Philosophical Transactions - Royal Society. Mathematical, Physical and Engineering Sciences* 368, no. 1914 (2010): 1191-1204. https://doi.org/10.1098/rsta.2009.0265.

Zghal, Mourad, Hamid-Eddine Bouali, Zohra Ben Lakhdar, and Habib Hamam. "The First Steps for Learning Optics: Ibn Sahl's, Al-Haytham's and Young's Works on Refraction as Typical Examples." *Education and Training in Optics and Photonics* (2007): 1-7. https://doi.org/10.1364/etop.2007.esb2.

BIOGRAPHY

LINA GHOTMEH
(b.1980, Beirut, Lebanon) leads her practice Lina Ghotmeh – Architecture in Paris, France and carries her works in the world spanning the realm of Art, Architecture & Design.

Having grown up and studied in Beirut, Ghotmeh's architecture draws inspiration from the diverse civilisations that have shaped the city's contours, resulting in designs deeply rooted in their surrounding land and environment. Confronting the challenges of climate change, she delves into the rich history of climatic architecture in the various regions, seamlessly integrating this knowledge into contemporary built environments. Today, she introduces a distinctive architectural posture with aesthetics undoubtedly tied to her heritage. Each of her designs represents an 'Archeology of the Future,' emerging in complete symbiosis with nature, guided by thorough historical and materially sensitive research.

Ghotmeh's projects include the acclaimed *Stone Garden* building, a crafted housing and gallery space in Beirut, Lebanon, dedicated to art in the Middle East and the Arab world (Dezeen 2021 Architecture of the Year Award); the future contemporary Art Museum of AlUla in Saudi Arabia, designed as a series of pavilions integrated in the oasis and showcasing art from the region; the Estonian National Museum (Grand Prix Afex 2016 & Mies van der Rohe Nominee); Ateliers Hermès in Normandy, first passive low-carbon workshops building in France & recently the 22nd Serpentine Pavilion in London a space fostering togetherness in a majlis-like assembly at Kensington Gardens.

Ghotmeh's influence extends beyond her designs, as she actively engages in discussions about the role of architecture in shaping society. She is engaged in the academic world and has lectured in institutions globally. She held the Kenzo Tange 2024 teaching position at Harvard; She was Louis I Khan 2021 visiting professor at Yale School of Architecture in the United States and Gehry Chair 2021–22 at the University of Toronto, Canada. She co-presides the Scientific Network for architecture in extreme climates and was a member of the Aga Khan Award for Architecture 2022 Jury. She is appointed professor member of the IAA International Academy of Architecture.

Recognitions for Ghotmeh's contributions include the 2023 Great Arab Minds Award, the 2020 Schelling Architecture Prize, the 2020 Tamayouz 'Woman of Outstanding Achievement', the French Fine Arts Academy Cardin Award 2019, the Architecture Academy Dejean Prize 2016 and the French Ministry of Culture Award in 2008.

Her work and research have been showcased at the Sharjah 2019 Architecture Biennale, the Cooper Hewitt Smithsonian Museum in New York, at the MAXXI in Rome (2021–22), in the Danish Architecture Institute and at the 17th Architecture Biennale in Venice (2021). Publications by Phaidon, RIBA, Domus and Architectural Record have featured her projects, solidifying her impact in the global architectural discourse.

IMPRINT

The Zumtobel Group aims to create well-being and improve people's quality of life through light as a group, and through all its individual brands, Thorn, Tridonic and Zumtobel. As a leading supplier of innovative lighting solutions, the Group offers its customers around the world a comprehensive portfolio, where the focus is invariably on people and their needs. The company's know-how about the effects of light on people, acquired over decades, forms the basis for future-oriented light-ing solutions that are increasingly energy- and resourceefficient while providing the best possible quality of light. The Group is based in Dornbirn in the Vorarlberg region of Austria.

The publication *Windows of Light* was initiated by the Zumtobel Group for the design of its Artistic Annual Report 2023/24.

INITIATOR	Zumtobel Group AG, Austria
PUBLISHER	Lars Müller Publishers, Switzerland
SPECIAL THANKS TO	Isabel Zumtobel (Zumtobel Licht AG)
AUTHOR	Lina Ghotmeh – Architecture
ARTWORK	Lina Ghotmeh – Architecture
PHOTOGRAPHY	Pages 194 - 233 © Laurian Ghinițoiu
	Pages 234 - 249 © Lina Ghotmeh
INK DRAWINGS	Pages 252 - 276 © Lina Ghotmeh
GRAPHIC DESIGN	Bruno Faivre, Lina Ghotmeh – Architecture
RESEARCH / TEXT	Sara Ibrahim, Lina Ghotmeh – Architecture
EDITOR	Claire Lubell, Canada
PROJECT MANAGEMENT	Bruno Faivre, Lina Ghotmeh – Architecture Agata Spatzek, Zumtobel Group
PROOFREADING	Christine Fitz, Austria Barbara Wrathall-Pohl, Austria
PRINTING & BOOKBINDING	Brizzolis, arte en gráficas, Spain
PAPERS	Munken Lynx 80 gsm Munken Lynx 130 gsm

© 2024 Lars Müller Publishers and Zumtobel Group AG

Reproduction and reprint only with express written approval of Zumtobel Group AG.

Zumtobel Group AG
Höchsterstrasse 8
6850 Dornbirn
Austria
T +43 5572 509-0
info@zumtobelgroup.com
www.z.lighting

Lars Müller Publishers
Zurich, Switzerland
www.lars-mueller-publishers.com

ISBN 978-3-03778-776-2

Distributed in North America, Latin America and the Caribbean by ARTBOOK | D.A.P.
www.artbook.com

Printed in Spain

The author and initiator have made every effort to clear all rights for image reproductions and identify all the owners of copyright. In case of doubt rights owners can contact the initiator.

Lina Ghotmeh — Architecture

Lina Ghotmeh — Architecture

75 rue Fontaine au Roi,
75011 Paris
France
T + 33 1 43 38 12 47
contact@linaghotmeh.com
www.linaghotmeh.com